AF511958

Indian Politics

Indian Politics

Author

Dr. Rutuja Holkar

ADROIT

Adroit Publishers

NEW DELHI • KATHMANDU

ISBN : 978-81-87393-86-3

2026

Copyright © : Dr. Rutuja Holkar

No part of this publication may be reproduced or transmitted in any form or by any means, electronic or mechanical, including photocopying, recording or any information storage and retrieval system, without permission in writing from the publisher & author.

Published by
ADROIT PUBLISHERS 4675/21, Ganpati Bhawan, Ansari Road,
Daryaganj, New Delhi-110 002 Phone : 011-23266030
adroitpublishers@gmail.com

Typeset in Garamond Premier Pro by Arun, Akriti Graphic
Solution, Delhi-110081 E-mail: arun263923@gmail.com,
Ph: 9999414390

Contents

Chapter One

Indian Constitution

The Constitution of India is the supreme law of India. The document lays down the framework that demarcates fundamental political code, structure, procedures, powers, and duties of government institutions and sets out fundamental rights, directive principles, and the duties of Citizens.

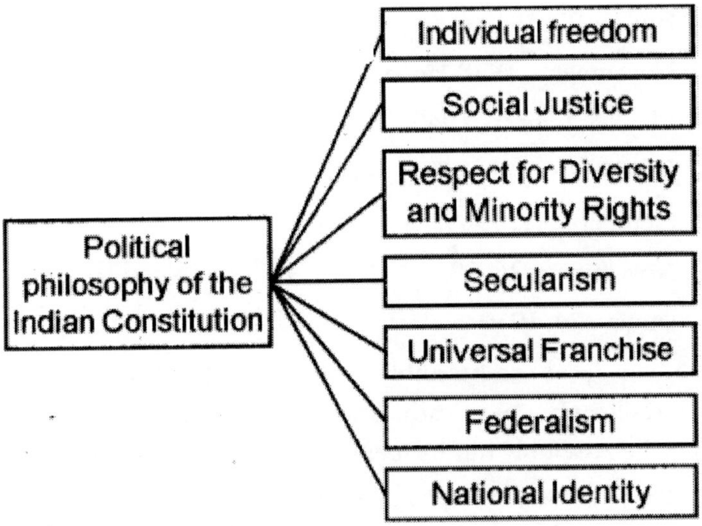

Salient Features of Constituent Assembly of India

- The Constituent Assembly of India came into existence as per the provisions of Cabinet Mission Plan of May 1946. Its task was to formulate constitution/s for facilitating appropriate transfer of sovereign power from British authorities to Indian hands.
- The Assembly was to have proportional representation from existing provincial legislatures and from various princely states. Bulk of these elections was completed by the end of July 1946, under the supervision of Reforms Office under Governor General (Viceroy).
- The Assembly was to have three sections: Punjab & North-West, Bengal-Assam and Rest of India. The Constitutions were to be formulated for Indian Union, each Section and for each of the Provinces therein. The Muslim League, which had won bulk of the 80 Muslim seats

and dominated two smaller Sections, chose not to participate so the Assembly never convened separately in sections.

- Assembly held 12 sessions, or rounds of sittings:
  1. December 9-23, 1946,
  2. January 20- 25, 1947,
  3. April 28- May 2, 1947,
  4. July 14- 31, 1947,
  5. August 14- 30, 1947,
  6. January 27, 1948,
  7. November 4, 1948-January 8, 1949,
  8. May 16- June 16, 1949,
  9. July 30-September 18, 1949,
  10. October 6-17, 1949,
  11. November 4-26, 1949,
  12. January 24, 1950.
- Membership of the Assembly kept varying for different reasons, other than resignation and death. Many public figures showed keenness to enter the Assembly but its membership was also denounced by certain groups like Muslim League, Communists and Socialists. These attitudes changed too. After passage of the Indian Independence Act by British Parliament it was decided that those members who wish to retain their seats in provincial legislature would vacate their seats in the Assembly. But several members of provincial legislature continued to come and partake in the Assembly until the provision against this was made in the Constitution itself. Biggest change in membership was caused by the declaration of Partition of India. Certain members like Dr. Ambedkar, who were elected from territories assigned to Dominion of Pakistan, lost their seats. Muslim League members elected from United Provinces, Bihar and elsewhere came to occupy their seats after partition. Such members were humiliated on many occasions and Patel even told them to go to Pakistan. After initial disinterest, the princely states started negotiating with a committee of the Assembly for their

representation. Over a period, hundreds of princely states were grouped into larger associations and provisions were made for them to elect their representatives to the Assembly. Till the last day of the Assembly, new members kept joining in. Hyderabad did not send any representative till the end. The total number of people who sat as members of the Assembly at any time has not been calculated by any official or scholar. Records show that maximum membership towards the end of tenure of Assembly was 307.

- The Assembly took help of several non-members in formulation of the Constitution. Eminent public figures outside the Assembly were requested to work as members of committees formed by the Assembly for focused deliberations on specific features or segments.
- Much of constitution-making took place in these committees, both from procedural and substantive viewpoint. Till date, no official report has appeared in public domain on the exact number of committees formed by the Constituent Assembly. Resolutions were moved for setting up committees as and when the need arose, and adopted after discussion. Depending on swiftness of nomination or election of members of respective committees, their formal appointment took few hours, days or weeks from the adoption of resolution.
- Some of the known committees were:

1. Organisational Committees

1.1. Rules of Procedure Committee (appointed on December 11, 1946. 15 members, Chairperson- Rajendra Prasad, ex-officio. Worked till 20 Dec. 1946)

1.2. Steering Committee (appointed on January 21, 1947. 19 members, Chairperson- Rajendra Prasad, ex-officio. Worked till the end.)

1.3. Staff and Finance Committee (appointed on December 23, 1946. 11 members, Chairperson- Rajendra Prasad, ex-officio. Worked till the end.)

1.4. Credentials Committee (appointed on December 23, 1946. 5 members, Chairperson- A.K. Ayyar. Worked till the end.

1.5. Order of Business Committee (appointed on January 25, 1947. 3 members, Chairperson- K.M. Munshi. Worked till July 14, 1947)

1.6. States (Negotiating) Committee (appointed on December 21, 1946. 6 members, Chairperson- J.L. Nehru. Worked till June 5, 1947)

1.7. Flag Committee (appointed on June 23, 1947. 12 members, Chairperson- Rajendra Prasad, ex-officio. Worked till July 22, 1947)

1.8. Committee on Functions of Constituent Assembly, under the Indian Independence Act (appointed on August 20, 1947. 7 members, Chairperson- G.V. Mavlankar. Worked till August 25, 1947)

2. Principal Committees and their sub-committees

2.1. Advisory Committee on Fundamental Rights, Minorities, Tribal Areas and Excluded Areas (appointed on 24 Jan. 1947. 57 members, Chairperson- Sardar Patel. Worked till 26 May 1949)

2.2. Union Powers Committee (appointed on 25 Jan, 1947. 12 members, Chairperson- J.L. Nehru. Worked till 26 Aug. 1947)

2.3. Union Constitution Committee (appointed on 4 May. 1947. 12 members, Chairperson- J.L. Nehru. Worked till 31 July, 1947.)

2.4. Provincial Constitution Committee (appointed on 4 May. 1947. 21 members, Chairperson- Sardar Patel. Worked till 21 July, 1947.)

2.5. Drafting Committee (appointed on 29 Aug. 1947. 8 members, Chairperson- Dr. Ambedkar. Worked till 17 Nov. 1949)

3. Other Sectoral Committees

3.1. Ad-hoc Committee on Citizenship (appointed on 30 April, 1947. 7 members, Chairperson- S. Varadachariar. Worked till 12 July. 1947)

3.2. Committee on Chief Commissioner's Provinces (appointed on 31 July, 1947. 7 members, Chairperson- N. Gopalaswami Ayyangar. Worked till 21 Oct. 1947)

3.3. Experts Committee on Financial Provisions of Constitution (appointed in Nov. 1947. 3 members, Chairperson- N.R. Sarkar. Worked between 17 Nov.- 5 Dec. 1947)

3.4. Sub-Committee on Minority safeguards for West Bengal and East Punjab (appointed on 24 Feb. 1948. 5 members, Chairperson- Sardar Patel. Worked till 23 Nov., 1948.)

- Curiously, the so-called Special Committee was constituted to decide the future course of action after comments had arrived in response to the Draft Constitution of February 1948. Neither a resolution for its constitution existed, nor anybody cared to inform the Assembly later on how and why this committee of great consequence was formed. In all, 32 members attended meetings of Special Committee on April 10-11, 1948, which were chaired by JL Nehru.
- Rajendra Prasad was the elected President of Constituent Assembly while VT Krishnamachari and HC Mookerji served as Vice-Presidents. HVR Iyengar was the secretary general of the Assembly, and SN Mukherji was the Chief Draftsman.
- After authentication of copies of the Constitution, the Constituent Assembly got naturally dissolved with its Chairperson having been elected the President of India, and its staff diverted to other avenues. But bulk of the Assembly continued functioning as provisional Parliament of India till first general elections were held. Indeed, the first amendment to the Constitution of India was made by this provisional Parliament in the summer of 1951.
- EVERY Constitution has a philosophy of its own.
- For the philosophy underlying our Constitution we must look back into **the historic Objectives Resolution of Pandit Nehru** which was adopted by the Constituent Assembly on January 22, 1947, and which inspired the shaping of the Constitution through all its subsequent stages. It reads thus -
- *"This Constituent Assembly declares its firm and solemn resolve to proclaim India as an Independent Sovereign Republic and to draw up for her future governance a Constitution:*
    1. *WHEREIN the territories that now comprise British India, the territories that now form the Indian States, and such other parts of India as are outside British India and the States as well as such other territories as are willing to be constituted into the Independent Sovereign india, shall be a Union of them all; and*
    2. WHEREIN the said territories, whether With their present boundaries or with such others as may be determined by **the**

Constituent Assembly and thereafter according to the law of the constitution, shall possess and retain the status of autonomous units, together with residuary powers, and exercise all powers and functions of Government and administration, save and except such powers and functions as are vested in or assigned to the Union, or as are inherent or implied in the Union or resulting therefrom; and

3. WHEREIN all powers and authority of the **Sovereign Independent India**, Its constituent parts and organs of Governments are derived from the people, and
4. Wherein shall be guaranteed and secured to all the people of India **Justice, social, economic and political; equality of status, of opportunity, and before the law; freedom of thought, expression, belief, faith, worship, vocation, association and action, subject to law and public morality** and
5. WHEREIN adequate safeguards shall be provided for **minorities, backward and tribal areas, and depressed and other backwards**; and
6. WHEREIN shall be maintained the **integrity of the territory of the Republic and Its sovereign rights on land, sea, and air according to justice and the law of civilized nations**
7. The ancient land attains Its rightful and honored place in the world and make its full and willing **contribution to the promotion of world peace and the welfare of mankind.**"

The Preamble

- The aforesaid Resolution was "something more than a resolution. It is a declaration, a firm resolve, a pledge, an undertaking and for all of us a dedication"
- It will be seen that the ideal embodied in the above Resolution is **faithfully reflected in the Preamble to the Constitution,** which, as amended in 1976, summarizes the aims and objects of the constitution
- The importance and utility of the Preamble has been pointed out in several decisions of our Supreme Court. **Though, by itself, it is not enforceable in a Court of law, the Preamble to a Written Constitution states the objects which the Constitution seeks to establish and**

promote and also aids the legal interpretation of the Constitution where the language is found to be ambiguous.

- The Preamble to our Constitution serves, two purposes:
  1. it indicates the source from which the Constitution derives its authority
  2. It also states the objects which the Constitution seeks to establish and promote.
- As has been already explained. the Constitution of India, unlike the preceding Government of India Acts, is not a gift of Sovereign the British parliament, **it is ordained by the people of India through their representatives assembled in a sovereign Constituent Assembly** which was competent to determine the political future of the country in any manner it liked.
- Sovereignty means the independent authority of a State. It means that it has the power to legislate on any subject; and that It is not subject to the control of any other State or external power.
- The Preamble declares, therefore in unequivocal terms that the source of all authority under the Constitution is the people of India and that there is no subordination to any external authority. **While Pakistan remained a British Dominion until 1956, India ceased to be a Dominion and declared herself a 'Republic' since the making of the Constitution in 1949.** It means a government by the people and for the people.

Membership of the Commonwealth of Nations

- On and from the 26th Jan, 1950, when the Constitution came into force, the Crown of England ceased to have any legal or constitutional authority over India and **no citizen of membership of the India was to have any allegiance to the British Crown.**
- But though India declared herself a Republic, she did not sever all ties with the **British Commonwealth as did Eire, by enacting the Republic of Ireland Act, 1948.**
- In fact, the conception of the Commonwealth itself has undergone a change owing to India's decision to adhere to the Commonwealth, without acknowledging allegiance to the Crown which was the symbol

of unity of the Old British Empire and also of its successor, the 'British Commonwealth of Nations'.

- It is this decision of India which has converted the 'British Common wealth', a relic of Imperialism, -into a free association of independent nations under the honorable name of the 'Commonwealth of Nations',
- This historic decision took place at the Prime Ministers' Conference at London on April 27, 1949 where our Prime Minister, Pandit Nehru, declared that notwithstanding her becoming a sovereign independent Republic. India will continue **her full membership of the Commonwealth of Nations and her acceptance of the King as the symbol of the free association of the independent nations and as such the Head of the Commonwealth."**
- It Is to be noted that this declaration is extra-legal and there is no mention of it in the Constitution of India. **It Is a voluntary declaration and indicates a free association and no obligation.**
- It accepts the Crown of England only as a symbolic head of the Commonwealth (having no functions to discharge in relation to India as belonged to him prior to the Constitution), and having no claim to the allegiance of the citizens of India.
- Even if the King or Queen of England visits India, **he or she will not be entitled to any precedence over the President of India.** Again though as a member of the Commonwealth, **India has a right to be represented on Commonwealth conferences decisions at Commonwealth conferences will not be binding on her and no treaty with a foreign power or declaration of war by any member of the Commonwealth will be binding on her without her express consent.**
- Hence, this voluntary association of India with the Commonwealth does not affect her sovereignty to any extent and it would be open to India to cut off that **association at any time she finds it not to be honorable or useful.**

Promotion of International Peace

- The great magnanimity with which India took this decision in the face of a powerful opposition at home which was the natural reaction of the manifold grievances under the imperialistic rule, and the great fortitude with which the association has still been maintained **under the pressure of repeated disappointments, the strain of baffling international alignments and the 1976 upsurge of racialism in England, speak volumes about the sincerity** of India's pledge to **contribute 'to the promotion of world peace' which is reiterated in Art. 51 of the Constitution:**

1. promote International peace and security;
2. maintain just and honorable relations between nations;
3. foster respect for International law and treaty obligations in the dealings of organized people with one another; and
4. encourage settlement of International disputes by arbitration."

- **The fraternity which is professed in the Preamble is thus not confined within the bounds of the national territory; it is ready to overflow them to reach the loftier ideal of universal brotherhood;** Thus, though India declares her sovereignty to manage her own affairs, in no unmistakable terms, the Constitution does not support **isolationism or Jingoism'**. Indian sovereignty is consistent with the concept of 'one world' international peace and amity.

Democracy

- The picture of a 'democratic republic' which the Preamble envisages is democratic not only from the political but also from the social standpoint; in other words, it envisages not only **a democratic form of government but also a democratic society**, infused with the spirit of **'justice, liberty, equality and fraternity'**.
- As a form of government, the democracy which is envisaged is, of course, **a representative democracy** and there are in Constitution no agencies of direct control by the people, such as **'referendum, or 'initiative'**.
- The people of India are to exercise their sovereignty through a Parliament at the Centre and a Legislature in each State, which is to be elected on adult franchise and to which the real Executive, namely, the Council of Ministers, shall be responsible.
- Though there shall be an elected President at the head of the Union and a Governor nominated by the President at the head of each State,

neither of them can exercise any political function without the advice of the **Council of Ministers, which is collectively responsible to the people's representatives in the respective Legislatures (excepting functions which the Governor is authorized by the Constitution itself to discharge in his discretion or on his individual responsibility)**, The Constitution holds out equality to all the citizens in the matters of choice of their representatives, who are to run the governmental machinery.

- Also known as parliamentary democracy, it envisages **(I) representation of the people, (ii) responsible government, and (ill) accountability of the Council of Ministers to the legislature.**
- The essence of this Is to draw a direct line of authority from the people through the legislature. The character and content of parliamentary democracy in the ultimate analysis depends upon the quality of persons who man the legislature as representatives of the people. **The members of the legislature, thus, must owe their power directly or indirectly to the people.**
- The ideal of a democratic republic enshrined in the Preamble of the Constitution can be best explained with reference to the **adoption of Government of the universal suffrage and the complete equality between the Sexes not only before the law but also In the political sphere. .**
- **Political Justice** means the absence of any arbitrary distinction between man and man in the political sphere. In order to ensure the **'Political' Justice** held out by the Preamble, it was essential that every person in the territory of India, irrespective of his proprietary or educational qualifications, should be allowed to participate in **the political system like any other person.**
- **Universal adult suffrage was adopted with this object in view.** This means that every five years, the members of the Legislatures of the Union and of each Stale shall be elected by the vote of the entire adult population, according to the **principle-'one man, one vote'.**
- The offering of equal opportunity to men and women, Irrespective of their caste and creed, in the matter of public employment also implements this democratic ideal. **The treatment of the minority, even**

apart from the constitutional safeguards, clearly brings out that the philosophy underlying the Constitution has not been overlooked by those in power.

- The fact that members of the Muslim and Christian communities are as a rule being included in the Council of Ministers of the Union as well as the States, in the Supreme Court, and even in Diplomatic Missions, without any constitutional reservation in that behalf, amply demonstrates that those who are working the Constitution have not missed Its true spirit, namely, **that every citizen must feel that this is country is his own.**
- That this democratic Republic stands for the good of all the people is embodied in the **concept of a 'Welfare State' which transpires the Directive Principles of State Policy.** The 'economic justice' assured by the Preamble can hardly be achieved if the democracy envisaged by the Constitution were confined to a 'political democracy'.

Economic Justice

- The State in a democratic society derives its strength from the cooperative and dispassionate will of all its free and equal citizens. Social and economic democracy is the foundation on which political democracy would be a way of life in the Indian polity
- The banishment of poverty, not by expropriation of **those who have wealth, but by the multiplication of the national wealth and resources and an equitable distribution thereof amongst all who contribute towards its production**, is the aim of the State envisaged by the **Directive Principles.**
- Economic democracy will be installed in our sub-continent to the extent that this goal is reached. In short. economic justice aims at establishing economic democracy and a 'Welfare State'.
- The ideal of economic justice is to make equality of status meaningful and life worth living at its best removing inequality of opportunity and of status--**social, economic and political.**

Social justice

- Social justice is a fundamental right, Social justice is the comprehensive form to remove social imbalance by law harmonizing the rival claims or the interests of different groups and/or sections in the social structure or individuals by means of which alone it would be possible to build up a welfare State.

- Liberty, equality and fraternity have to be secured and protected with economic empowerment and political justice to all the citizens under the rule of law.
- **Liberty:** Democracy, in any sense, cannot be established unless certain minimal rights, which are essential for a free and civilized existence, are assured to every member of the community. **The Preamble** mentions these essential individual rights as 'freedom of thought, expression, belief, faith and worship' and these are guaranteed against all the authorities of the State by **Part III of the Constitution subject, of course, to the implementation of the Directive Principles, for the common good and the 'fundamental duties', introduced [Art. 51A]. by the 42nd Amendment, 1976.**
- **'Liberty' should be coupled with social restraint and subordinated to the liberty of the greatest number for common happiness.**

Equality

- Guaranteeing of certain rights to each individual would be meaningless unless all **Inequality is banished from the social structure and each individual is assured of equality of status and opportunity for the development of the best In him and the means (or the enforcement of the rights guaranteed to him.**
- This object is secured in the body of the Constitution, by making illegal all discriminations by the State between citizen, simply on the **ground of religion, race, caste, sex or place of birth by throwing open 'public places' to all citizens by abolishing untouchability , by abolishing titles of honor; by offering equality of opportunity in matters relating to employment under the State; by guaranteeing equality before the law and equal protection of the laws, as justiciable rights**
- In addition to the above provisions to ensure **civic equality the Constitution seeks to achieve political equality** by providing for universal adult franchise [Art. 326] and by reiterating that no person shall be either excluded from the general electoral roll or allowed to be

Included in any general or special electoral roll, only on the ground of his religion, race, caste or sex.

- The realization of so many objectives would certainly mean an expansion of the functions of the State. The goal of Society envisaged by the Constitution, therefore, is that of a **'Welfare State, and the establishment of a 'socialist state'**.
- That the goal of the Indian polity is socialism was ensured by inserting through the 42 Amendment the word 'socialist' in the Preamble. It has been inserted "to spell out expressly the high ideals of socialism".
- It is to be noted, however, that the 'socialism' envisaged by the Indian Constitution is not the usual scheme of State socialism which involves 'nationalization' of all means of production, and the abolition of private property.
- Though the word 'Socialism' is vague, our Supreme Court has observed that Its **principal aim is to eliminate inequality or income and status and standards of life**, and to provide a decent standard of life to the working people.
- The Indian Constitution, therefore, does not seek to abolish private property altogether but seeks to put **it under restraints so that it may be used in the interests of the nation, which includes the upliftment of the poor.**
- Instead of a total nationalization of all property and Industry, it envisages a **'mixed economy', but aims at offering 'equal opportunity' to all, and the abolition of 'vested Interests'.**
- **From 1992 onwards the trend is now away from socialism to privatization.**
- Investment in many public enterprises has been divested in favor of private persons and many industries and services which were reserved for the government sector have been thrown open for private enterprise.
- This is in keeping with the worldwide trend after the collapse of socialism in the U.S.S.R, and East European countries. But the constitutional obligation to pay compensation to the private owner for State acquisition has been taken away by repealing **Art. 31, by the Constitution (44th Amendment) Act, 1978.**

Need for Unity and integrity of the Nation - Part of the basic structure of the Constitution

- Unity amongst the inhabitants of this vast sub-content, torn asunder by a multitude of problems was the first requisite for maintaining the independence of the country as well as to make the experiment of democracy successful.
- But neither the integration of the people nor a democratic political system could be ensured without confusion a **spirit of brotherhood amongst the heterogeneous population, belonging to different races, religions and cultures.**
- The 'Fraternity' cherished by the framers of the Constitution will be achieved not only by abolishing untouchability amongst the close aspects of the same community, but **by abolishing all communal or sectional or even local or provincial anti-social feelings which stand in the way of the unity of India.**
- Democracy would indeed be hollow if it fails to generate this spirit of brotherhood amongst all sections of the people - a feeling that they are all children of the same soil, of the same Motherland.
- The unity and fraternity of the people of India, professing numerous, Faiths, has been sought to be achieved by enshrining guaranteeing the ideal of a 'secular State" which means that the State **protects all religions equally and does not itself uphold any religion as the State religion.**
- The question of Secularism is not one of sentiments, but one of law. The secular objective of the State has been specifically **expressed by 42nd Amendment inserting the word 'secular' in the Preamble by the in 1976**
- There is no provision in the Constitution making any religion the 'established Church' as some other Constitutions do. On the other hand, the liberty of 'belief, faith and worship' promised in the Preamble is implemented by incorporating the fundamental rights of all citizens relating to **'freedom of religion'** in Arts. 25-28, which guarantee to **each individual freedom to profess, practice and propagate religion, assure strict Impartiality on the part of the State and its institutions towards all religions.**

Dignity of the Individual

- A fraternity cannot, however, be installed unless the dignity of each of its members Is maintained. The Preamble, therefore, says that the State, in India, will assure the dignity of the Individual. Our Supreme Court has come to hold that the right to dignity is a fundamental right,
- The Constitution seeks to achieve this object by guaranteeing equal fundamental rights to each individual, so that he can enforce his minimal rights, if invaded by anybody in a court of law.
- Seeing that these Justiciable rights may not be enough to maintain the dignity of an individual if he Is not free from wants and misery, a number of Directives have been molded in Part IV of the Constitution, exhorting the State so to shape its **social and economic policies that, inter alia., "all citizens, men and women equally, have the right to an adequate means of livelihood" [Art. 39(a)], "Just and humane conditions of work" [Art. 42], and "a decent standard of life and full enjoyment of leisure and social and cultural opportunities".**
- **In order to remove poverty and to bring about a socio-economic revolution,** the list of Directives was widened by the Constitution (42nd Amendment) Act, 1976, and it was provided that - in order that such welfare measures for the benefit of the masses may not be defeated any measure for the implementation of any of the **Directives shall be immune from any attack in the Courts on the ground that such measure contravenes any person's fundamental rights under Art. 14 or 19.**

Fundamental Duties

- The philosophy contained in the Preamble has been further highlighted by emphasizing that each individual shall not only have the fundamental rights in Part III of the Constitution to ensure his liberty of expression, faith and worship, equality of opportunity and the like, but also a **corresponding fundamental duty, such as to uphold the sovereignty, unity and Integrity of the nation, to maintain secularism and the common brotherhood amongst all the people of India.**
- This has been done by inserting Art, 51A, laying down ten 'Fundamental Duties', by the Constitution (42nd Amendment) Act, 1976

- Combining the ideals of political, social and economic democracy with that of equality and fraternity, the Preamble seeks to establish what Mahatma Gandhi described as **"the India or My Dreams"**

Introduction

Lengthiest written constitution: 465 articles [25 parts] and 12 schedules. This can be due to vast geographic factors, vast historical factors, single constitution for Centre and States, dominance of legal luminaries in the assembly.

Drawn from various constitutions of the world: Structural part [GoI Act, 1935], political part [British constitution].

Partly rigid and flexible

Federal with unitary bias: There are certain federal features of the constitution viz. Two governments, separation of powers, bicameralism, written constitution – rigid and supreme, independent judiciary. The nonfederal features are strong Centre, singe constitution, single citizenship, no equal representation to states in upper house, destructible states, states can't cede from union, integrated audit, election machinery. All India service, appointment of governor and veto over state bills.

Parliamentary form of government: Indian democracy is based on Westminster model i.e. Leadership of PM, dissolution of lower house, dual membership of Executive, Legislature is supreme, Majority party rule. However, some differences between Indian and British systems are Indian Parliament isn't sovereign body unlike British and President isn't a hereditary head but elected.

Balance between Judicial and Parliamentary supremacy: Indian constitution has mentioned "Procedure established by law" which reduces judicial review by courts unlike in USA ["due process of law"]. Thus Indian courts can invalidate laws only if they are unconstitutional, but parliament can use its constituent power to amend the constitution.

Integrated and independent judiciary: A single system of courts enforces for both union and state laws. Independence of courts is ensured by security of tenure, protection against arbitrary removal, all expense charged on the consolidated fund, ban on employment after retirement, contempt of court.

Fundamental rights: Justifiable by courts. Guarantee political democracy. Inspired by USA constitution. Protect against arbitrary laws of legislature and tyranny of executive. The courts can issue writs to enforce these rights. These can be suspended during emergency. However reasonable restrictions can be placed on these rights.

Directive principles of state policy: These are non-justifiable, non-enforceable by courts. They are meant to promote social, economic democracy. They are inspired by Irish constitution. They are also part of Instrument of instructions in GoI Act, 1935.

Fundamental duties: These were added by the 42nd amendment. They are inspired from Russian constitution. They are non-justifiable and non-enforceable by courts.

Secular state: This word was added to the preamble by 42nd amendment. Western concept of secularism "Separation of church and state" doesn't apply to India due to its multi-religious nature. Indian secularism is positive "State shall treat all religions equally".

Universal franchise: This was unanimously agreed by the constituent assembly. All people above age 18 [reduced from 21 by 61st constitution amendment] can vote. This ensures broad based participation in the democracy.

Single citizenship: Irrespective of state in which they are born or reside all people enjoy same political rights.

Independent bodies: Certain bodies have been created like CAG, EC, and UPSC etc.

Emergency provision: To protect sovereignty, security, integrity, unity constitution has certain emergency powers. During emergencies, Centre becomes all powerful and states go into its total control. This converts federal structure into unitary without formal amendment to the constitution [unique feature].

Constitutional recognition to local governments [73rd, 74th **amendment**] **is also unique to India.**

Inspired from other constitutions

- Fundamental rights – USA
- Fundamental duties – USSR
- Directive principles – Irish

- Procedure established by law – Japan
- Scheme of Indian federation, residuary powers – Canada
- Procedure to amend constitution – South Africa
- Emergency powers – Germany
- Concurrent list – Australia
- Liberty, equality, fraternity – French

Directive Principles of State Policy (DPSP)

Articles 36-51 under Part-IV of Indian Constitution deal with Directive Principles of State Policy (DPSP). They are borrowed from the Constitution of Ireland, which had copied it from the Spanish Constitution. This article will solely discuss the Directive Principles of State Policy, its importance in the Indian Constitution and the history of its conflict with Fundamental Rights. This topic is important for UPSC Mains GS-II and also for political science optional papers and aspirants can also download the DPSP notes.

Indian Constitution has not originally classified DPSPs but on the basis of their content and direction, they are usually classified into three types-

- **Socialistic Principles,**
- **Gandhian Principles** and,
- **Liberal-Intellectual Principles.**

The details of the three types of DPSPs are given below:

DPSP – Socialistic Principles	
Definition: They are the principles that aim at providing social and economic justice and set the path towards the welfare state. Under various articles, they direct the state to:	
Article 38	Promote the welfare of the people by securing a social order through justice—social, economic and political—and to minimize inequalities in income, status, facilities and opportunities
Article 39	Secure citizens: ❖ Right to adequate means of livelihood for all citizens ❖ Equitable distribution of material resources of the community for the common good ❖ Prevention of concentration of wealth and means of production ❖ Equal pay for equal work for men and women ❖ Preservation of the health and strength of workers and children against forcible abuse ❖ Opportunities for the healthy development of children

Article 39A	Promote equal justice and free legal aid to the poor
Article 41	In cases of unemployment, old age, sickness and disablement, secure citizens: ❖ Right to work ❖ Right to education ❖ Right to public assistance,
Article 42	Make provision for just and humane conditions of work and maternity relief
Article 43	Secure a living wage, a decent standard of living and social and cultural opportunities for all workers
Article 43A	Take steps to secure the participation of workers in the management of industries
Article 47	Raise the level of nutrition and the standard of living of people and to improve public health

DPSP – Gandhian Principles	
Definition: These principles are based on Gandhian ideology used to represent the programme of reconstruction enunciated by Gandhi during the national movement. Under various articles, they direct the state to:	
Article 40	Organize village panchayats and endow them with necessary powers and authority to enable them to function as units of self-government
Article 43	Promote cottage industries on an individual or co-operation basis in rural areas
Article 43B	Promote voluntary formation, autonomous functioning, democratic control and professional management of co-operative societies
Article 46	Promote the educational and economic interests of SCs, STs, and other weaker sections of the society and to protect them from social injustice and exploitation
Article 47	Prohibit the consumption of intoxicating drinks and drugs which are injurious to health
Article 48	Prohibit the slaughter of cows, calves and other milch and draught cattle and to improve their breeds

DPSP – Liberal-Intellectual Principles	
Definition: These principles reflect the ideology of liberalism. Under various articles, they direct the state to:	
Article 44	Secure for all citizens a uniform civil code throughout the country
Article 45	Provide early childhood care and education for all children until they complete the age of six years

Article 48	Organize agriculture and animal husbandry on modern and scientific lines
Article 49	Protect monuments, places and objects of artistic or historic interest which are declared to be of national importance
Article 50	Separate the judiciary from the executive in the public services of the State
Article 51	Promote international peace and security and maintain just and honorable relations between nations Foster respect for international law and treaty obligations Encourage settlement of international disputes by arbitration

Directive Principles of State Policy's notes about its classification is important for UPSC 2021 and aspirants should learn these with articles mentioned.

What are the new DPSPs added by the 42nd Amendment Act, 1976?

42nd Amendment Act, 1976 added four new Directive Principles in the list:

S. No	Article	New DPSPs
1	**Article 39**	To secure opportunities for the healthy development of children
2	**Article 39A**	To promote equal justice and to provide free legal aid to the poor
3	**Article 43A**	To take steps to secure the participation of workers in the management of industries
4	**Article 48A**	To protect and improve the environment and to safeguard forests and wildlife

Fundamental Duties of Indian Citizens

Fundamental Duties were incorporated in the Indian Constitution by the 42nd amendment. There are 11 Fundamental Duties for Indian Citizens drafted on the lines of moral, ethical and culture code of conduct followed by people. The duties are educative in nature and direct the citizens to behave in a virtuous and honorable manner.

1. Abide by the Constitution and respect national flag & National Anthem
2. Follow ideals of the freedom struggle
3. Protect sovereignty & integrity of India
4. Defend the country and render national services when called upon
5. Sprit of common brotherhood
6. Preserve composite culture

7. Preserve natural environment
8. Develop scientific temper
9. Safeguard public property
10. Strive for excellence
11. Duty for all parents/guardians to send their children in the age group of 6-14 years to school.

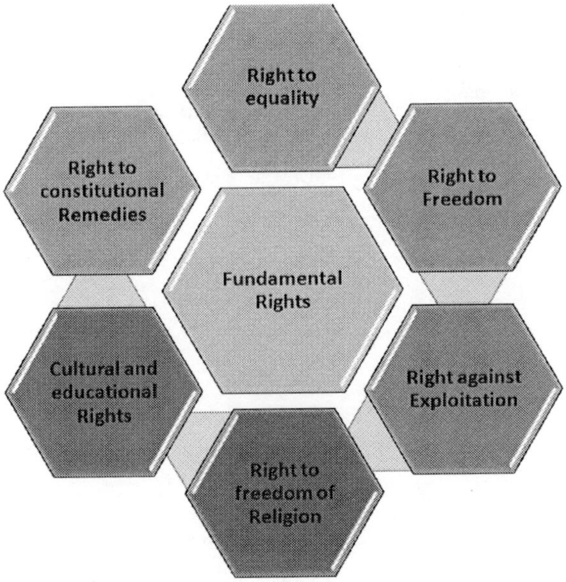

CLASSIFICATION OF DIRECTIVE PRINCIPLES OF STATE POLICY

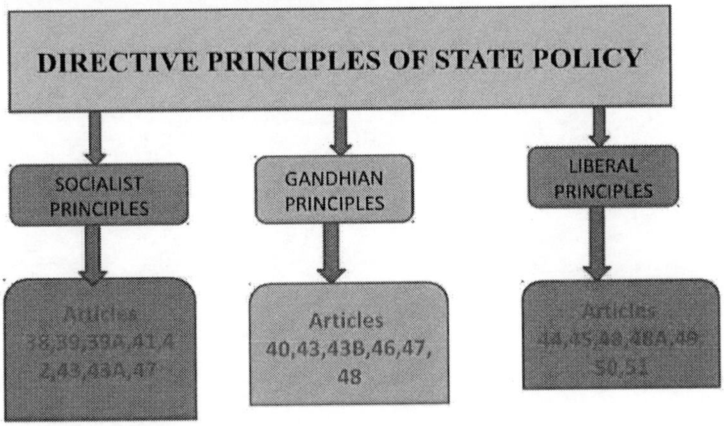

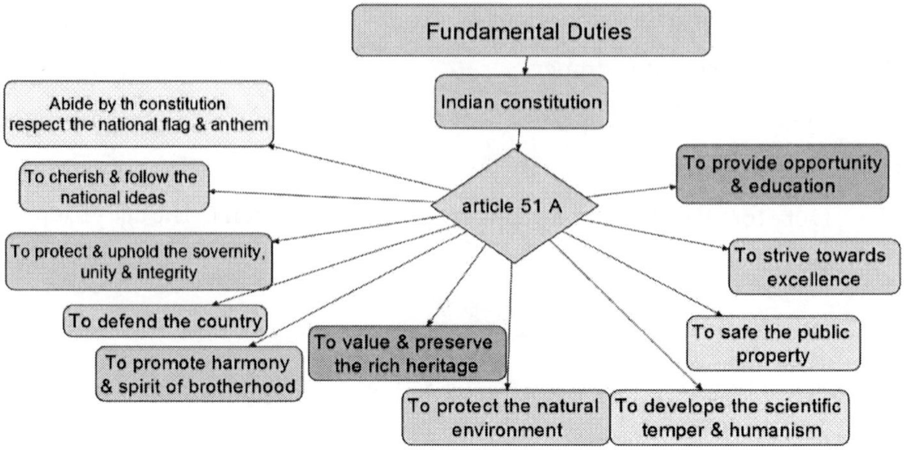
Fundamental Duties
Indian constitution
article 51 A
Abide by th constitution respect the national flag & anthem
To cherish & follow the national ideas
To protect & uphold the sovernity, unity & integrity
To defend the country
To promote harmony & spirit of brotherhood
To value & preserve the rich heritage
To protect the natural environment
To develope the scientific temper & humanism
To safe the public property
To strive towards excellence
To provide opportunity & education

Chapter Two

Three branches of government

- Legislative
- Executive
- Judiciary

The modern India Government was originally formed through the Constitution of India. The Constitution was approved by India's law making officials, officially known as the Constituent Assembly, on November 26, 1949 and went into effect on January 21, 1950. The reason this important document was created such as short time ago, is because India was ruled by the British and British approved princely states for the time period prior to the constitution's creation. The government of India is officially known as the Union Government, but is also sometimes referred to as the Central Government as well. Whatever you call it; it is the powerful governing authority of the Indian union, which is made up of 28 states and seven union territories. Together, these states and union territories are known as the Republic of India.

The India Government leaders are located in New Delhi, which is the capital of India. It's what Washington, DC is to the United States. Like the United States, there are three branches of the government in India that were established in order to check and balance the overall government. These three branches of government are the executive, the legislative and the judiciary branches, just like in the United States.

The executive branch is led by the President; he is Head of State and either exercises his powers directly, or through officers that rank beneath him. One difference in the government of India's executive branch versus the United States executive branch is that India's also has a Prime Minister, similar to Britain's.

The President selects a Prime Minister that he believes will be able to successfully lead the Lok Sabha, which is the Lower House of the People in India, representing the greater population. The person selected for this important role is usually the same person that leads India's majority party. This is one of the most powerful positions in the India Government.

The President also appoints the members of the Council of Ministers and he delivers instructive portfolios to these members based on the direction or opinion of the Prime Minister. The Council of Ministers stays in power during the President's term, but the Council of Ministers has to remain in the favor of the Lok Sabha. The President cannot dismiss Council Ministers on his own because it could lead to a constitutional crisis. So, the Council of Ministers cannot be dismissed as long as they have the support of the majority in the Lok Sabha.

1Save

The Legislative branch, or Parliament, includes the lower house, called the Lok Sabha, and the upper house, called the Rajya Sabha. The president works with the house to make, change and enforce policies over the Republic of India. The Lower House and the Upper House are similar to the Congress and the Senate of the United States, as far as their role to the Republic of India.

The Judicial branch is led by India's Supreme Court and it includes 21 High Courts, and numerous civil, criminal and family courts at the district level. The primary civil and criminal laws that govern India are written in the legislation of the Parliament. Indian Civil Procedure Code, Indian Penal Code, and the Criminal Procedure Code are examples of these. Each union and individual state government includes its own executive, legislative and judicial branches too. Thus, the India Government is duplicated on a more local level to the people who reside in each district of India.

India's legal system applies to both the federal and individual state governments. It's based on the English Common and Statutory Law, which was directly influenced through the British Occupation. India does accept International Court of Justice jurisdiction, with several reservations, and is now an independent nation. In recent years, India has bulked up its military weaponry and army to address China, who became its biggest threat in the region after tension between India and Pakistan recently died down.

Indian Legislature

PARLIAMENT OF INDIA

Legislature of the Union, which is called Parliament, consists of **the President and two Houses**, known as Council of States (Rajya Sabha) and House of the People (Lok Sabha). Each House has to meet within six months of its previous sitting. A joint sitting of two Houses can be held in certain cases.

Rajya Sabha

The Constitution provides that the Rajya Sabha shall consist of 250 members, of which 12 members shall be nominated by the President from amongst persons having special knowledge or practical experience in respect of such matters as literature, science, art and social service; and not more than 238 representatives of the States and of the Union Territories.

Elections to the Rajya Sabha are indirect; members representing States are elected by elected members of legislative assemblies of the States in accordance with the system of proportional representation by means of the single transferable vote, and those representing Union Territories are chosen in such manner as

Parliament may by law prescribe. The Rajya Sabha is not subject to dissolution; one-third of its members retire every second year.

Rajya Sabha, at present, has 245 seats. Of these, 233 members represent the States and the Union Territories, and 12 members are nominated by the President.

Lok Sabha

The Lok Sabha is composed of representatives of people chosen by direct election on the basis of adult suffrage. The maximum strength of the House envisaged by the Constitution is now 552 (530 members to represent States, 20 to represent Union Territories, and not more than two members of the Anglo-Indian community to be nominated by the President, if, in his opinion, that community is not adequately represented in the House). The total elective membership of the Lok Sabha is distributed among States in such a way that the ratio between the number of seats allotted to each State and population of the State is, as far as practicable, the same for all States. The Lok Sabha at present consists of 545 members. Of these, 530 members are directly elected from the States and 13 from Union Territories, while two are nominated by the President to represent the Anglo-Indian community. Following the Constitution 84th Amendment Act, the total number of existing seats as allocated to various States in the Lok Sabha on the basis of the 1971 census, shall remain unaltered till the first census to be taken after the year 2026.

The term of the Lok Sabha, unless dissolved earlier, is five years from the date appointed for its first meeting. However, while a proclamation of emergency is in operation, this period may be extended by Parliament by law for a period not exceeding one year at a time, and not extending in any case, beyond a period of six months after the proclamation has ceased to operate. Fourteen Lok Sabha have been constituted so far.

Qualification for Membership of Parliament

In order to be chosen a member of Parliament, a person must be a citizen of India and not less than 30 years of age in the case of Rajya Sabha and not less than 25 years of age in the case of Lok Sabha. Additional qualifications may be prescribed by Parliament by law.

Functions and Powers of Parliament

As in other parliamentary democracies, the Parliament in India has the cardinal functions of legislation, overseeing of administration, passing of the Budget, ventilation of public grievances and discussing various subjects like development plans, national policies and international relations. The distribution of powers between the Union and the States, followed in the Constitution, emphasizes in many ways the general predominance of Parliament in the legislative field. Apart from a wide-range of subjects, even in normal times, the Parliament can, under certain circumstances, assume legislative power with respect to a subject falling within the sphere exclusively reserved for the States. The Parliament is also vested with powers to impeach the President and to remove the Judges of Supreme Court and High Courts, the Chief Election Commissioner and the Comptroller and Auditor General in accordance with the procedure laid down in the Constitution.

All legislation require consent of both the Houses of Parliament. In the case of money bills, however, the will of the Lok Sabha prevails. Delegated legislation is also subject to review and control by Parliament. Besides the power to legislate, the Constitution vests in Parliament the power to initiate amendment of the Constitution.

Executive

The Union executive consists of the President, the Vice-President, and the Council of Ministers with the Prime Minister as the head to aid and advise the President.

President

The President is elected by members of an electoral college consisting of elected members of both Houses of Parliament and Legislative Assemblies of the states in accordance with the system of proportional representation, by means of single transferable vote. To secure uniformity among state inter se, as well as parity between the states as a whole, and the Union, suitable weightage is given to each vote. The President must be a citizen of India, not less than 35 years of age, and qualified for election as member of the Lok Sabha. His term of office is five years, and he is eligible for re-election. His removal from office is to be in accordance with procedure prescribed in Article 61 of the Constitution. He may, by writing under his hand addressed to the Vice-President, resign his office.

Executive power of the Union is vested in the President, and is exercised by him either directly or through officers subordinate to him in accordance with the Constitution. Supreme command of defense forces of the Union also vests in him. The President summons, prorogues, addresses, sends messages to Parliament and dissolves the Lok Sabha, promulgates Ordinances at any time, except when both Houses of Parliament are in session, makes recommendations for introducing financial and money bills and gives assent to bills, grants pardons, reprieves, respites or remission of punishment or suspends, and remits or commutes sentences in certain cases. When there is a failure of the constitutional machinery in a state, he can assume to himself all, or any of the functions of the government of that state. The President can proclaim emergency in the country if he is satisfied that a grave emergency exists, whereby security of India or any part of its territory is threatened, whether by war or external aggression or armed rebellion.

Vice-President

The Vice-President is elected by members of an electoral college consisting of members of both Houses of Parliament in accordance with the system of proportional representation by means of single transferable vote. He must be a citizen of India, not less than 35 years of age, and eligible for election as a member of the Rajya Sabha. His term of office is five years, and he is eligible for re-election. His removal from office is to be in accordance with procedure prescribed in Article 67 b.

The Vice-President is ex-officio Chairman of the Rajya Sabha and acts as President when the latter is unable to discharge his functions due to absence, illness or any other cause, or till the election of a new President (to be held within six months when a vacancy is caused by death, resignation or removal or otherwise of President). While so acting, he ceases to perform the function of the Chairman of the Rajya Sabha.

Council of Ministers

There is a Council of Ministers headed by the Prime Minister to aid and advise the President in exercise of his functions. The Prime Minister is appointed by the President, who also appoints other ministers on the advice of Prime Minister. The Council is collectively responsible to the Lok Sabha. It is the duty of the Prime Minister to communicate to the President all decisions of Council of

Ministers relating to administration of affairs of the Union and proposals for legislation and information relating to them.

The Council of Ministers comprises Ministers who are members of Cabinet, Ministers of State (independent charge), Ministers of State and Deputy Ministers.

Judiciary System in India

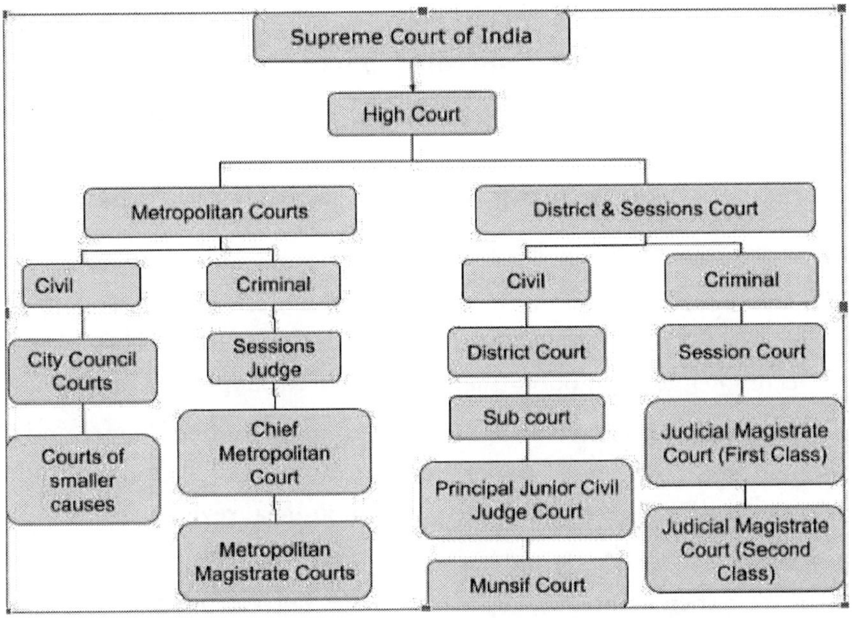

The **Supreme Court of India** (IAST: *Bhāratīya Ucchatama Nyāyālaya*) is the supreme judicial body of India and the highest court of India under the constitution. It is the most senior constitutional court, and has the power of judicial review. The Chief Justice of India is the head and chief judge of the Supreme Court, which consists of a maximum of 34 judges and has extensive powers in the form of original, appellate and advisory jurisdictions. It is regarded as the most powerful public institution in India.

As the apex constitutional court in India, it takes up appeals primarily against verdicts of the high courts of various states of the Union and other courts and tribunals. It is required to safeguard the fundamental rights of citizens and settles disputes between various government authorities as well as the central government vs state governments or state governments versus another state government in the country. As an advisory court, it hears matters which may specifically be referred to it under the Constitution by President of India. The law declared by the Supreme Court becomes binding on all courts within India and also by the union and state governments. As per the Article 142 of the Constitution, it is the duty of the President of India to enforce the decrees of the Supreme Court and the court is conferred with the inherent jurisdiction to pass any order deemed necessary in the interest of justice. The Supreme Court has replaced the Judicial Committee of the Privy Council as the highest court of appeal since 28 January 1950.

Eligibility of a judge of the Supreme Court

A citizen of India not exceeding 65 years' age per Article 124 of the Constitution who has been:

- a judge of one high court or more (continuously), for at least five years,
- an advocate there, for at least ten years,
- a distinguished jurist, in the opinion of the president, power conferred by clause 2 of article 124 of the Constitution of India is eligible to be recommended for appointment, a judge of the Supreme Court.
- The **Supreme Court of India** is the **highest judicial court** and the **final court of appeal** under the Constitution of India, the **highest constitutional court,** with the power of **judicial review.**
- India is a federal State and has a **single and unified judicial system** with **three tier structure,** i.e. Supreme Court, High Courts and Subordinate Courts.

Important Institution Supreme Court of India

- 11 Sep 2019
- 23 min read

Tags:

GS Paper - 2

Judiciary

The **Supreme Court of India** is the **highest judicial court** and the **final court of appeal** under the Constitution of India, the **highest constitutional court,** with the power of **judicial review.**

- India is a federal State and has a **single and unified judicial system** with **three tier structure,** i.e. Supreme Court, High Courts and Subordinate Courts.

Brief History of the Supreme Court of India

- The promulgation of **Regulating Act of 1773** established the **Supreme Court of Judicature at Calcutta** as a **Court of Record, with full power & authority.**
- **It was established** to hear and determine all complaints for any crimes and also to entertain, hear and determine any suits or actions in **Bengal, Bihar and Orissa.**
- The **Supreme Courts at Madras and Bombay** were established by **King George – III** in **1800 and 1823 respectively.**
- The **India High Courts Act 1861** created High Courts for various provinces and **abolished Supreme Courts at Calcutta, Madras and Bombay** and also the **Sadar Adalats in Presidency towns.**
- These High Courts had the distinction of being the highest Courts for all cases till the creation of **Federal Court of India** under the **Government of India Act 1935.**
- The **Federal Court** had jurisdiction to solve disputes between provinces and federal states and hear appeal against Judgements from High Courts.
- After India attained independence in 1947, the Constitution of India came into being on **26 January 1950.** The **Supreme Court of India** also came into existence and its first sitting was held on 28 January 1950.
- The law declared by the Supreme Court is **binding on all Courts** within the territory of India.
- It has the power of **judicial review** – to strike down the legislative and executive action contrary to the provisions and the scheme of the constitution, the distribution of power between Union and States or inimical to the fundamental rights guaranteed by the Constitution.

Constitutional Provisions

- The Indian constitution provides for a provision of Supreme Court under **Part V (The Union)** and **Chapter 6 (The Union Judiciary).**

- **Articles 124 to 147 in Part V** of the Constitution deal with the organization, independence, jurisdiction, powers and procedures of the Supreme Court.
- The Indian constitution under **Article 124(1)** states that there shall be a Supreme Court of India constituting of a Chief Justice of India (CJI) and, until Parliament by law prescribes a larger number, of not more than seven other Judges.
- The Jurisdiction of the Supreme Court of India can broadly be categorized into **original jurisdiction, appellate jurisdiction and advisory jurisdiction.** However, there are other multiple powers of the Supreme Court.

Organization of Supreme Court

- At present, the Supreme Court consists of thirty-one judges (one chief justice and thirty other judges).
    - **Supreme Court (Number of Judges) Bill of 2019** has added four judges to strength. It increased the judicial strength from 31 to 34, including the CJI.
- Originally, the strength of the Supreme Court was fixed at eight (one chief justice and seven other judges).
- The Parliament is authorized to regulate them.

Seat of Supreme Court

- The **Constitution declares Delhi as the seat of the Supreme Court.** It also authorizes the **CJI** to appoint other place or places as seat of the Supreme Court.
- He can take decision in this regard only with the approval of the President. **This provision is only optional and not compulsory.** This means that no court can give any direction either to the President or to the Chief Justice to appoint any other place as the seat of the Supreme Court.

Appointment of Judges

- The **judges of the Supreme Court** are appointed by the **President.** The CJI is appointed by the President after **consultation with such judges of the Supreme Court** and high courts as he deems necessary.

- The other judges are appointed by the President after **consultation** with the CJI and such other judges of the Supreme Court and the high courts as he deems necessary. The consultation with the chief justice is **obligatory** in the case of appointment of a judge other than Chief justice.
- **Appointment of Chief Justice from 1950 to 1973:** The practice has been to appoint the senior most judge of the Supreme Court as the chief justice of India. This established convention was violated in 1973 when **A N Ray** was appointed as the **Chief Justice of India by superseding three senior judges.** Again in 1977, M U Beg was appointed as the chief justice of India by superseding the then senior-most judge.
    - This discretion of the government was curtailed by the Supreme Court in the **Second Judges Case (1993)**, in which the Supreme Court ruled that **the senior most judge of the Supreme Court** should **alone be appointed to the office of the Chief Justice of India.**

Controversy over Consultation and Evolution of Collegium system

- The Supreme Court has given different interpretations of the word 'consultation' in the above mentioned provisions.
    - In the **First Judges case (1982)**, the Court held that consultation does not mean concurrence and it only implies exchange of views.
    - In the **Second Judges case (1993)**, the Court reversed its earlier ruling and changed the meaning of the word consultation to **concurrence.**
    - In the **Third Judges case (1998)**, the Court opined that the consultation process to be adopted by the **Chief Justice of India** requires '**consultation of plurality judges**'.
- The sole opinion of the CJI does not constitute the consultation process. He should consult a **collegium of four senior most judges of the Supreme Court** and even if two judges give an adverse opinion, he should not send the recommendation to the government.
- The court held that **the recommendation made by the chief justice of India** without complying with the norms and requirements of the consultation process are not binding on the government.

Collegium System

- Collegium system was born through **"three judges case"** and it is in practice since 1998. It is used for appointments and transfers of judges in High courts and Supreme Courts.
- There is no mention of the Collegium either in the original Constitution of India or in successive amendments

Working of Collegium System and NJAC

- The collegium recommends of the names of lawyers or judges to the Central Government. Similarly, the Central Government also sends some of its proposed names to the Collegium.
- Collegium considers the names or suggestions made by the Central Government and resends the file to the government for final approval.
    - If the **Collegium resends** the same name again then the government has to give its assent to the names. But **time limit is not fixed** to reply. This is the reason that appointment of judges takes a long time.
- Through the 99th **Constitutional Amendment Act, 2014 the National Judicial Commission Act (NJAC)** was established to replace the collegium system for the appointment of judges.
- However, the Supreme Court **upheld the collegium system and struck down the NJAC as unconstitutional** on the grounds that the involvement of **Political Executive** in judicial appointment was **against the "Principles of Basic Structure". I.e.** the **"Independence of Judiciary".**

Qualifications of Judges

- A person to be appointed as a judge of the Supreme Court should have the following qualifications:
    - He should be a **citizen of India.**
    - He should have been a **judge of a High Court** (or high courts in succession) **for five years;** or
    - He should have been an advocate of a High Court (or High Courts in succession) for ten years; or

- He should be **a distinguished jurist in the opinion of the president.**

❖ The Constitution **has not prescribed a minimum age** for appointment as a judge of the Supreme Court.

Oath or Affirmation

❖ A person appointed as a judge of the Supreme Court, before entering upon his office, has to make and subscribe to an **oath or affirmation before the President,** or some other person appointed by him for this purpose. In his oath, a judge of the Supreme Court swears:

- to bear true faith and allegiance to the Constitution of India;
- to uphold the sovereignty and integrity of India;
- to duly and faithfully and to the best of his ability, knowledge and judgement to perform the duties of the Office without fear or favor, affection or ill-will; and
- to uphold the Constitution and the laws.

Tenure of Judges

❖ The Constitution has not fixed the tenure of a judge of the Supreme Court. However, it makes the following three provisions in this regard:

- He holds office until he attains the age of 65 years. Any question regarding his age is to be determined by such authority and in such manner as provided by Parliament.
- He can resign his office by writing to the President.
- He can be removed from his office by the President on the recommendation of the Parliament.

Removal of Judges

❖ A judge of the Supreme Court can be removed from his office by an **order of the President.** The President can issue the removal order only after an address by Parliament has been presented to him in the same session for such removal.

❖ The address must be supported by a **special majority** of each House of Parliament (ie, a majority of the total membership of that House and a majority of not less than **two-thirds of the members** of that

House present and voting). The grounds of removal are two—**proved misbehavior or incapacity.**

- **The Judges Enquiry Act (1968)** regulates the procedure relating to the removal of a judge of the Supreme Court by the process of impeachment:
  - **No judge of the Supreme Court has been impeached** so far. Impeachment motions of Justice V Ramaswami (1991–1993) and the Justice Dipak Misra (2017-18) were defeated in the Parliament.

Salaries and Allowances

- The salaries, allowances, privileges, leave and pension of the judges of the Supreme Court are **determined from time to time by the Parliament.** They cannot be varied to their disadvantage after their appointment except during a financial emergency.

Acting Chief Justice

- The President can appoint a judge of the Supreme Court as an acting Chief Justice of India when:
  - the office of Chief Justice of India is vacant; or
  - the Chief Justice of India is temporarily absent; or
  - the Chief Justice of India is unable to perform the duties of his office.

Ad hoc Judge

- When there is a **lack of quorum** of the permanent judges to hold or continue any session of the Supreme Court, **the Chief Justice of India** can **appoint a judge of a High Court as an ad hoc judge of the Supreme Court** for a temporary period. He can do so only after consultation with the Chief Justice of the High Court concerned and with the previous consent of the president.
- The judge so appointed should be **qualified for appointment as a judge of the Supreme Court.** It is the duty of the judge so appointed to attend the sittings of the Supreme Court, in priority to other duties of his office. While so attending, he enjoys all the jurisdiction, powers and privileges (and discharges the duties) of a judge of the Supreme Court.

Retired Judges

- At any time, the **CJI can request a retired judge** of the Supreme Court or a retired judge of a high court (who is duly qualified for appointment as a judge of the Supreme Court) to act as a judge of the Supreme Court for a temporary period.
- He can do so only with the **previous consent of the President** and also of the person to be so appointed.
    - Such a judge is entitled to such allowances as the president may determine. He will also enjoy all the jurisdiction, powers and privileges of a judge of the Supreme Court. But, he will not otherwise be deemed to be a judge of the Supreme Court.

Jurisdiction and Powers of Supreme Court

Original Jurisdiction

- As a Federal court, the Supreme Court decides disputes between different units of the Indian Federation. More elaborately, any dispute between:
    - the Centre and one or more states; or
    - the Centre and any state or states on one side and one or more states on the other; or
    - between two or more states.
- In the above federal disputes, the Supreme Court has **exclusive original jurisdiction.**
- Further, this jurisdiction of the Supreme Court **does not extend** to the following:
    - A dispute arising out of any pre-Constitution treaty, agreement, covenant,
    - engagement, sanad or other similar instrument.
    - A dispute arising out of any treaty, agreement, etc.,which specifically provides that the said jurisdiction does not extent to such a dispute.
    - Inter-state water disputes.
    - Matters referred to the Finance Commission.

- Adjustment of certain expenses and pensions between the Centre and the states.
- Ordinary dispute of Commercial nature between the Centre and the states.
- Recovery of damages by a state against the Centre.

Writ Jurisdiction

❖ The Supreme Court is empowered to issue writs, including **habeas corpus, mandamus, prohibition, quo-warranto and certiorari** for the enforcement of the fundamental rights of an aggrieved citizen.

- In this regard, the Supreme Court has **original jurisdiction** in the sense that an aggrieved citizen can go directly to the Supreme Court, not necessarily by way of appeal.
- However, the writ jurisdiction of the Supreme Court is not exclusive. The High Courts are also empowered to issue writs for the enforcement of the Fundamental Rights.

Appellate Jurisdiction

❖ The Supreme Court is primarily a court of appeal and hears appeals against the judgements of the lower courts. It enjoys a wide appellate jurisdiction which can be classified under four heads:

- Appeals in constitutional matters
- Appeals in civil matters
- Appeals in criminal matters
- Appeals by special leave

Advisory Jurisdiction

❖ The Constitution **under Article 143** authorises the President to seek the opinion of the Supreme Court in the two categories of matters:

- On any question of law or fact of public importance which has arisen or which is likely to arise.
- On any dispute arising out of any pre-constitution treaty, agreement, covenant, engagement, sanad or other similar instruments.

A Court of Record

- As a Court of Record, the Supreme Court has two powers:
  - The judgements, proceedings and acts of the Supreme Court are recorded for perpetual memory and testimony. These records are admitted to be of evidentiary value and cannot be questioned when produced before any court.
  - They are **recognized as legal precedents and legal references.**
  - It has power to **punish for contempt of court,** either with simple imprisonment for a term up to six months or with fine up to 2,000 or with both.

Power of Judicial Review

- Judicial review is the power of the Supreme Court to examine the constitutionality of legislative enactments and executive orders of both the Central and state governments.
  - On examination, if they are found to be **violate of the Constitution (ultra-vires)**, they can be declared as **illegal, unconstitutional and invalid (null and void)** by the Supreme Court. Consequently, they cannot be enforced by the Government.

Recent issues in Supreme Court

- **Master of Roster:** It refers to the privilege of the Chief Justice to constitute Benches to hear cases.
  - The controversy has emerged in the Supreme Court over **absolute power of Chief Justice** on the judicial administration.
  - The SC has upheld a number of times that "the Chief Justice is the master of the roster and he alone has the prerogative to constitute the Benches of the Court and allocate cases to the Benches so constituted."
  - Be it the Chief Justice of India or Chief Justice of any high court it is he or she who heads the **administrative** side. This includes allocation of matters before a judge as well.
- So, no Judge can take up the matter on his own, unless allocated by the Chief Justice of India.

HIGH COURTS:

The **High courts of India** are the principal civil courts of original jurisdiction in each state and union territory. However, a high court exercises its original civil and criminal jurisdiction only if the subordinate courts are not authorized by law to try such matters for lack of pecuniary, territorial jurisdiction. High courts may also enjoy original jurisdiction in certain matters, if so designated Specially in a state or federal law.

Basically, the work of highest courts primarily consists of appeals from lower courts and writ petitions in terms of Articles 226 and 227 of the constitution. Writ jurisdiction is also an original jurisdiction of a high court.

Each state is divided into judicial districts presided over by a district and sessions judge. He is known as district judge when he presides over a civil case, and session's judge when he presides over a criminal case. He is the highest judicial authority below a high court judge. Below him, there are courts of civil jurisdiction, known by different names in different states. Under Article 141 of the constitution, all courts in India — including high courts — are bounded by the judgments and orders of the Supreme Court of India by precedence.

Judges in a high court are appointed by the President of India in consultation with the Chief Justice of India and the governor of the state. High courts are headed by a chief justice. The chief justices rank fourteenth (within their respective states) and seventeenth (outside their respective states) on the Indian order of precedence. The number of judges in a court is decided by dividing the average institution of main cases during the last five years by the national average, or the average rate of disposal of main cases per judge per year in that High Court, whichever is higher.

The **High courts of India** are the principal civil courts of original jurisdiction in each state and union territory. However, a high court exercises its original civil and criminal jurisdiction only if the subordinate courts are not authorized by law to try such matters for lack of pecuniary, territorial jurisdiction. High courts may also enjoy original jurisdiction in certain matters, if so designated Specially in a state or federal law.

Basically, the work of high courts primarily consists of appeals from lower courts and writ petitions in terms of Articles 226 and 227 of the constitution. Writ jurisdiction is also an original jurisdiction of a high court.

Each state is divided into judicial districts presided over by a district and sessions judge. He is known as district judge when he presides over a civil case, and session's judge when he presides over a criminal case. He is the highest judicial authority below a high court judge. Below him, there are courts of civil jurisdiction, known by different names in different states. Under Article 141 of the constitution, all courts in India — including high courts — are bounded by the judgments and orders of the Supreme Court of India by precedence.

Judges in a high court are appointed by the President of India in consultation with the Chief Justice of India and the governor of the state. High courts are headed by a chief justice. The chief justices rank fourteenth (within their respective states) and seventeenth (outside their respective states) on the Indian order of precedence. The number of judges in a court is decided by dividing the average institution of main cases during the last five years by the national average, or the average rate of disposal of main cases per judge per year in that High Court, whichever is higher.

PUBLIC INTERST LITIGATION

Judiciary, being the sentinel of constitutional statutory rights of citizens has a special role to play in the constitutional scheme. It can review legislation and administrative actions or decisions on the anvil of constitutional law. For the enforcement of fundamental rights one has to move the Supreme Court or the High Courts directly by invoking Writ Jurisdiction of these courts. But the high cost and complicated procedure involved in litigation, however, makes equal access to jurisdiction in mere slogan in respect of millions of destitute and underprivileged masses stricken by poverty, illiteracy and ignorance. The Supreme Court of India, pioneered the Public Interest Litigation (PIL) thereby throwing upon the portals of courts to the common man.

Chapter Three

Local Self Government

73rd & 74th Amendmet & their implementation

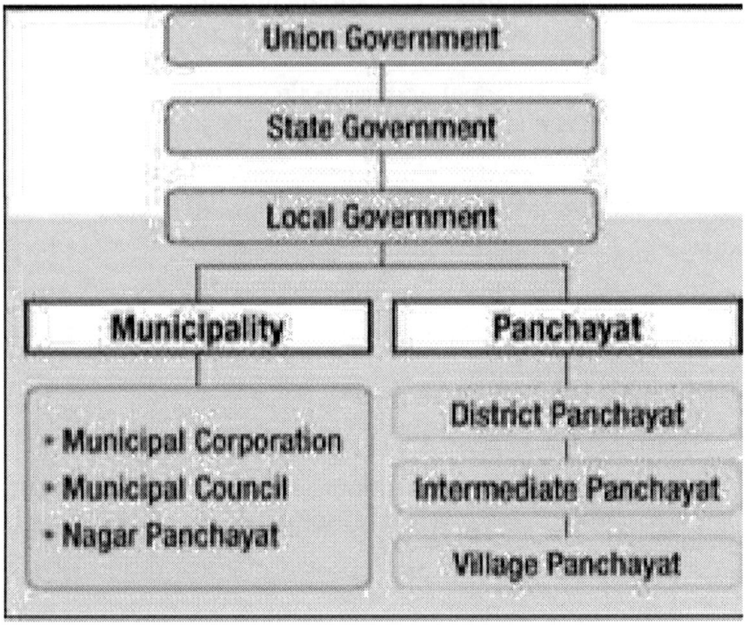

Local Self Government is **the management of local affairs by such local bodies who have been elected by the local people.** PRI was constitutionalized through the 73rd Constitutional Amendment Act, 1992 to build democracy at the grass roots level and was entrusted with the task of rural development in the country.

73rd and 74th Constitutional Amendments were **passed by Parliament in December, 1992.** Through these amendments local self-governance was introduced in rural and urban India.

Local government in India refers to governmental jurisdictions below the level of the state. India is a federal republic with three spheres of government: central, state and local. The 73rd and 74th constitutional amendments give recognition and protection to local governments and in addition each state has its own local government legislation. Since 1992, local government in India takes place in two very distinct forms. Urban localities, covered in the 74th amendment to the Constitution, have Nagar Palika but derive their powers from the individual state governments, while the powers of rural localities have been formalized under the *panchayati raj* system, under the 73rd amendment to the Constitution.

Within the Administrative setup of India, the democratically elected Local self-governance bodies are called the *"municipalities"* (abbreviated as the *"MC"*) in urban areas and the *"Panchayati Raj Institutes (PRI)"* (simply called the *"panchayats"*) in rural areas. There are 3 types of municipalities based on the population, Municipal Corporation (Nagar Nigam) with more than 1 million population, Municipal Councils (Nagar Palika) with more than 25,000 and less than 1 million population, and Municipal Committee (Nagar Panchayat) with more than 10,000 and less than 25,000 population. PRIs in rural areas have 3 hierarchies of panchayats, Gram panchayats at village level, Mandal or block panchayats at block level, and Zilla panchayats at district level.

Panchayats cover about 96% of India's more than 5.8 lakh (580,000) villages and nearly 99.6% of the rural population. As of 2020, there were about 3 million elected representatives at all levels of the panchayat, nearly 1.3 million are women. These members represent more than 2.4 lakh (240,000) gram panchayats, about over 6,672 were intermediate level panchayat samitis at the block level and more than 500 Zila Parishads at district level. Following the 2013 local election, 37.1% of Councillors were women, and in 2015/16 local government expenditure was 16.3% of total government expenditure.

Various committees were formed to study the issues and make recommendations for the implementation of local self-governance in India.

The Balwant Rai Mehta Committee (1957)

In 1957, a committee led by Balwant Rai Mehta Committee studied the Community Development Projects and the National Extension Service and assessed the extent to which the movement had succeeded in utilizing local initiatives and in creating institutions to ensure continuity in the process of improving economic and social conditions in rural areas. The Committee held that community development would only be deep and enduring when the community was involved in the planning, decision-making and implementation process. The suggestions were for as follows:

- an early establishment of elected local bodies and devolution to them of necessary resources, power, and authority,
- that the basic unit of democratic decentralization was at the block/samiti level since the area of jurisdiction of the local body should neither be too large nor too small. The block was large enough for efficiency and economy of administration, and small enough for sustaining a sense of involvement in the citizens,
- such body must not be constrained by too much control by the government or government agencies,
- the body must be constituted for five years by indirect elections from the village panchayats,
- its functions should cover the development of agriculture in all its aspects, the promotion of local industries and others
- services such as drinking water, road building, etc., and
- the higher-level body, Zilla Parishad, would play an advisory role.

Ashok Mehta Committee (1977)

The PRI structure did not develop the requisite democratic momentum and failed to cater to the needs of rural development. There are various reasons for such an outcome which include political and bureaucratic resistance at the state level to share power and resources with local-level institutions, the domination of local elites over the major share of the benefits of welfare schemes, lack of capability at the local level and lack of political will.

It was decided to appoint a high-level committee under the chairmanship of Ashok Mehta to examine and suggest measures to strengthen PRIs. The Committee had to evolve an effective decentralized system of development for PRIs. They made the following recommendations:

- the district is a viable administrative unit for which planning, coordination, and resource allocation are feasible and technical expertise available,
- PRIs as a two-tier system, with Mandal Panchayat at the base and Zilla Parishad at the top,
- the PRIs are capable of planning for themselves with the resources available to them,

- district planning should take care of the urban-rural continuum,
- representation of SCs and STs in the election to PRIs on the basis of their population,
- four-year term of PRIs,
- participation of political parties in elections,
- any financial devolution should be committed to accepting that much of the developmental functions at the district level would be played by the panchayats.

The states of Karnataka, Andhra Pradesh and West Bengal passed new legislation based on this report. However, the flux in politics at the state level did not allow these institutions to develop their own political dynamics.

G.V.K. Rao Committee (1985)

The G.V.K. Rao Committee was appointed by Planning Commission to once again look at various aspects of PRIs. The Committee was of the opinion that a total view of rural development must be taken in which PRIs must play a central role in handling people's problems. It recommended the following:

- PRIs have to be activated and provided with all the required support to become effective organizations,
- PRIs at district level and below should be assigned the work of planning, implementation and monitoring of rural development programs, and
- the block development office should be the spinal cord of the rural development process.
- district development commissioner to be introduced.
- election should conduct regularly.

L. M. Singhvi Committee (1986)

A committee led by Laxmi Mall Singhvi was constituted in the 1980s to recommend ways to revitalize PRIs. The Gram Sabha was considered as the base of a municipality decentralized, and PRIs viewed as institutions of self-governance which would actually facilitate the participation of the people in the process of planning and development. It recommended:

- local self-government should be constitutionally recognized, protected and preserved by the inclusion of new chapter in the Constitution,

- non-involvement of political parties in Panchayat elections.

The suggestion of giving panchayats constitutional status was opposed by the Sarkaria Commission, but the idea, however, gained momentum in the late 1980s especially because of the endorsement by the late Prime Minister Rajiv Gandhi, who introduced the 64th Constitutional Amendment Bill in 1989. The 64th Amendment Bill was prepared and introduced in the lower house of Parliament. But it got defeated in the Rajya Sabha as non-convincing. He lost the general elections too. In 1989, the National Front introduced the 74th Constitutional Amendment Bill, which could not become an Act because of the dissolution of the Ninth Lok Sabha. All these various suggestions and recommendations and means of strengthening PRIs were considered while formulating the new Constitutional Amendment Act.

Legal framework

Following laws and subsequent amendments were passed to implement the selected recommendations of various committees.

The 73rd Constitutional Amendment Act (1992)

The idea which produced the 73rd and Amendment was not a response to pressure from the grassroots, but to an increasing recognition that the institutional initiatives of the preceding decade had not delivered, that the extent of rural poverty was still much too large and thus the existing structure of government needed to be reformed. This idea evolved from the Centre and the state governments. It was a political drive to see PRIs as a solution to the governmental crises that India was experiencing.

The Constitutional (73rd Amendment) Act, passed in 1992 by the Narasimha Rao government, came into force on April 24, 1993. It was meant to provide constitutional sanction to establish "democracy at the grassroots level as it is at the state level or national level". Its main features are as follows:

- The Gram Sabha or village assembly as a deliberative body to decentralized governance has been envisaged as the foundation of the Panchayati Raj System.73rd Amendment of the Constitution empowered the Gram Sabhas to conduct social audits in addition to its other functions.
- A uniform three-tier structure of panchayats at village (Gram Panchayat — GP), intermediate or block (Panchayat Samiti — PS) and district (Zilla Parishad — ZP) levels.

- All the seats in a panchayat at every level are to be filled by elections from respective territorial constituencies.
- Not less than one-third of the total seats for membership as well as office of chairpersons of each tier have to be reserved for women.
- Reservation for weaker castes and tribes (SCs and STs) have to be provided at all levels in proportion to their population in the panchayats.
- To supervise, direct and control the regular and smooth elections to panchayats, a State Election Commission has The Act has ensured constitution of a State Finance Commission in every State/UT, for every five years, to suggest measures to strengthen finances of panchayati raj institutions.
- To promote bottom-up-planning, the District Planning Committee (DPC) in every district has been accorded to constitutional status.
- An indicative list of 29 items has been given in Eleventh Schedule of the Constitution. Panchayats are expected to play an effective role in planning and implementation of works related to these 29 items.

97th Constitutional Amendment Act (2011)

Cooperative Societies are taken under "Local Government" after 97th Constitutional Amendment act 2011,under Dr Manmohan Singh's Govt. Part-IX of Indian Constitution is related to Local Government, under which Panchayt Raj was defined, then after 74th amendment Municipal Corporation and council were included and defined by inducing Part IX-A, and in 2011,Cooperative Societies were included in Local Government by inducing PartIX-B in the Constitution. The 97th Constitutional Amendment Act, 2011 provided for amendment in following things: 1. It amended article 19(1)c by inserting after the word 'or unions' the words 'or Co-operative Societies'. 2. It also inserted Article 43B in part IV of the Constitution as "The State shall endeavor to promote Voluntary formation, autonomous functioning, democratic control and professional Management of the Co-operative Societies" and 3. After Part IX-A of the Constitution Part IX-B was inserted. Part IX-B extended from Article 243ZH to Article 243ZT.

Types of local governance entities

The local governance entities are broadly classified into urban and rural, which are further sub-divided based on the size of population in case of the urban bodies and based on the size of population and hierarchy in case of the rural bodies.

Urban local governance bodies

3 types of MCs

The following 3 types of democratically elected urban local governance bodies in India are called municipalities and abbreviated as the *"MC"*. These are classified based on the size of the population of the urban settlement.

Municipal Corporation, also called the *"Nagar Nigam"*, of cities with more than 1 million populations.

Municipal Councils, also called the *"Nagar Palika"*, of cities with more than 25,000 and less than 1 million populations.

Municipal Committee, also called the *"Town Council"* or *"Nagar Panchayat"* or *"Town Panchayat"* or *"Notified Area Council"* depending on the state within which they lie, these are in the town with more than 10,000 and less than 25,000 populations.

Functions of MCs

All municipal acts in India provide for functions, powers and responsibilities to be carried out by the municipal government. These are divided into two categories: obligatory and discretionary.

The mandatory functions of MC include the supply of pure and wholesome water, construction and maintenance of public streets, lighting and watering of public streets, cleaning of public streets, places and sewers, regulation of offensive, dangerous or obnoxious trades and callings or practices, maintenance or support of public hospitals, establishment and maintenance of primary schools, registration of births and deaths, removing obstructions and projections in public streets, bridges and other places, naming streets and numbering houses, maintenance of law and public order, etc.

The discretionary functions of MC include the laying out of areas, securing or removal of dangerous buildings or places, construction and maintenance of public parks, gardens, libraries, museums, rest houses, leper homes, orphanages and rescue homes for women, public buildings, planting of trees and maintenance of roads, housing for low income groups, conducting surveys, organizing public receptions, public exhibitions, public entertainment, provision of transport facilities with the municipality, and promotion of welfare of municipal employees.

Some of the functions of the urban bodies overlap with the work of state agencies. The functions of the municipality, including those listed in the Twelfth Schedule to the Constitution, are left to the discretion of the state government. Local bodies have to be bestowed with adequate powers, authority and responsibility to perform the functions entrusted to them by the Act. However, the Act has not provided them with any powers directly and has instead left it to state government discretion.

Rural local governance bodies

The democratically elected local self-governance bodies in the villages of rural India are called Panchayati Raj Institutions (PRIs) which are based on the vedic era native democratic panchayat (Council of five officials) system.

3 hierarchies of PRI panchayats

The following 3 hierarchies of PRI panchayats exist in states or Union Territories with more than two million inhabitants:

Gram Panchayats at village level

Panchayat Samiti at Community Development Block level and Zila Parishad at district level.

The Panchayati Raj system is a three-tier system with elected bodies at the village, taluk and district levels. The modern system is based in part on traditional {Panchayati Raj, Panchayat governance}, in part on the vision of (Mahatma Gandhi) and in part by the work of various committees to harmonize the highly centralized Indian governmental administration with a degree of local autonomy. The result was intended to create greater participation in local government by people and more effective implementation of rural development programs. Although, as of 2015, implementation in all of India is not complete, the intention is for there to be a gram panchayat for each village or group of villages, a tehsil level council, and a Zilla Panchayat at the district level.

Functions of PRIs

Defined in the Part IX of the Indian Constitution, these are responsible for the 29 subjects listed in the Eleventh Schedule including the "economic development, and strengthening social justice."

Local bodies by states

The Constitution of India visualizes panchayats as institutions of self-governance. However, giving due consideration to the federal structure of India's polity, most of the financial powers and authorities to be endowed on panchayats have been left at the discretion of concerned state legislatures. Consequently, the powers and functions vested in PRIs vary from state to state. These provisions combine representative and direct democracy into a synergy and are expected to result in an extension and deepening of democracy in India. Hence, panchayats have journeyed from an institution within the culture of India to attain constitutional status.

Chapter Four

Social Dynamics of Indian Politics

- GENDER AND POLITICS
- RELIGION AND POLITICS
- CASTE AND POLITICS

Indian political life is firmly embedded in the regular rhythm of the electoral cycle. All that matters in India's political system is the next election and recent experience is highlighting the permanence of electoral politics, continuing immediately after the conclusion of the tumultuous national parliamentary election of 2019. This latter phenomenon is the result of dramatic shifts in the balance of political power in India, in the first instance to regional parties and, second, the rise of the BJP to build a large enough political footprint to dominate national politics, if not the nation's destiny. It indicates major socio-political changes in the country and the retreat of the GOP and elites associated with it and their intransigent refusal to accept their political repudiation by voters. Another obvious immediate reason for the overriding focus on elections is that for political parties losing them on two successive occasions spells likely doom and certainly the prospect of a change in its political leadership. The threat of the loss of personal political power predisposes parties to opt for a dynastic configuration of leadership. As a result, electioneering and the quest for personal political pre-eminence outweigh issues of governance and even vital national security goals. Simply put, once out of power nothing matters. To paraphrase the renowned economist, John Maynard Keynes in another context, "in the long run we are all dead" and immediate political power alone truly matters to participants in Indian political life.

These principles of political life apply mutatis mutandis elsewhere too. However, the absence of a truly stable inter-generational political class, which endures as a viable feature in Indian political life, creates the kind of destructive competition for power and position that impacts its governance and national security negatively. The competition for political power influences virtually all aspects of social life in India, from the media, certainly, to academic discourses and the very attempt to define the historical identity of the nation. The media in India is often an appendage to political interests, although there are occasional exceptions that, however, do not always enjoy a mass audience. Academic discourses have unashamedly espoused the vocabulary of political competition, defining social reality in terms of its grammar. Ideas like "pluralism", "diversity" and "human rights" that do not have their genuine authentic meaning in India have become embroiled in the cut and thrust of political debate and point scoring. In fact, so great is the impact of domestic political competition for power that a huge proportion of all academic research globally on India is obsessively preoccupied with caste issues, a critical variable in its electoral dynamics, in the process often fabricating and deepening its malign impact on Indian society.

The decline of a more national-minded politics and retreat of the momentary identification of a nascent all-India elite with the nation after 1947 began during the ascent of Indira Gandhi in 1969. It paradoxically, underlined India's democratization and the rise of a popular political consciousness that was unavoidably local and regional. Mrs Indira Gandhi responded to the evident changed circumstances and her personal differences vis-à-vis a pan Indian Congress leadership by trying to go over their heads to voters. She adopted the slogan of "removing poverty", the one common denominator among the majority of Indians and with particular appeal to the disadvantaged. A predictable corollary was the mobilization of the minority vote and the unerring attempt since, by all regional caste-based political parties, to forge an alliance with a religious political constituency. The intensification of caste divisions and antagonisms is the inescapable expression of political mobilization along caste identities, with the incitement of supposed ancient divisions and contrivance of fresh grievances on a prodigious scale.

Regional caste political mobilization is ineluctably parochial, stoking linguistic allegiances and the poisonous potent theory of race. The notion of an Aryan invasion of the south from the north was implanted by imperial British administrators in the consciousness of many in India. The identity of a shared civilizational ethos, common experiences and imperatives of collective action, in relation to the predatory wider world, have become overlaid with sentiments that prefer a potentially calamitous national setback to joint endeavor with one's fellow Indians. Once the monstrous genie of identity politics was out of the bottle, political parties engaged in regional rivalries vied with each other to pose more and more extreme versions of the miasma of purported injustices to appeal to local emotional sensibilities and resentments. The resulting spiral of an implosive descent had the strong likelihood of ending in fratricidal conflicts between regions and the Centre, though the latter is but only a symbol of the political identity of the other regions that constitute any national government. These deep fissures have been self-evident in some states and only simmer below the surface elsewhere in many parts of India, with a proposed "southern federation", no longer unspoken, to end the unity of the Indian Union. Little new needs be said of the politics of India's Northeast and the only recently quiescent paroxysm of regional militancy. The politics of the Bengal government's increasing truculent rejection of all manifestations of Constitutional central authority is merely an expression of regionalism as well that earlier masqueraded in the faux garb of radicalism. But its principal expression for many decades has always been bitter antagonism towards the Centre regardless of the extraordinary price paid by the state and its hapless people as a consequence. This forbidding reality has now assumed a distinctive wider guise of communal political mobilization in West Bengal that could have momentous implications for the future of the Indian Union.

The centrality of Muslim political enlistment in India was recognized early by the British imperial power, which initially patronized a Hindu revival, having just ousted Muslim rule in Bengal in 1757. But the British later facilitated both the rise of the Deobandi movement and the ardently collaborationist Ahmadiyya variant, as an insurance policy, to exercise influence in India after the 1860s. The Viceroy's imperial office in Delhi subsequently underwrote and celebrated the creation of the Muslim League in 1906 as a game changer to stem the nationalist tide sweeping Bengal. It had been preceded by the failed attempt to partition Bengal in 1905 that presaged the eventual creation of Pakistan in 1947, receiving its strongest support from the Bengal Presidency. Secessionist demands were to become the backdrop to Indian nationalism for much of the first half of the twentieth century and the eventual bloody partition of the country, which few have understood has remained unfinished business after August 1947 from a Pakistani perspective. Indeed, Mohammed Ali Jinnah and the Muslim League leadership viewed their own community as the legitimate successor to British imperial overlordship, once even suggesting to Winston Churchill to "cut out the Hindus" and ruling together.

The challenge posed by such thinking to India's durability as a state was to become a permanent external and internal feature, requiring major budgetary commitments to deal with both foreign aggression and internal security. The latter alone reputedly consumes 2% of GDP in addition to the cost of the national defense budget. The issue has continued to haunt India, with separatist aspirations informing segments of regional politics in various parts of the country and posing further challenges to India's territorial and geographical identity and integrity. The post-Independence hiatus in Muslim League-inspired political pugnacity, in the aftermath of the apocalyptic partition of India in 1947, turned out to be transitory, coinciding with the decline of the all-India reach of the Congress party by the early 1970s. It was rapidly accentuated by India's domestic political divisions and dynamics of the demographic transformation of various Indian states, not least Assam and West Bengal, subject to a tsunami of illegal migration from neighboring East Pakistan and later the successor state of Bangladeshi.

In competing for the minority vote, Indian political parties have descended into a destructive competitive whirl, trying to outdo each other with outlandish pledges to such constituents, some of which they themselves concoct, without any prompting from the intended beneficiaries. The rampant incitement of extravagant sectarian ambitions by India's political parties and intensification of its radicalization, owing to the unconstrained competition for their political support, is creating fertile ground for the grafting of a nihilistic ISIS ideology. A catalogue of the inflammatory and grotesquely anti-national appeals directed by Indian political parties towards Muslim constituents is deeply alarming and endangers the fundamental security interests of India. An especially troubling outcome of appeasement politics in India is the ability of criminal cliques to exploit caste and regional sentiments to form political parties that get elected by making crude appeals to minority constituents. It has become a recurrent phenomenon in some states like Bihar and UP, though the rampant criminalization of politics is the norm rather than the exception across India. Concerns of Muslim voters are sought to be narrowly focused, for instance, to prevent the BJP from achieving electoral success. In addition, these voters are being mobilized by the oft-repeated historic pretext that "Islam is in danger", which could not be further from reality in India.

The extent of appeasement was underlined in recent years by one prominent political leader appealing for Pakistani help to settle domestic political scores, virtually signaling the need for its violent intervention. The supreme leader of the same political party defended SIMI, since banned as a terror front, at an Oxford University lecture and allegedly wept when terrorists were killed in an encounter at Delhi's Batla House with India's security services, without condoling the death of one of its officers. Even more shocking is the allegation, by a former home ministry official and two leading London journalists, of the complicity of senior ministers of the national government in the 26/11 Mumbai terrorist assault. A top Indian intelligence officer has also confirmed that the terrorists who bombed New Delhi in 2005 enjoyed an escort into the capital from a regional political party. The list goes on and on, with the sitting Prime Minister of the country announcing, in the run up to the 2014 national general elections, that Muslims had first claim to national resources. India also experiences the uninterrupted entry into its territory of millions of illegal migrants from neighbouring countries. They apparently enjoy the open support of political parties who hurriedly ensure their legitimacy by issuing identity documents to them in the expectation of adding to their vote bank.

In recent years, at least three regional states have espoused a mode confrontational political autonomy that verges on quasi-independence from the Indian Union and a fourth barely accepts the legitimacy of its inclusion within it. Indian democracy, with the backing of its innumerable adversaries abroad and cynical "frenemies", is being wielded against it and threatens the political unravelling of India. A major well-funded political association in Bangladesh is known to be attempting to sponsor a demand at the UN for a plebiscite in the Indian state of West Bengal. Only approximately 11% of registered Hindu voters supported the ruling TMC in the April-May 2021 Assembly elections, which nevertheless won by a handsome margin and is poised to enjoy a majority nearing 80% if rumored defections occur.

India's Constitution needs far-reaching reform. Despite all the attendant dissent, this will have to be contemplated if a national party comes to power with the appropriate majority. It needs to be borne in mind that Constitutions are the product of the emergence of an historic consensus in a polity, often after the cessation of domestic conflicts, like civil war, after which the erstwhile protagonists decide on a shared concord for the future. In India's case, the national Constitution was the product of an imitative intellectual exercise before a societal consensus had occurred. In fact, societal consensus was being grimly contested for preceding decades and ended in bloody partition. And the framing of the Indian Constitution after Independence was a case of hope triumphing over experience, a "constructivist" exercise in essence. In the final analysis, the Indian Constitution put the horse before the cart, so to speak, hoping the Constitution itself would create the consensus it visibly preceded. Frequent amendments to it only highlighted the fragile tentativeness of parts of it. Implacably hostile editorialists abroad should not now be permitted to dictate India's willingness to use force to survive as a united country, unless they wish for the country to suffer the fate of the once mighty USSR.

Gender and Politics

Gender studies is an interdisciplinary academic field devoted to analyzing gender identity and gendered representation. It includes women's studies, men's studies and queer studies. Its rise to prominence, especially in Western universities after 1990, has been noted as a success of deconstructionism.

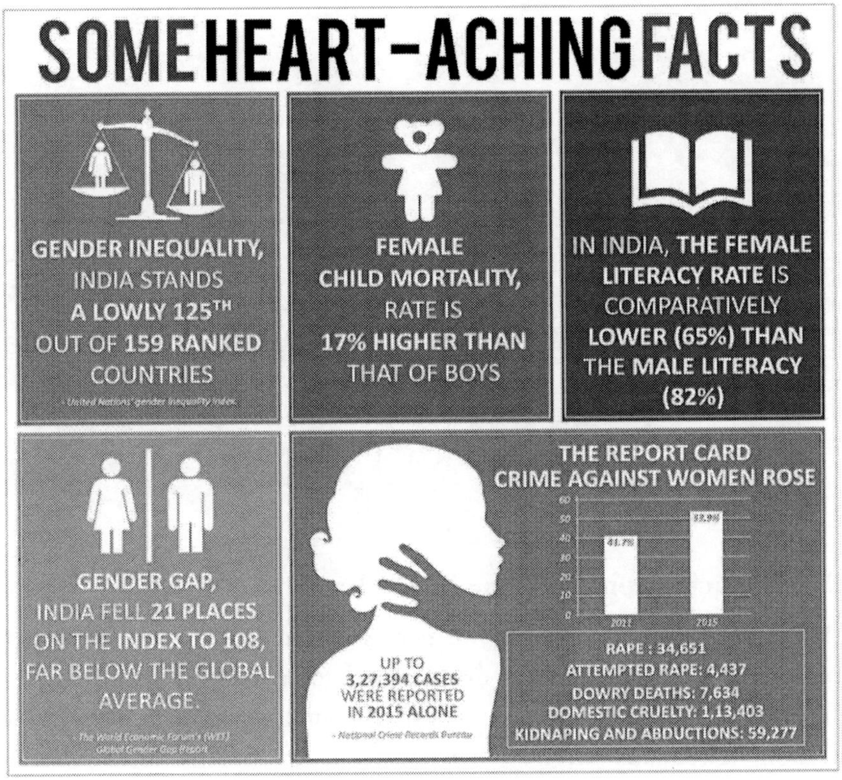

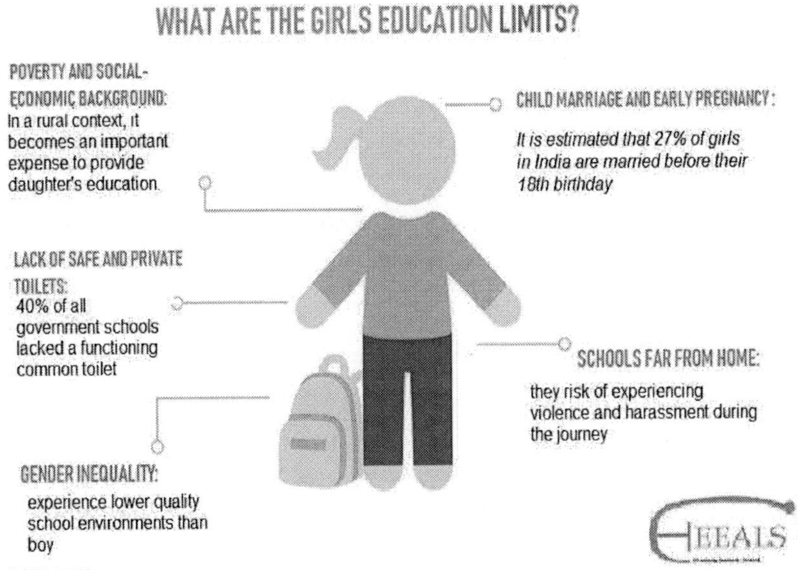

by Elisa Stucchi

Political Participation of Women in India

In India, political participation of women is not impressive when compared with men. This is the case in most of the countries across the world. However, women's political participation now is quite encouraging compared to the older times. Today it remains stronger than ever. But, in India, women who have decision making powers invariably hail from urban and elite groups. Even today, representation of women in Indian Parliament is far from satisfactory. Women have been demanding for more space in legislative bodies.

Political participation

Political participation means exercising the right to vote, power sharing, membership of political parties, electoral campaigning, attending party meetings, holding party positions, contesting elections, co-decision making, co-policy making at all levels of governance of the state. Simply put, it is a process through which individuals plays a role in political life deciding the common goals of the society and determining the best way to achieve it.

The root of political participation of women can be traced back to 19th century reform movements. Social reformers like Rajaram Mohan Roy, Ishwar Chandra Vidyasagar, Mahadeva Govinda Ranade, Behramji Malabari believed that social evils could be eradicated by raising consciousness and educating women.

Pre independent political participation of women

The late 19th and early 20th centuries witnessed the establishment of women's associations all over the country. These organizations took up the issues concerning women like right to vote etc. Three main organizations were established during this period. They are:

- The Women's Indian Association (WIA): WIA concentrated its work over religion, education, politics and philanthropy. Annie Besant became the first president of WIA along with Margaret Cousins.
- The National Council of women in India (NCWI): it was established in 1925 as a national branch of the International Council of Women. Due to its elitist nature, the NCWI failed to become a vital national organization.
- The All India Women's conference (AIWC): AIWC materialized due to the dedicated work of Margaret Cousins and other women of WIA and it first met in Poona in January 1927. It worked for female education and opposed social customs that restricted female education such as child marriage and purdah.

Participation of Women in post independent period

The foundation formed during the national movement helped women to participate in democratic process after independence. Various legal, social and economic measures were taken by the government of India to raise the status of women in India after independence. Women also began to participate in national and state politics.

The first assembly after independence saw the presence of very few women (about 2%). Women members included Masuma Begum, who later on became the Minister of Social Welfare, Renuka Ray, veteran social worker; Durgabai, a veteran Gandhian, Radhabai Subbarayan, who was appointed as a delegate to the first Round Table Conference. As per various accounts, men in the assembly listened carefully to the speeches made by women. Rajkumari Amrit Kaur became Union Health Minister in 1947. Sucheta Kriplani became the general secretary of Congress in 1959, labour minister of Uttar Pradesh in 1962 and subsequently Chief Minister of United Province in from 1963 to 1967. Vijayalakshmi Pandit was selected as a delegate to the UN and was appointed as ambassador to the erstwhile USSR in 1947 and later as ambassador to the US. She was also elected as president of the United Nations General Assembly in 1953.

In the subsequent elections, women started to hold 4-5% seats in the Lok Sabha till 1980s after which their numbers increased to 7-8%. In Rajya Sabha, women have held 7-10% of seats.

Representation of women in 16th Lok Sabha is 61. This is the highest in history. Presenttly, Rajya Sabha has 29 women members. Six of the 23 Cabinet ministers in the present government are women, claiming almost a 25 per cent share.

Constitutional provisions

The Constitution of India guaranteed justice-social, economic and political, liberty of thought, and equality to all citizens. Constitution provided for equality of women and called State to take measures to neutralize the socio-economic, educational and political disadvantage faced by women.

- Article 14: It guarantees equality before law and equal protection of law with in the territory of India.
- Article 15: It prohibits discrimination on the basis of religion, race, caste, sex, place of birth. According to article 15(3), State can make special provisions for the benefit women and children.
- Article 16: Equality of opportunity for all citizens in matter relating to employment. No citizen can be denied employment on grounds of religion, race, cast, sex, decent, place of birth residence or any of them.
- Article 39: Article 39(a) provides for an adequate means of livelihood for all citizen. Article 39 (b) has provisions for equal pay for equal work for both men and women. Article 39 (c) has provisions for securing the health and strength of workers, men and women, and not to abuse the tender age of children.
- Article 42: It guarantees just and humane condition of work and maternity relief. Article 42 is in accordance with Article 23 and 25 of Universal Declaration of Human Rights.
- Article 325 and 326: They guarantee political equality, equal right to participate in political activity and right to vote, respectively.

Article 243 (D): It provides for the political reservation to women in every panchayat election. It has extended this reservation to elected office as well.

In spite of the above provisions, participation of women in politics has not improved significantly. These are contradictory to the aims of the constitution.

Challenges

Women who demonstrated their bravery during freedom movement found it difficult to make the gain ground in electoral politics due to the following reasons:

- Problem of party backing. The political parties are reluctant to provide more seats to women candidates. Women are not able to change social attitudes about women.
- Women have begun to dislike the rough life offered by politics. While many are ready to endure the hardships provided by the political life, they have not been able to change the social stereotypes and attitudes about women's place in the society. Many women have expressed their dislike for political process and has opted for the gentler working atmosphere provided by social welfare work.
- Cultural environment puts maximum emphasis on men. Apart from it criminalization of politics and the political environment of instability and personality traits are the primary causes for marginal participation of women in politics.

Need for political participation of women

UNICEF cites the following reasons for the political participation of women:

- Political participation of women has the potential to change societies.
- It can have impact on outcomes for women and children especially in the distribution of community resources.
- Their participation in peace negotiations and post-conflict reconstruction is important to ensure the safety and protection of children and vulnerable sections of populations.

Global scenario

At the global level also, only a few countries have equal participation of women in par with men in politics. In countries like Germany, Sweden, Norway, Denmark and Finland, women's participation in the decision making process is substantial. Sweden with 47% female participation has almost equal participation of women in Parliament followed by Cuba and Iceland.

Women's presence in parliament is highest in Nordic countries (42.5%), followed by America (22%), Europe (19.5%), Asia (18%), Sub-Saharan Africa (18%), the Pacific (15%) and lastly in Arab states (9.4%).

Global debate

The issue of political empowerment of women has become the agenda of various international conferences and symposiums. The issue came at the forefront at the time of the Fourth World Conference on Women held at Beijing in 1995. At the conference, it was declared that women's political participation is crucial for the general process of the advancement of women. This conference stressed the importance of women's political participation not only because of their points of view and talents, but also as a matter of their human rights.

Way forward

- Political parties should come forward to increase women representatives. The absence of critical mass of women representatives has pushed women to the fringes in power sharing and has adverse impacts on thire overall political status.
- Gender stereotypes which perceive women as weak representatives should be changes through awareness and education. Efforts need to be taken to enhance the participation of women in governance in large numbers.

Women's Reservation Bill which reserves 33% of seats for Indian women at the legislatures has to be passed soon in the Parliament.

Women's leadership and communication skills need to be enhanced by increasing female literacy especially in rural areas. They should be empowered in order to break socio-cultural barriers and improve their status in the society.

- Women panchayat members have to be trained to analysis and understand their roles and responsibilities given in the 73rd amendment act.

Initiatives of government for empowering women

- Mahatma Gandhi National Rural Employment Guarantee Act (MGNREGA)
- Swayam Siddha

- Scheme for Working Women Hostel
- STEP (Support to Training and Employment Programme for Women)
- Swarnjayanti Gram Swarozgar Yojana
- Sarva Shiksha Abhiyan
- Indira Gandhi Matritva Sahyog Yojana (IGMSY)
- Rajiv Gandhi Scheme for Empowerment of Adolescent Girls (RGSEAG)—Sabla
- Janani Suraksha Yojana
- Integrated Child Protection Scheme
- Swadhar
- Targeted Public Distribution System (TPDS)
- Antyodaya Anna Yojna (AAY)
- Ujjawala

Religion and Politics

In August 1947, India was finally freed from its prolonged era under British colonial rule, winning independence, albeit as a self-governing member of the British Commonwealth. Independence, however, was accompanied by a very painful division into two separate states within its borders, the Dominion of India and the Dominion of Pakistan. That separation became the source of great turmoil to follow in Indian history.

Independence itself did not involve bloody struggles with the former suzerain, Great Britain, but a series of hideous massacres occurred between Muslims and Hindus, who had lived together as compatriots under British rule. Partition into the two independent states led to the largest-scale mass migration of religious groups in the history of the Indian subcontinent.[1] Muslim refugees headed for Pakistan, and Hindu and Sikh refugees for India. As they met midway, many cases of bloodshed occurred on a scale comparable to war.[2] This tragedy was caused when religion became linked with the modern territorial state. The dogmatism that brought about such conflict and disputes between religious groups has been called 'communalism' or religious confrontations.

One may be inclined to think that 'communalism' between Hindus and Muslims has prevailed since Muslims took over India (dating back as far as the tenth century, during the Ghaznavid dynasty, when Muslims became the suzerains of northern India). As recent historical research has pointed out, however, there are strong indications that it was during the British colonial rule – that brought India into the modern age – that rigid boundaries were established between Hindus and Muslims.[3] In other words, the unambiguous articulation of religious groups assumed primary importance under the modern governing system, and confrontation became palpable along those articulated lines.

Colonial rule brought unprecedented radical change and reorganization to the various societies it encountered in the Indian subcontinent. How to control many different peoples of the land and incorporate them into the structure of rule was the unavoidable task of the colonial administration. Over time, there emerged a public view of society that divided the peoples of India using religion and caste as the yardsticks of division. The division of people by religion, especially, was in accord with the Western-type secularism (separation of religion and politics) that, beginning with the separation of Church and State, constituted the basic policy of administration of colonial states. This political stance gave rise to a rigid communalism that split Muslims and Hindus. That was the source of 'the twisted relationship between secularism and communalism' in India, as shall be discussed later. This 'twisted relationship' continued even after Independence, and still haunts people, causing new problems under the phenomenon of globalization today. The aim of this paper is to present – while mindful of the modern period since the start of colonial rule – a framework for adequately understanding the thorny problem of contemporary communalism in India since the end of the twentieth century. There is no quick remedy for this extremely complex problem. What is important above all is a careful diagnosis of the problem, which will be the first step toward correct treatment. For such a diagnosis, it is imperative at first to precisely identify the problem.

Formation and Limitation of Secularism

It is simplistic to describe the construction of modern (or colonial) India as a result of the one-way introduction of modern achievements of the West by the British. As Edward Said's *Orientalism*[4] has shown, Occident and Orient shaped the image of the self and the image of the other in their relationship of mutual reflection and, accordingly, created ruler-ruled ideas and institutions. The eighteenth century, when Britain began controlling India, and the nineteenth century, when it won firm control of the territory, coincided with the time during which the West came to establish the ideology of rule by reason, or reason-centered thought.[5] The idea that even religion could be incorporated into the system of reason emerged in nineteenth-century currents of thought. It was also believed that reason brought progress, and that because the vessel of reason could breed anti-rational attitudes, it was the job of reason to choose between reasonable and unreasonable acts. This system of thought in the nineteenth century, when people lived within a reason-governing autistic space, represented a major philosophical shift from the eighteenth century, when reason was in its inception in milieus dominated by religion. The colonial era unfolded in these eighteenth and nineteenth centuries, and as can readily be imagined, the Western experience of encounter with the non-western world worked as the experience of concretely corroborating the philosophical shift, that is, the establishment of reason-centered thought within the West. Reason with which to ascertain a reason vs. anti-reason picture in its totality, is homologous with the transcendental quality of the 'knower' in 'Orientalism' as referred to by Said. It was produced simultaneously with the development of colonial rule over Asia and Africa. The separation of Church and State in the seventeenth-century West did not necessarily mean separation of the state as reason versus religion as antithetical to reason. It was not until the appearance of Hegel in the nineteenth century that the view of the state as the perfection of reason on earth was established (which led to the concept of state sovereignty). Only then did there come into being the idea that the state conducting politics and serving as the embodiment of judgement by reason, made possible the separation of politics and religion.

Philosophical change in the nineteenth century paved the way for market economy, democracy and secularization in the twentieth century. Modern nation-states, thus, made it a basic policy to pursue separation of politics and religion.[6] In the name of modernization, nation-states also took it for granted that economic development and democracy were inseparable as the two wheels of a cart. Today, especially since the collapse of the Cold War structure, a good deal of soul-searching is going on about the once-firm conviction that the market-oriented capitalist system – a product of Western modernization – would guarantee limitless progress. The increasingly felt impossibility of such progress has thrown the world into a deadlock. People now labor between the unwillingness to abandon the idea of progress and the reality of the earth's limited resources and irreversibility of environmental changes. This is not simply\ a matter of material limits. Post-World War II democracy, advocating freedom and equality for the individual, was undergirded by the ideology of progress, which became a device for continually putting off attainment of freedom and equality to a future time. Once doubts are raised about such democracy, the inequities and absence of freedom in reality loom up as unendurable. The people of the modern era who have sought their identity in never-ending growth and progress have been assaulted with the puncturing of the growth myth with identity crisis and a wave of uncertainty. As if in response to a sense of deadlock of the times, religious revival movements have arisen and ethnic conflicts have flared in places throughout the world. The simplistic expectation that democracy would be attained and religion would go into decline have thus been frustrated. The advance of the era of reason has provoked anti-reason, igniting chaotic conditions in the form of religious and ethnic strife.

Under these circumstances, some advocate 'sustainable development' as the assurance for a soft-landing of development monism, but the challenge is how to come up with ideas and techniques of identity-building that are free from the established images of development. Seeing religious fundamentalism or revival as a threat to democracy, some call for cultural pluralism on the basis of the spirit of tolerance. But again, the challenge is, to what extent are the voices of anti-reason that demand attention for the communality to be heeded. These voices have long been suppressed by modernistic reason, and are closely related to identity building. One must be aware, above all, that the problems we face today are so difficult that they cannot be solved by merely expedient revamping of modern reason and its applications. Modern reason views independent individuals as good and envisions a free society as made up of such individuals. But the fact is that such reason, in reality, suppresses people and leads them to turn away from freedom and bury themselves in communality. This irony, as represented by the rise of Nazism, is by no means a thing of the past. The foisting of reason upon people produces anti-reason, which strikes back. Calling this the 'other of reason' issue, I have addressed the significance of the problem elsewhere.[7] This is because I believe that we must face the difficult issues that have remained unresolved since the issue of 'overcoming the modern' (*kindai no chôkoku*) was proposed in the dangerous shape of fascism. Looking back over the past one hundred years, we can consider the twentieth century as a century of democracy versus fascism and light versus shadow. Post-World War II democracy, in the wake of the storm of fascism, "discarded (fascism) as an 'irrational' ideology that would hobble the emergence of modern democratic states and independence."[8] In other words, "postwar democracy, while ignoring the trap of modern rationalism, its very premise, cast aside as irrational the legitimacy of addressing the challenge, though prematurely, by fascism to 'overcome the modern.'"[9] The concept of 'overcoming the modern' was discussed directly in the context of Japanese modern and contemporary history, but I think it can be applied much more generally. The religious 'fundamentalist' movements emerging in connection with politics in contemporary history, especially from the 1980s onward, can be seen as replay of fascism in the broad sense. This problem is not something we could settle by simply affirming or rejecting it. We must face it as an unsettled challenge for overcoming the modern. We must, moreover, conquer it as a philosophical challenge for building our individual identities. This 'other of reason' issue has to be seen as an objection to the market economy (development monism), democracy (civil society), and secularization (rationalism), the values taken for granted by modernization advocates in the latter half of the twentieth century dreaming of limitless progress, values premised upon independent, reason- oriented individuals (persons whose identity is so strong that they can remain unperturbed even when isolated; such a way of living is actually impossible). What is called for today is the formulation of a more profound and more realistic image of humanity and society.

The Legacy of British Colonial Rule: Twisted Relations between Secularism and Communalism

The problem identified in the previous section shows the essence of a thorny issue imbedded in the process beginning with the advent of British colonial rule in India, through the post-independence era, and continuing till today. This problem, in India's context, can be described as characterized by a twisted relationship between secularism and communalism. There is considerable debate over the usage and definitions of these terms, but this paper will not go into these matters in detail.[10] Suffice it here simply to call attention to two points. First, viewing a different religious group as an enemy involves an attempt to absolutize religious differences, ignoring various other cultural elements, and the term communalism, which is translated as religious confrontations, is valid as long as it discusses this subjective viewpoint.[11] Second, as for secularism, which means separation of religion and politics, studies have been done of the distinctively Indian usage of secularism that is different from secularism in its original

Western sense, as well as of the distinction between secularism in its narrow, political sense and secularism with more positive implications.[12] The complex character of secularism is itself a topic of discussion in this paper. Neither of the two terms, communalism and secularism, can be used simplistically, but let me say in advance, that with such reservations, I use them to begin dealing with the essence of the issues facing modern Indian society. In this section, the paper focuses on how the contradictory structure of the twisted relationship between secularism and communalism was fundamentally formed during the British colonial era.

The British rule of India, beginning during the eighteenth-century enlightenment period, was fraught with internal conflict between the Orientalist stance of non-intervention (represented by the East India Company, rightist Tories), which affirmed the distinctiveness of Indian society and culture; and the Anglicist stance of intervention, which sought to universalize the values of British society and apply them to India (represented by evangelists, Utilitarian's and free traders). Both shared some universalism, in that they primarily considered modern Western values to be superior. The Orientalists, however, were closer to cultural relativism than the Anglicists, because the former tried to understand the qualities inherent in Indian society, albeit in a distorted way. Implemented amid such discord between the two camps, actual colonial policy vacillated between intervention and non-intervention. The governing policy, therefore, was a compromise mix of 'transcendental' and 'inherent' standpoints.

The British colonial government's basic understanding of Indian society was expressed in its broad division of the Indian population into Muslims, Hindus, and tribal peoples and further dividing the majority Hindus into castes.[13] Division between Muslims and Hindus according to religious differences; separation of tribal peoples from the Hindus as a result of the combining of the myth of the 'noble savage' with anti-Hinduism; and caste social stratification on the basis of the idea of Varna categories – in all these divisions, identity was provided through classification from above, the *transcendental* position of the ruler. Once the division was made, however, homogeneity of each group was assumed, and its objectification led to the creation of 'an imagined community' within the *inherent* viewpoint of each group.[14] There emerged a cultural pluralism in which standardized social customs were approved for each group, and it became necessary to deal with the new situation.

Specifically, the principle of personal law, respecting the customary law of each of the separate groups, was introduced to the courts by the Governor of Bengal, Warren Hastings, in 1772. This allowed the law of Hinduism to be applied to Hindus and the law of Islam to apply to Muslims. Because, such customary law was made part of the framework of the modern judiciary, coordinating customary law and modern judicature later became a very difficult task. In other words, a contradictory structure of 'non-intervention within intervention' was incorporated on a practical level into the governing system. It should be kept in mind that relative independence was accorded to religious groups (as with the case of introduction of personal law) by the political philosophy of secularism that separated state politics from religion, as well as by the presence of the colonial ruler, Great Britain, as the pressure that kept inter- group violence from erupting. Serious contradictions thus became endemic, contradictions originating from transforming religious groups into social units and building a ruling structure on the basis of the separation of politics and religion. As long as relative independence was officially provided to religious groups, potential communalism was inevitably involved. This situation is what this paper calls 'twisted relations between secularism and communalism.'

This framework, shaped by colonial rule, continued to primarily determine the social conditions of independent India in the post-colonial era. In that sense, we cannot summarily reject those who blame British colonial rule for the communalism plaguing India at the end of the twentieth century. It is a fact that during the colonial rule a possible path toward communalism was constructed.

Religion in pre-colonial, pre-modern society was naturally different from religion in the modern era, when separation between the spiritual and secular, between politics and religion, was promoted. Under the rule of pre-modern divine kingship, religion must have permeated the entirety of people's daily lives. In the modern period brought by colonial rule, by contrast, the diffusion of dualism that divided people's way of living into spiritual and secular made it possible to separate religion from worldly affairs and to see it at a certain distance. Religion, in other words, became an object of conscious manipulation and choice. Here paradoxes occurred. At the time when the system dividing the Indian population into Hindus and Muslims – a system that made religion look as if it were the most important element of people's identity – became established, a secularization of religion, that is, religion no longer coinciding with the entire identity of the people, was also in progress. Secularization, needless to say, reduces religion to just a part of life. People are thus placed in a double bind religiously. They are suspended between the basic proposition of secularism – that religion should withdraw from government (a state that does not intervene in matters of religion) – and the proposition that religion is employed as the criterion for division into social groups (a state that intervenes in religion). In a secular state, a solution to this double-bind situation is generally to divide the life of a person into private life and public life, and to allot religion to private life. Implementation of this solution, however, inevitably leaves people with a sense of oppression, because it is unnatural that a person should draw such a clear line between the private and public aspects of life. In India, this general solution can work all the less, because the official recognition of religious division is institutionalized. Thus, British colonial rule in India brought into being a secular state system which used religion institutionally for its own ends and in which it was difficult to maintain a balanced administration.

Through the medium of this double-bind state system, secularism paved the twisted path to communalism. The formidable problems that faced the anti-British nationalist movement that rose up for independence toward the end of the nineteenth century can be attributed to the nature of a secular state that utilized religion.[15] The problem was that anti-British nationalism was twisted into anti-Muslim communalism, as seen in the case of Hindu nationalist Bal Gangadhar Tilak.[16] The development of Indian nationalism proceeded side by side with the Hindu purification movement. This combination of nationalism with communalism was a projection of the victim consciousness that surfaced under British rule, and back to the time of the Muslim conquest of India. This stretch of imagination was basically accelerated by the British policy of rule by religious division. It strengthened religious divisions to such an extent that nationalist leaders reacted sensitively to the demarcated religious borders of government and eventually led to Partition (independence of two separate states).

Let us outline, drawing on the work of Naitô,[17] the birth and growth of the Hindu nationalist forces that fought against Muslims under the anti-colonial movement. Stimulated by the Bengal Partition in 1905, a blatant manifestation of the colonial government's utilization of religion, and by the formation in 1906 of the Muslim League, Hindus organized the Hindu Maha Sabha (HMS) in

1915 through the medium of the Punjab-Hindu Sabha set up in 1907. Initially, the HMS had close ties with the Indian National Congress Party, but in the 1920s it parted with the Congress, attacking Mohandas Karamchand Gandhi ((Mahatma Gandhi) and other Congress Party leaders' Muslim leanings (as exemplified by their approval of Muslim partition election and the development of the Khilafat Movement). Then, together with the Arya Samaj ('society of Aryans'), HMS launched a forceful re-conversion movement.

By that time, Hindu-Muslim communal conflicts had spread widely. Under these circumstances was born a communal organization called Rashtriya Swayamsevak Sangh (RSS or, literally, Association of National Volunteers) in September 1925. RSS was founded by K B Hedgewar and its philosophical basis was the idea of *sangatan* (organising), aimed at forging a unity among Hindus that sustained HMS. The idea is epitomised in *Hindutva* (The Essence of Hinduism), one of Vinayak Damodar Savarkar's major works. The concept of *hindutva* is based on Hinduism, but goes beyond it. By 'Hindus', Savarkar means people born in the 'land of India' (Hindustan), who recognise the land as the holy place of their ancestors. They make up an ethnic entity united by the love for this common homeland and by common blood. The goal of the idea is, therefore, to establish the ethnic entity, Hindu *Rashtriyatva*. The *hindutva* doctrine defines Muslims, Christians and other 'heretical' minority groups as those whose land of origin is elsewhere and who, therefore, cannot love the land of India, thereby providing communalists with a rationale for expelling them from Indian society. By extension of that rationale, it came to be argued that if they remained in India, they could not be on an equal footing with Hindus.

The RSS, which defined itself as a cultural organisation, expanded to 500 local branches with a total of 60,000 members by the end of the 1930s. Many (most) RSS activists were upper caste members and middle-class people in urban areas. In 1940, Hedgewar died and M S Golwalkar became president, and the RSS movement directed its efforts toward Indian independence. In 1941, in rivalry with Hindu nationalist activities like those of the RSS, a Muslim communal organisation, the Jamaat-e-Islami, was established. The development and radicalisation of such communalism eventually resulted in Partition. The Partition was particularly humiliating to Hindus, whose sense of communalism was strong, based on their reverence for the entire land of India as Hindustan. Indian independence, thus, left in its wake further heightened communalism, for the presence of Muslims within India after Partition always reminds Hindu nationalists of the humiliating sense they bitterly felt at the time of independence, and of their powerlessness.

It should be kept in mind that resistance in the form of anti-colonial movements are apt to follow the framework of the governing structure. Resistance activists thus tend to form their organizations along the lines of religious divisions when the ruling side utilizes religion, and along the lines of caste divisions when the ruling side utilizes the caste system. As in the case of the escalation of Hindu nationalism from anti-British to anti-Muslim, the energy of resistance accepts group divisions from above and assumes an immediate foe therein, projecting a false image. Consciously or unconsciously, politicians make effective use of this mechanism of false projection in mobilizing people. This is how ideologies religion encouraged by nationalism takes shape.

Amid the dynamic intersection of differences between religious groups, between castes, and between regions (languages), anti-colonial nationalism has been twisted in various ways. To cite but one easily visible example in history is sufficient to surmise the complexity of the situation. Westernized Indian elites, who received their education in Britain, experienced inner struggle over the question of how to build India as an independent modern state against colonial forces. Jawaharlal Nehru is an example *par excellence*. A man whose mind worked like a modern Western rationalist, Nehru must have been annoyed by his spiritual attraction to Mahatma Gandhi, who seemed irrational, even unrealistic. Things were complicated because Gandhi was torn within himself between ideal and reality and between Hindus and Muslims. Such inner split developed in the face of the twisted secularism-communalism relations that were rooted in the double-bind governing structure discussed earlier. Those twisted relations were carried over to post-independence India, and have been reproduced.

Religion and Politics in Post-independence India: Communalism Today

When the Indian Constitution came into force on January 26, 1950, India became a republic and the Congress Party came to power with Nehru as India's Prime Minister. A great challenge for independent India was how to cope with the volatile situation caused by continuation of the social structures based on castes and religious division established under the colonial rule, once the colonial weight from above, which had kept violence from erupting among different groups, was lifted.

The political history of India after World War I has been divided by Hiroshi Satô into three periods: the first period, leading up to independence in 1947; the second period from 1947 to the fourth general election thereafter, held in 1967, in which the Congress Party suffered a crushing defeat; and the third period from then onward.[18] According to Satô, the first period can be represented by Mahatma Gandhi, the second by Jawaharlal Nehru, and the third by Indira Gandhi.

Mahatma Gandhi, an ardent advocate of *Swaraj* (home rule) for India, mediated between radicals demanding early independence and moderates who attached more importance to social reform, and succeeded in involving not only the urban middle class but *kisans* (peasants) in the nationalist movement. He also played a leading role in expanding the support base of the Indian National Congress Party, organised as an appeasement measure under colonial rule, into a nation-wide organisation of Indians themselves.[19] Through the Congress Party, the three classes – peasants, middle class, and capitalists – united forces, paving the way for a system of parliamentary democracy led by the Congress Party in post-independence India. Gandhi himself, however, saw the realities of post-independence Congress Party politics as anti-democratic and called for reform to nurture a Lok Sevak Sangh (People's Voluntary Service Association). However, in 1948, amid the upsurge of communal sentiments in the wake of the Partition, he was fatally shot by a young man who belonged to the RSS, the Hindu communalist organization.

Built on the legacy of the first period was the 'Nehru democracy' of the second period (which was launched after the Congress Party's victory in the first general election in 1952). There were two major factors that sustained the Indian people's dreams for democracy, development, and progress during this period: the presence of a social consensus for nation building through modernization and the practical possibility of realizing a socialist society embodied in a mixed economy. Because of this consensus and vision, in the early stages of independence, India was able to deal with the issue of communalism with relative ease, bringing it under control.

In the third period, communalism-prompted riots quickly became widespread under the influence of the second and third India-Pakistan wars in 1965 and

1971, on the one hand, and strife between the Congress Party and the Janata Party, on the other. The Jan Sangh (JS, literally, People's Association; formed in 1951), the predecessor of the Hindu communalist Bharatiya Janata Party (BJP, literally, Indian People's Party, formed in 1980) joined the Janata Party, in power between 1977 and 1980 after an overwhelming victory in the 1977 election over the Congress Party led by Indira Gandhi. The merging of the Jan Sangh and the Janata Party was a result of the fact that the RSS, which had remained a cultural organization until the end of the term of its second president Golwalkar, began to actively engage in political activities under its third president M D Deoras. The RSS also has close ties with the religious organization, the Vishwa Hindu Parishad (VHP, World Hindu Council), organized in 1964 as a union of India-wide Hindu groups aimed at strengthening the bonds of Hindu society at home and abroad. The emergence of diverse Hindu communalist groups, mainly during the third period, forming what is known as the Sangh Parivar (RSS Family) centering on the RSS, VHP, and BJP, was not unrelated to the outbreak of frequent communal riots. A communal incident that symbolized the period was occasioned by the massive conversion to Islam of former untouchables in the village of Minakshipuram, in the State of Tamil Nadu in southern India, in February 1981. In response, a Hindu communalist organization in the Tamil area linked to the Sangh Parivar launched a movement to convert them back to Hinduism. This case indicates the early pattern in which Hindu communalist organizations began to spread throughout India.

To bring the account up-to-date to the present day, we may add one more period to Sato's three-period scheme. This is the period of communalism we see today. The events that ushered in the fourth period occurred between 1984, when Indira Gandhi was assassinated (igniting communal clashes between Hindus and Sikhs mainly in the capital city of New Delhi) and her son Rajiv Gandhi succeeded her as Prime Minister, and 1989, when the Cold War structure collapsed. In terms of the domestic political phenomena of contemporary India, the fourth-period upsurge of communalism is characterized by the political instability caused by the rise of Hindu nationalists coinciding with the advent of the multi-party era following the end of prolonged single-party rule by the Indian National Congress Party. That upsurge can also be seen, in broader perspective, as linked to the religious revitalization sweeping the world today. In Iran, Ayatollah Khomeini's 1979 revolution marked the starting point of the religious revival movement that is often called Islamic fundamentalism. In India around that time, after the Indira Gandhi administration lost in the 1977 election, the Janata Party was in power. This indicates that the dreams of modernization and the forces of political ideology were completely frustrated as the third period came to an end. In that sense, one can say that India entered an era of 'reflexive modernization' – to paraphrase sociologist Ulrich Beck – contrasting with the 'simple modernization' of the Nehru democracy period that Indians had pursued while they shared the belief in socialism and modernization. In the unsettled period of reflexive modernization,[20] as people began realizing that their dreams were illusory, the insecure and delicate relationship between religion and politics began to take belligerent forms. In other words, the contradictory structure inherent in the twisted relationship between secularism and communalism began to resurface in new forms.

On December 6, 1992, riots fanned by BJP and other Jan Sangh members destroyed the Babri Masjid (Babri mosque, built by the first Mughal emperor Babur) in Ayodhya, the sacred birthplace of Hindu deity Rama. This means that, although the Hindu-Muslim confrontation over the holy city of Ayodhya had already begun during the colonial period, Hindu nationalists took the dangerous, dramatic first step toward communalism that we see currently. The incident was widely reported in the media and was instantly known within and outside India, sparking violent reactions in various areas, including Bombay (now Mumbai). In Bombay, two major waves of riots followed the toppling of the Babri Masjid. The first, which flared as a more-or-less spontaneous reaction, only a day later, lasted until December 17, 1992, leaving 227 people dead. The second case of violence, which occurred the following year, March 12, 1993, was planned in advance and the toll was much higher (approximately 500 dead). This series of communal riots provided a decisive turning point. The crescendo of communalism and the crisis of secularism became a serious plague in India. Notwithstanding, the BJP, the political arm of the Jan Sangh, rapidly increased its support base in the 1990s, and eventually took over the central government in 1998, albeit by allying itself with other parties.

Hindu nationalists have long been hostile, primarily towards Muslims, but over the last several years, their offensive against Christians has grown intense as well. More recently, their attacks on Christians in the State of Gujarat, commencing towards the end of year 1998, drew much attention, and all of India was shocked when an Australian missionary and his two children were killed on the night of January 22, 1999, in a village in the State of Orissa.[22]

These incidents seem to be the result of fervor for expulsion of minority religious groups deemed strangers in the holy land of India, probably inspired by the ideology of *Hindutva.* The idea alone, however, cannot fully explain why Christians are targets of Hindu attacks at present. Anger on the part of Hindus over conversion of Indians to Christianity may be one reason, but it cannot be the complete answer. Their attacks on Christians cannot be sufficiently explained on the grounds of advancing their noble cause. Dipankar Gupta argues that Muslims and Sikhs, who once suffered Hindu assaults without much resistance, are now fighting back, making the defenseless and weak Christians easier targets of Hindu rage. Naming VHP, RSS, and Bajrang Dal among others, he asserts that such Hindu nationalist fanatics, who kill but avoid self-sacrifice, should be distinguished from fundamentalists who are ready to die for great causes. He denounces the corruption of VHP leaders, mentioning them by name, and declares that they have grown jealous and frustrated because of their inability to fulfil their own ideals. They are quick to identify objects of harassment in an attempt to justify their inglorious lives by sacrificing others. Gupta's analysis is helpful in attempting to understand the communalism of today. His view echoes Ashis Nandy's assertion that communalism, contrary to its superficial appearance, is moving further and further away from religion in the true sense.[23] Gupta's distinction between fanatical nationalists and fundamentalists is close to Nandy's distinction between 'religion as ideology,' that is a communalist sense of religion, on the one hand and 'religion as faith' that comes alive in people's everyday lives, on the other.[24] It is also similar to the contrast Imtiaz Ahmad sees between communalism and religion.[25] There is no doubt that in Nandy's mind, 'religion as ideology' is associated with the communalism of the Jan Sangh and 'religion as faith' with religion as aspired to by Mahatma Gandhi. Be that as it may, what is the crucial issue posed by today's daily intensifying communalism?

Misunderstanding of the Communalism vs. Secularism Scheme

Worried about the current upsurge of communalism, many argue that secularism should be protected in order to defend democracy. This approach, needless to say, places communalism in antithesis to secularism. But can such an approach really give us any insight about the future? Can it deal soundly with the problems thrust before us by the tide of religious revivalism and communalism today?

There are facts that undermine the conventional view that secularism and communalism are at opposite poles. Attainment of 'genuine secularism' is included among the planks of the ruling BJP government agenda. Some may say that such a statement should be ignored because it is simply part of the glib rhetoric of politicians. But it is quite intriguing: a communalist party advocating 'genuine secularism.' What circumstances does this paradoxical rhetoric reflect? One is forced to re-examine the relationship between secularism and communalism, which on the surface seem to be opposites, because the former calls for separation of religion and politics and the latter for unity of religion and politics.

To state my conclusion at the outset, it may be argued that the difference between the two positions is not one between dualistic elements that have nothing in common, but a distinctive opposition between two elements that share the same ground, like the binary opposition of structuralism.[26] If that is so, it is not without reason that the BJP advocates 'genuine secularism.' Let me elucidate this in detail. In the secularism-communalism confrontation, it does appear that culturally relativistic secularism, which refrains from making judgements about religious values, is threatened by an absolutist communalism that asserts a specific religion as a universal value. In actuality, however, both secularism and communalism have a relative understanding of the coexistence of various religious groups in the world, and are premised upon a modern consciousness of homogeneous space that allows the drawing of a sectional religious map. In other words, epistemologically, both secularism and communalism are relativistic. In that sense, they share a secularized understanding of the world, a modern thought that enables them to view religion as an object, that is, to separate religion from politics. It is on this shared ground that the differences of secularism from communalism must be considered.

The difference is found at the level of value judgements. Secularism embraces moral relativism while communalism takes the stance of moral absolutism. The latter approach leads to separatism, abandoning any constructive effort at internalized or empathetic understanding of others. The narrow-minded separatism of communalism is a product of the marriage of epistemological relativism and moral absolutism. Seen in this way, the BJP's 'genuine secularism' can be interpreted as follows: 'secularism' indicates secular epistemological relativism and 'genuine' means moral absolutism as expressed in the idea of *Hindutva*. The phrase in the BJP's government agenda, therefore, can be considered a very candid expression of the BJP's ideology. Theoretically (due to its relativist position), it is impossible to easily add 'genuine' to secularism, because this would throw secularism into a very difficult position *vis-à-vis* communalism.

Partha Chatterjee, for example, points out that, because right-wing Hindus do not challenge the idea of a secular state, they cannot be denounced as a means of defending secularism. Generally, secularism has two constituent aspects:

1. the modern state is strictly separated from religion; and
2. the modern state always observes a neutral stand toward religion.[27] Especially in India, where religious groups are utilized in the official structure of society, the second aspect of secularism arises as a realistic problem in dealing with strife among religious groups. Communalism, which takes tactical advantage of these two aspects of secularism, is hard to bring under control. In an extreme case, when a majority religious group takes the helm of national government, it can suppress minority religious groups in the name of a modern state.

The situation may be easier to understand by looking at Imtiaz Ahmad's discussion, which rejects the belief that communalism and secularism are in direct opposition, and astutely argues that the real discord is between religion and communalism as mentioned above.[28] In Ahmad's view, the state-religion relationship as stipulated in the Indian Constitution is a product of the 'compromise' of two constituent aspects of secularism (a compromise that is not necessarily negative). Secularism as defined in the Constitution connotes two simultaneous positions (stipulations). From the viewpoint of the Early-Nehru-style or Western-style secularism, it states that the government is separated from religion (referred to hereafter as stipulation A); on the one hand, and, from a Gandhi-style standpoint, it states that the central government equally supports all religions (referred to hereafter as stipulation B).[29]

There is a possibility that the two positions may make different assertions relying on these stipulations as their basis of argument, and because of this possibility, it is necessary to identify a point of compromise. In other words, the first position (stipulation A) may lead to an assertion that the nation's goal should be to make it possible for people, regardless of religious difference, to have equal duties and rights under non-religious, unified laws. This stance is oriented toward unification, giving consideration to people before religious groups. The second position (stipulation B), on the other hand, tends toward pluralism, approving the existence of any religious group (religious community) and granting them the right to pursue their respective creeds and practices. Although this stance guarantees freedom of religion, it also reserves room for the interpretation that religious groups may come before the people affiliated with them. The two opposite stipulations, one oriented toward unification of the state and the other toward religious pluralism, coexist in the Indian Constitution. Religious groups have tried to utilize this compromise constitution to their own advantage, and that, argues Ahmad, is the history of independent India.

A serious problem arises when a majority religious group takes advantage of the law, as is the case with the issue over adoption of the uniform civil code. The results completely differ, depending upon whether the uniform civil code subordinates 'stipulation B' to 'stipulation A' or subordinates 'stipulation A' to 'stipulation B'. The former would be attainment of law as a forging of consensus among religious groups, an ideal desired in the materialization of secularism in the future, while the latter corresponds to the behavior of communalists who forcefully and hastily demand a uniform civil code.

A case in point is the advocacy of a uniform civil code by the nationalist BJP, whose support base is made up of majority Hindus. The party tries to utilize the two stipulations to its advantage, with emphasis on 'stipulation B', and seeks to make the voices of Hindus sound like the voice of the Indian nation. This position exploits two misguided attitudes. One is seen in the tendency to utilize officially accepted religious divisions so as to advance the views of some nationalists as if they represented Hindus in general. The other is in introducing the idea of *Hindutva* to assert the association of Hinduism with the Indian state. This is how the phoney phrase 'genuine secularism' came into being. As discussed thus far, it is clear that the contradictory structure of a secular state made up of religion-based social groups – 'the twisted relationship between secularism and communalism' – cannot be rectified from the simplistic perspective of secularism versus communalism.

The De-Modernization Dilemma: 'Religion and Human Life' Reconsidered

Assuming that the secularism–communalism confrontation is not a real problem to be tackled, then where does the real problem lie? To find it out, Ahmad focuses on the difference between 'religion' and 'communalism,' as mentioned earlier. The importance of this shift or leap in perspective lies in seeing the twisted relationship between secularism and communalism as revealing the limits of the modern system (perceptions and institutions). That is to say, placing 'communalism' as antithetical to 'religion' is oriented toward the overcoming of the modern-de-modernization – as is Nandy's distinction between 'religion as ideology' and 'religion as faith.' The approach is derived from the anticipation that an emphasis on the defense of secularism alone may fail to resolve the real problem of 'overcoming the modern,' the issue addressed by communalism, and may suppress the problem and delay its solution.

In the sense that the urgent issue of anti-communalism is understood in greater depth as necessary for de-modernization, the perspective from which this paper tries to address the problem is very close to that of Ashis Nandy. Nandy is often criticised as an anti-modernist, but if one grasps his true meaning, one may well call him a spokesperson for de-modernisation. In Nandy's view, secularism, together with democracy, are part of the greater Western modernist project, and communalism came into being as the evil by-product of Western modernism or secularism, namely as the shadow delineating the limits of modernism. Nandy says that the shadow is especially evident, not among the elite or the lower classes, but among the middle class. This is because the middle class has experienced the most drastic social changes with the globalization of the economy and information.

In the face of the phenomena of communalism, people of the modern era, who were taught of the dangers of allowing religion into the official arena because it might be incapable of carrying on rational argument, usually think it advisable to return to the secularism that confines religion to the private realm. While cognizant of this danger, Nandy emphasises that it is time to abandon that approach. The modern cannot conceal the defects of the modern. As discussed in this paper, post-independence India, which sought to modernize itself, adopted Western-style secularism as a basic policy. It is becoming evident that adherence to this basic principle has not had the expected result, and it is time to face this problem squarely, because in reality religion enters into the official realm from the back door in the form of communalism.[31] According to Nandy's analysis, the actual situation in which religion can be officially talked about only via the back door under Western-style secularism works to aggravate the feelings of frustration and helplessness of the religious faithful and fuels fanaticism among them. He emphasizes that the fundamental path for dissolving the phenomenon of communalism is to adequately meet the needs of those who cannot but enter through this back door. Because communalism, or religion as ideology, was the result of the attempt to seal off religion with Western-style secularism, dualistic approaches such as politics versus religion, or secular versus spiritual, will not work. It is crucial to build a path of tolerance and harmony by attaching more importance to 'religion as faith' that embraces the entirety of people's everyday lives. For Nandy, an advocate of the de-modernization project, this both anti-secularist and anti-communalist proposal also means a call for fundamental reforms in the way the modern state system has clung to science and development.[32]

Outward appearances aside, the phenomena of communalism today have grown less and less religious in the true sense and grown more and more secular. As Nandy sees it, contemporary Hindu nationalists (communalists) are secular modernists who manipulate 'religion as ideology,' as for example the concept of *Hindutva*. They are like merchants dealing in packaged Hinduism (as opposed to a packaged Islam), making ideology a uniformly standardized commercial commodity. 'Religion as faith,' on the other hand, is religion as it shaped the Indian life style before such modernization or secularization. Religion in that sense is not self-righteous or monolithic, but pluralistic in practice. Religion in this sense is premised not upon the rigid and close-minded individual but upon the mobile and open-minded individual, and has its own principles about tolerance and intolerance.

By introducing the above distinction into religion, Nandy clearly shows:

1. it is difficult (for Indian people at least) to imagine human life that rejects the presence of religion; and
2. the highly flexible religious tradition that once endowed human life with the meaning of life is actually abused as an ideology for secular benefit.

By separating the two different types of religion, he calls for conscious efforts to explore and restore the profound meaning of 'religion as faith.' From this dimension, he urges reestablishment of religious tolerance so that all religions can respect one another.

Among Indian intellectuals, many criticize the Nandy-style anti-modernism as an anachronistic throw-back to Mahatma Gandhi, declaring that modern secularism itself should be strengthened. (In fact, these people are Nandy's targets, and *vice versa*.) They are essentially advocates of Nehru-style secularism based on Western-style secularism, but it is also true that they feel acutely the necessity to rectify the defects of secularism and reinvigorate it. They reflect that Nehru-style secularism and Congress Party politics, propelled by favorable circumstances of the times, grew transcendental and dogmatic, failing to develop the pluralism that allows for constructive dialogue among different groups. That failure resulted in the deadlock and decline of the Congress Party-led politics that had sustained Indian democracy. Despite such reflection, they (Amartya Sen, for example) argue that as long as there is no better alternative, secularism cannot easily be abandoned. From this viewpoint, they are concerned that the Nandy-like stance of criticizing secularism and communalism at the same time may turn out to support the communalists' criticism of Congress Party secularism.

This concern is somewhat understandable, but is a totally off-the-mark criticism of Nandy. An attempt to explore the intersection of modern reformists and de-modernists, like Rajeev Bhargava's work, is valuable, but the reason this paper devotes much space to Nandy's argument is because its generally believes that, unless people change their perceptions so as to awaken thinking and the institutions bound by the spell of the modern, it will be impossible to attain a forum of plurality where dialogue to bridge the gap between the self and others is made possible.

In that sense, this author's interpretation of Nandy's argument is different from that of the advocates of modernist secularism. Modern reformists, who try to act within the framework of modern secularism, tend to criticise Nandy's approach as a revivalist anachronism, seeing his division of religion into two types as an attempt to contrast Western modernity with Indian tradition. But, this is a very shallow understanding of Nandy.

The distinction between *Hindutva*, which is 'religion as ideology,' and Hinduism in the realm of people's everyday life ('religion as faith'), can be expressed as follows, borrowing literary critic Karatani Kojin's analytical concepts, 'individuality as particularity' ('I' that can be compared with others) and 'individuality as singularity' (the 'none other than I' that cannot be compared with others). It is possible to make a distinction between 'religion as particularity,' in which religions can be compared and often used as a means of discrimination, and 'religion as singularity,' in which the differences of the secular 'costumes' worn by religions are meaningless, and only deep faith in the absolute other, regardless of religious differences, is focused upon. The latter, or 'religion as singularity,' can only exist on the peripheral border of the social space of secular modern society, where 'religion as ideology' is dominant. Only there, does the world of faith open to others, and , which should be the core of religion, unfold. This is because, that place borders on the outside (the other). On the surface, the place seems to be where 'traditional' or 'indigenous' culture is being lost under the impact of a dominant culture. But in fact, the place is where the closed space of modern secular society borders on the outside. It is the scene of plurality where 'dialogue' is possible between the self and others, and 'tolerance' (not that advocated by modern humanism) that belongs in Nandy's 'religion as faith' can be materialized.

The passions of communalism are erupting on the oppressive periphery of the modern secular social space dominated by reason. This is occurring in reaction to the act of attempting to immediately throw into the secular prison of reason (closed space) all encounters with the outside (the other of reason), which results in violence and sacrifices of the other. At the same time, this volatile peripheral place is the very place where it is possible to reform the modern, a place suitable for thinking about the 'other of reason.' In other words, the place where communalism is occurring can become a place where a homicidal religion is transformed into religion that brings people alive. When violence that sacrifices others in the name of religion is transformed into acts of the self-sacrifice which is the core of faith, it will become a force that makes people spontaneously accept others. Nowhere, except at this border (periphery) where reason encounters the outside, can such genuine faith emerge.

The realities of human existence now challenge the validity of modernity; under which it has been believed that reason can control even religion. The phenomena of communalism can be interpreted as an immature form of the challenge. The issues they raise seem unclear and even retrogressive, but what is called for now is reform of perceptions that will allow people to firmly grasp the true meaning of those issues. This paper is a step toward that reform.

Caste and Politics

Emergence of electoral democracy in India created a very fertile ground. Caste system is a closed system but it's still evolving. British saw caste as a prism to understand India's social reality- "White man's burden".

Caste became a tool for justifying their rule in India. It led to caste conflicts among people. Caste also started churning in social consciousness. Therefore caste started evolving in Indian society. Modern Constitution abolished untouchability, also in 1976 (the Protection of Civil Rights Act), reservation of seats which ultimately resulted in further concretization of caste. Caste and casteism never disappeared in India. Myron Weiner's concept of "political co-optation" became very relevant. The policy of political mobilization followed by Congress and other parties also resulted in co-optation many lower castes into the party. With the erosion of the moral basis of caste, the self-imposed barrier to protest by the lower castes was also eroded. Therefore, some middle and lower castes sought equality with the upper castes through the process of sanskritisation (by emulating the orthopraxy of the higher castes), thus claiming more political power.

Thus according to Rajni Kothari, politicization of caste in India played a very important role in developing party politics. He proved how politicization of caste is a double process. Caste needs politics as much as politics need caste. When caste groupings make politics their sphere of activities. Caste groups then also gets a chance to assert their identity and to strive for position. MN Srinivas also used the concept of dominant caste. A dominant caste is a caste which dominates numerically, due to its numeric preponderance it enjoys political power. Politicians find caste a handy and convenient instrument for use during elections. Politics in Indian states had also been viewed in terms of competition among major caste groups for political power. Caste is also said to fractionalize national politics.

The previously excluded political leaders now enter the sphere. Srinivas also talked about 'dominant caste' which gained political and economic power through sensitization. Thus the intermediate castes also aspire for dominant position in every sphere due to the development of adult franchise and Panchayati Raj System. Although it is true that caste system had been strengthened rather than weakened by all these.

Caste based reservations came with the Article 15 of the Indian Constitution which prohibits discrimination of Indians on basis of religion, race , caste, sex or place of birth. But Article 15 (4)modified by asserting that nothing in this article shall prevent the state from making any special provision for the advancement of any socially and educationally backward of citizens or for the SC's and ST's.

Thus the constitution simultaneously embodies two conflicting notions of equality, one bases on individual rights and the other based on group rights. Also the Mandal Commission, or the Socially and Educationally Backward Classes Commission(SEBC), was established in 1979 by the Janata Party government under Prime minister Morarji Desai with a mandate to "identify the socially or educationally backward classes" of India. It basically defined backward classes in terms of caste . The caste membership rather than individual class characteristics became the matter of importance. Thus low social ranking in the class rather than average per capita income became the criteria for inclusion in the OBC list. Thus it made possible for caste membership to become responsible for identifying class benefits, thus social ranking became a matter of perception rather than a average per capita income. Thus caste and class became cross cutting identities.

Also with time as stated by Christophe Jaffrelot , class started transforming caste relations in India. Thus class and caste started coexisting in Indian society. Caste in India, thus slowly got converted into class plus status (social stigma of being pure and impure). Reservation helped certain jatis within dalits to catch up with OBC's and other dominant castes in terms of acquiring revenues. Thus within caste group due to reservation, people started leaving their jobs thus creating a socio economic differentiation within their caste groups.

Thus caste continues to be a 'lived in social reality' as stated by Myron Weiner. Orthopraxy still continued although ideological basis of caste is undermined. Still caste became an instrument of social change which resulted in rise of 'casteism', there also happened co-optation of previously excluded groups and this political mobilization gave rise to 'messy identity politics'. Thus sharpening of group identities, also the scheme of reservations 'taken hold as a mantra'(Marc Galanter) facilitated the lower caste groups to rise to political power.

The relation between class and caste is complex and 'cross cutting ' (Myron Weiner), overlapping identities so the struggle for status and the quest for equality continued. So caste became a far more potent form of social identity than class so social order remained in egalitarian. Also Mandal framework led 'egregious consequences' (Marc Galanter) because it identified Other Backward Classes in terms of caste . It created a heterogeneous vast diverse category of OBC's. Thus caste became the basis of a scheme of permanent protection.

'Curious Cognitive hiatus' as stated by Rajni Kothari, which explained the dichotomy between tradition and modernity, also the symbolism of caste for social and economic positions of different groups. Thus caste as a traditional social structure has changed its functions and roles, maintaining itself in the process. Thus like caste has been changing and influencing politics, politics has also been influencing and changing the caste system. Sanskritisation as status urge turned as a 'mirage' (Kothari) , status became ambivalent, unsettled also Westernization and secularization led for economic well-being, liberal education gave rise to rationality and also political power for more institutions drew caste into politics. Thus caste identities took to new form of articulation thus changing the very ethics of the social system and diminished the very importance of inscriptive and ritualistic basis on the other hand the process of 'ethnicization' (Christophe Jaffrelot) and positive discrimination of caste has been the result of transformation of caste into interest groups.

Chapter Five

Indian Foreign Policy

Foreign Policy of India

Foreign policy refers to the sum total of principles, interests and objectives which a country promotes while interacting with other countries. Even though there are certain basic features of a foreign policy it is not a fixed concept.

The thrust of foreign policy keeps on changing according to changing international conditions. India's foreign policy is shaped by several factors including its history, culture, geography and economy.

Panchsheel

- Panchsheel was born fifty years ago in response to a world asking for a new set of principles for the conduct of international relations that would reflect the aspirations of all nations to co-exist and prosper together in peace and harmony.

- India's desired peaceful and friendly relations with all countries, particularly the big powers and the neighbouring nations, while signing an agreement with China, on April 28, 1954, India advocated adherence to five guiding principles known as Panchsheel for the conduct of bilitral relations.

It includes the following:

Mutual respect for each other's territorial integrity and sovereignty.

Mutual non-aggression.

Mutual non-interference in each other's internal affairs.

Equality and mutual benefit.

Peaceful co-existence.

Non-alignment

- Non-alignment has been regarded as the most important feature of India's foreign policy.
- Non alignment aimed to maintain national independence in foreign affairs by not joining any military alliance formed by the USA and Soviet Union in the aftermath of the Second World War.
- Non-alignment was neither neutrality nor non-involvement nor isolationism. It was a dynamic concept which meant not committing to any military bloc but taking an independent stand on international issues according to the merits of each case.
- The policy of non-alignment won many supporters in the developing countries as it provided an opportunity to them for protecting their sovereignty as also retaining their freedom of during the tension ridden cold war period.
- India played an important role in forging the non-aligned movement (NAM). The concept of NAM emerged through a gradual process. Nehru took the initiative to convene the Asian Relations Conference in New Delhi in 1947. Later on a Conference, of 29 countries of Asia and Africa was held in Bandung (Indonesia) in 1955. This was the first gathering of its kind which pledged to work together for colonial liberation, peace, cultural, economic and political cooperation.

- Bandung to Belgrade in 1961 where the first NAM conference was held was a logical process to project an alternative to cold war bloc politics and assertion of newly independent countries of their independent and sovereign rights.
- The Non-Aligned Movement is providing all member states, regardless of size and importance, an opportunity to participate in global decision making and world politics.
- India hosted the Seventh NAM Summit at New Delhi in 1983. India hoped NAM take up the cause of development, disarmament and the Palestine question.
- Since NAM was a product of the cold war scenario and the bipolar world, many scholars have questioned the relevance of NAM after the end of cold war and demise of the Soviet Union.
- NAM has a significant role to play, First, with the disintegration of Soviet Union, the world faces threat from unipolar world. The NAM can act as a check against US dominance.

  Secondly the developed (North) and developing (South) world are divided over several economic issues. The NAM remains a very relevant forum for third world countries to engage the developed nations in a productive dialogue.

  The NAM can prove to be powerful instrument for South-South cooperation. Such a thing is essential if the third world countries are to increase their bargaining power vis-a-vis the developed world.

  Finally, the developing countries united under the forum of NAM have to fight for the reform of UN and change it according to the requirements of 21st century

Anti Imperialism, Anti Racism, Anti Colonialism

- India has always opposed colonialism and racism. Whenever any injustice happened, India raised her voice, for instance in favor of Indonesia's nationality fighting the Dutch colonialism in 1947, against South Africa's illegal occupation of Namibia and the infamous apartheid policy in South Africa India fully supported inclusion of communist China in the United Nations.

Anti Imperialism, Anti Racism, 3nti Colonialism

- India has always opposed colonialism and racism. Whenever any injustice happened, India raised her voice, for instance in favour of Indonesia's nationality fighting the Dutch colonialism in 1947, against South Africa's illegal occupation of Namibia and the infamous apartheid policy in South Africa India fully supported inclusion of communist China in the United Nations.

Strengthening of UN

- India has always viewed UN as a vehicle for peace and for peaceful change in world politics. Apart from this, India has always expected UN to actively involve countries to moderate their differences through talks or negotiations. Further, India has advocated active role for UN in development effort of Third World countries. India has pleaded for a common united front of the third world countries in the UN. It believes that the nonaligned world by virtue of its massive number could play a constructive and meaningful role in the UN by stopping the superpowers from using this world body for their own designs. As early as 1950 India linked the reduction of armaments with the larger goal of development. The UN has in fact played a key role in preserving world peace by helping in the decolonization process, by providing humanitarian and developmental assistance and through peacekeeping. Decolonization - refers to achievement of independence from colonial rule. After the Second World War many colonies of achieved freedom in Asia and Africa.

Major Concerns in India's Foreign Policy in the Post Cold War Period

- For India, disintegration of the Soviet Union has meant uncertainty on several aspects viz. supply of weapons system, supply of spare parts, diplomatic support on Kashmir and other politico-strategic issues in and outside the United Nations and as a counter weight to US in South Asia
- The cold war has ended, the world has become unipolar, a number of states have disintegrated, cold war military blocs have lost their significance, some such blocs have dissolved and new regional economic blocs are shaping up.

- Globalization has given rise to new set of problems such as terrorism, money laundering, proliferation of weapons, global warming etc. These problems are not endemic to any region but affect all the countries to some extent or the other.
- Militancy in Kashmir has emerged as the foremost challenge to our foreign policy. Pakistan and the Western countries blamed India for violating human rights and denial of rights to self-determination. Gradually, India brought the situation under control.

Major Concerns in India's Foreign Policy in the Post Cold War Period

- For India, disintegration of the Soviet Union has meant uncertainty on several aspects viz. supply of weapons system, supply of spare parts, diplomatic support on Kashmir and other politico-strategic issues in and outside the United Nations and as a counter weight to US in South Asia.
- The cold war has ended, the world has become unipolar, a number of states have disintegrated, cold war military blocs have lost their significance, some such blocs have dissolved and new regional economic blocs are shaping up.
- Globalization has given rise to new set of problems such as terrorism, money laundering, proliferation of weapons, global warming etc. These problems are not endemic to any region but affect all the countries to some extent or the other.
- Militancy in Kashmir has emerged as the foremost challenge to our foreign policy. Pakistan and the Western countries blamed India for violating human rights and denial of rights to self-determination. Gradually, India brought the situation under control.
- Because of the Kashmir dispute, India's relations with Pakistan sharply deteriorated. India accused Pakistan of fanning trouble through cross border terrorism in Kashmir and other parts of our country.
- India conducted nuclear weapon tests in 1998, followed by Pakistan's tests. Pakistan resorted to further mischief by secretly sending its soldiers into Kargil in India and the World order to cut off the Kashmir valley from the rest of India. India handled the challenge firmly and

effectively. Now engaging Pakistan in a constructive and composite dialogue process remains a challenge to India's foreign policy, because there is a great deal of push from the United States.

- Spread of terrorism to corners beyond Kashmir is a challenge as well as opportunity for our foreign policy now a day. India is interested in forging anti-terrorism coalition with as many countries as possible.
- Keeping old friendship and looking for new friendships is another challenge for our foreign policy after the cold war has ended.

India and the United Nations

- India's Contribution to UN Efforts for Peace and Disarmament is limitation, reduction and possible elimination of dangerous (like nuclear) weapons. Since independence, India has consistently pursued the objective of global disarmament based on the principles of non-discrimination.
- Given the destructive capacity of nuclear weapons, India has always believed that a world free of nuclear weapons would enhance global security.
- India has contributed to UN significantly on disarmament in terms of ideas, resolutions, initiatives and bridging differences through action plans.
- In 1948, India had proposed limiting the use of atomic energy to peaceful purposes and elimination of nuclear weapons from national arsenals.
- In 1950, India suggested formation of a UN Peace Fund created through peaceful reduction of arms and directing the amount thus released towards development purposes.
- In 1984, India launched a Six-Nation Five Continent Peace Initiative along with Argentina, Greece, Mexico, Sweden and Tanzania. Four years later in a joint declaration issued on the occasion of visit of President Gorbachev of Soviet Union
- India is also an original signatory to the Chemical Weapons Convention, having signed it on Jan. 14, 1993 and was among the first 65 countries to have ratified the treaty. In 1993 India sponsored a resolution on

comprehensive test ban along with the US within the overall framework of advancing towards nuclear disarmament.

India's participation in UN peacekeeping

- In UN India's contribution has been acknowledged by members of the international communities.
- Peace keeping stands for prevention, containment and termination of hostilities between or within states through the non offensive activities of multinational forces of soldiers, police and civilian people sent unto the authority of the United Nations with the consent of the countries concerned. Peacekeeping nations changed in its scope and nature according to needs of a conflict situation.
- India has taken part in 35 of UN peacekeeping operations in four continents. Its most significant contribution has been to peace and stability in Africa and Asia. Presently India is ranked as the largest troop contributor to UN.
- The saga of India's role in UN peace keeping began with the establishment of the United Nation's Emergency Force (UNEF) in the Gaza strip and the Sinai in 1956 after Israeli war against Egypt ended. The Congo in Africa benefitted significantly from troop presence. India's contributed to keep unity and integrity of that history in 1960s.
- After the end of cold war, India's contribution to UN peacekeeping remains significant equally, if not more, military personal at the request of the United Nations Secretary General to Angola, Cambodia, Somalia, El Salvador and Sierra Leone etc. Many of these countries were victims of chaos caused by civil wars. No government machinery collapsed or was discredited. India sent not just troops, but police, doctors, engineers and administrators.

India's Case for a permanent Seat in the Security Council

- The efficiency of peace maintenance in the world depends on the effectiveness of the Security Council but the Council has suffered in this regard due to its outdated, unchanged membership.
- Presently the permanent membership of the Security Council is confined to US, Russia, Great Britain, France and China. However,

such composition of the Security Council does not take into account the current global power configuration which has changed since the days when these countries were inducted as permanent members.

- Since India has emerged as the fourth fastest growing economy and also because of the leadership it has provided in all international fora, its contribution to UN peacekeeping, its track record in espousing the cause of the third world,
- India has a strong case for a permanent seat in the Security Council. We are getting support from many friendly countries. A final decision on the matter is likely to take some time, because of its complexity.

India and BRIC

- For India, these two groups are extremely important, considering that both aim to collectively boost bargaining power and clout on global issues, and also strengthen economic and political ties among the member countries on the lines of South-South co-operation.
- Co-operation on the economic front is one of the focus areas of India's policy towards BRIC. It believes that global challenges can only be addressed by co-operative effort, with the full and equal participation of major and emerging powers and economies.
- Since they share common challenges as developing countries and global challenges often affect them in a similar way. In addition to discussions about how to respond to the financial crisis, India exchanged ideas and experiences on food security, agriculture, disease, foreign aid, energy and global warming.
- Sharing these experiences not only helps the BRIC member-states themselves, it also allows them to share experiences and "best practices" with the developing world and thereby expand South-South cooperation.
- India has also tried to use BRIC as a forum to engage China as the latter has become the largest market for the fast-industrializing countries of East Asia. The volume of China-India trade has soared in recent years, and is likely to reach $60 billion by the end of 2010.
- India seeks co-operation in with Russia to devise effective countries-terror strategies by co-coordinating intelligence and information gathering systems between the two countries.

- On the other hand, there are immense opportunities to expnd trade, investment and technology flow between the two countries. Ci-operation in the fields of energy, number energy program and defense are the other import aspects of co-operation between the two countries, besides shared views on issues like economic slowdown, climate change and global governance.
- With Brazil, India has a unique partnership arrangement that has attracted international attention. Both countries have directly challenged western nations over free trade during various rounds of WTO negotiations, most notably at the 2003 Cancun meeting.

Conclusion

- India has followed certain basic principles in the conduct of its foreign policy from which it has not deviated much. In fact some of its basic features such as non-alignment still remain significant and relevant. The proof of the durability of some decades old principles lie in the efforts of India and China to revive the fifty year old Panchsheel as the basis of bilateral relations. India has contributed significantly to UN efforts for peace and disarmament and to UN peacekeeping operations. Even as India is poised to become an economic superpower in the coming times, it always has and in future too will take necessary steps to further its national interest in every respect i.e. political, strategic and economic terms.

Basic Objectives of Indian Foreign Policy

The foreign policy of India aims to maintain international peace and security, to oppose imperialism, to stand against the apartheid policy, to propagate the peaceful and political settlement of international disputes, to foster peaceful coexistence, to remain non-aligned and non-committed, and to maintain the unity and solidarity of the Third World.

The important objectives of India's foreign policy include preservation of national interest, achievement of world peace, disarmament, independence for Afro-Asian nations. These objectives are sought to be achieved through some guiding principles such as Panchsheel, NAM, and others

Major Objectives of India's Foreign Policy

The major objectives governing India's Foreign policy are detailed below:

The preservation of India's territorial integrity and independence of foreign policy:

- The territorial integrity and protection of national boundaries from foreign aggression is the core interest of a nation.
- India had gained hard-earned independence from foreign rule after a long time. Thus, it was natural for her to give due emphasis on the independence of foreign policy.
- India's effort to strengthen Afro-Asian solidarity endorsement of principles of non-interference, in the internal affairs of other nations and finally the adoption of the policy of non-alignment should be seen in this light.
- To sustain the country's growth trajectory, India needs to interact with its foreign partners to bring in Foreign Direct Investments, financial assistance, and transfer of technology for schemes and programs like Make in India, Skills India, Smart Cities, infrastructure development, Digital India, Clean India etc. Therefore, it can be noted that in recent years, India's foreign policy adopted an approach by integrating economic diplomacy with political diplomacy.
- India has the largest diaspora in the world, comprising about 20 million Non-Resident Indians and Persons of Indian Origin, spread all over the world. Therefore, one of the major objectives is to engage them and derive maximum benefits from their presence abroad, while at the same time protecting their interests to the extent possible.
- To summarize, four important goals of India's Foreign Policy are:
    - To protect India from traditional and non-traditional threats;
    - To create an external environment that is conducive for inclusive development of India so that the benefits of growth can reach the poorest of the poor in the country;
    - To make sure that India's opinions are heard on global platforms and that India is able to influence world opinion on issues of global dimensions such as terrorism, climate change, disarmament, reforms of institutions of global governance;
    - To engage and protect the Indian Diaspora.

Promoting international peace and security:

- India as a 'newly independent and developing country rightly realized that international peace and development are correlated.

- Her emphasis on disarmament and the policy of keeping away from military alliances is intended to promote global peace.

The economic development of India:

- The fast development of the country was the fundamental requirement of India at the time of independence.
- It was also required to strengthen democracy and freedom in the country
- In order to gain financial resources and technology from both blocks and to concentrate her energy on the development, India opted away from the power bloc politics, which was the defining feature of Cold War international politics.
- The foreign policy practice of India also reveals its two other objectives:
  - Elimination of colonialism and racial discrimination
  - Protection of the interests of people of Indian origin abroad.
- An official statement of the Ministry of External Affairs (2010) notes that India's foreign policy seeks to safeguard her enlightened self-interest.
- Its primary objective is to promote and maintain a peaceful and stable external environment in which the domestic tasks of inclusive economic development and poverty alleviation can progress rapidly.
- Thus, India seeks a peaceful periphery and works for good neighborly relations in her extended neighborhood. India's foreign policy also recognizes that issues such as climate change, energy, and food security are crucial for India's transformation. Since these issues are global in nature, they require global solutions.

Determinants of Foreign Policy

Each nation has the right and power to secure the goals of her national interest in international relations. It is her supreme duty to satisfy the needs of her people. Each nation wants to be self-reliant in all areas of activity. However, in reality no nation can achieve cent per cent self-reliance and self-sufficiency.

Nations have always been interdependent and these are bound to remain so even after attaining high levels of development. "Interdependence has been an incontrovertible fact of international relations." It compels every nation to get essentially involved in the process of establishing and conducting relations with other nations. Each nation establishes diplomatic, economic, trade, educational, cultural and political relations with other nations.

What is Foreign Policy?

Foreign Policy can be defined as a set of principles, decisions and means, adopted and followed by a nation for securing her goals of national interest in international relations. Foreign Policy defines the goals of national interest and then tries to secure these through the exercise of national power.

George Modelski defined foreign policy as *"Foreign Policy is the system of activities evolved by communities for changing the behaviour of other states and for adjusting their own activities to the international environment."*

In simple words, it can be observed that Foreign Policy is a set of principles and decisions, a plan of action and a thought out course of action adopted and used by a nation for conducting relations with other nations and all international actors with a view to secure the preferred and defined goals of her national interest.

The Foreign Policy Contains

- A set of principles, policies and decisions adopted and followed by the nation in international relations.
- Objectives, goals or aims of national interest which are to be secured.
- Means to be used for achieving the goals of national interest.
- Broad policy principles and decisions for conducting international relations.
- Assessment of the gains and failures of the nation in respect of its goals of national interest.
- Policies, decisions and action-programs for maintaining continuity or change or both in international relations.

Common objective of foreign policy

- Protecting national prestige and developing national power, and
- Maintaining the integrity of state
- Promoting common interest

- Providing for national security
- Maintaining world order.

Determinants of Foreign Policy:

The foreign policy of a nation is formulated and implemented by its policy makers. In doing so they take into account the national interest of the nation, the internal and external environment, the national values, the foreign policy goals and decisions of other nations and the nature of international power structure.

1. Size of State Territory:

The size of a state is an important factor of its Foreign Policy. Size influences the psychological and operational environment within which the foreign policy-makers and public respond. It includes both human and non-human resources. Nations with large human and non-human resources always try to be big powers and they have better chances of becoming big powers in international relations.

Size has been a factor in the foreign policies of the U.S.A., Russia, China, India, Brazil, France and others. Large sized states, with few exceptions, always formulate and use an active Foreign Policy and through it these play an active role in international relations.

However, size alone is not an independent determinant of foreign policy. Resources and capabilities of the state are not always dependent upon size. The countries of the Middle East, even with small sizes but with the largest quantity of oil resources, have been playing quite an active role in international relations. Japan is relatively a small sized state and yet its role in international relations has been active and influential.

Israel, despite being a small sized state has been influencing the course of politics among nations. Before 1945, Britain, with a small size, could play the role of a world power. Large size poses the problem of defense, security and maintenance of communications. In the absence of natural boundaries, the large size of a nation very often creates the problem of relations with neighboring states. Despite being the large sized states, Australian and Canadian foreign policies have not been very active. Russia is a large sized state but its role in contemporary international relations continues to be weak.

2. Geographical Factor:

Geography of a state is relatively the most permanent and stable factor of its foreign Policy. The topography of land, its fertility, climate and location are the major geographic factors which influence the Foreign Policy of a nation.

Suitable geographical factors can help and encourage the nation to adopt and pursue higher goals. The role played by English Channel in the development of Britain as a major naval power and consequently as an imperial power is well known. The influence of the Atlantic Ocean on the US Foreign Policy has been always there. Indian Foreign Policy now definitely bears the influence of the geographical location of India as the largest littoral state of the Indian Ocean.

The natural resources and the food production capacity of a nation is directly linked with its geography. These factors are also important factors in the formulation and implementation of foreign policy. Adequate existence of vital natural resources minerals, food and energy resources have been helping factors of the US and Russian foreign policies.

Food shortage was a source of limitation on Indian Foreign Policy in the 1950s & 1960s. Consumer goods shortage have been hitting hard the foreign policy and relations of Russia. Large quantities of oil have made it possible for the West Asian and Gulf nations to adopt oil diplomacy as a means of their foreign policies.

Geography, as such is an important and permanent factor of foreign policy, yet it is not a deterministic factor. The revolutionary developments in communications and modern warfare, and the ability of nations to overcome geographical hindrances have tended to reduce the importance of geography.

3. Level and Nature of Economic Development:

One of the main reasons why the US Foreign Policy has been very often successful in securing its national objectives, particularly in relation to the poor and economically lowly placed states of the world is the high degree of its economic development. The developed countries of our times are highly industrialized and economically developed states. These can use foreign aid as a tool for securing their foreign policy goals.

The level of economic development also determines the scope of relations that a nation wishes to establish with other nations. The Foreign Policy of Japan in the contemporary times is directly and fundamentally related to its economic development. The military preparedness and military capability of a nation is again directly related to the factor of economic development and industrialization. Only industrially and economically developed nations can hope to become major and stable military powers.

Economic power constitutes a fundamental dimension of national power in contemporary times and at present; it can be used more effectively for securing foreign policy goals. The US economic power has been a major instrument of its foreign policy. Economic weakness of Russia has forced it to change its policy towards the U.S.A. and other countries. Steadily developing India economy has definitely given a boost to India's foreign relations. Thus, the level and nature of economic development, industrialization and modernization are important factors of foreign policy. The rise of India and China as economic power has shaped the foreign policy in not only Indo-Pacific regions but world as well.

4. Cultural and Historical Factors:

The cultural heritage and the history of a nation are again important and valuable factors of its Foreign Policy. The norms and traditions that characterize the life of the people of a state are highly influential factors of its foreign policy.

Strong cultural unity of the people is always a source of strength for them. It materially influences their ability to secure the objectives of national interest during the course of international bargaining. Historical experiences and cultural links further help them to analyze and assess the nature and scope of relations with other nations. Indeed, the weakness of the foreign policies of most of the Asian and African states has been largely due to the presence of internal dissensions and conflicts among their peoples.

Bitter experiences with the policies of imperialism and colonialism have been a determining factor of the anti-imperialist and anti-colonial contents of the foreign policies of most of the new sovereign states. History is an important factor in determining the relations among the neighboring nations. Foreign policy interactions between India and Pakistan are mostly the legacies of past history. The shadow of the history of 1962 still influences the course of Sino-Indian relations.

However, cultural values and links are always subject to perpetual changes and adjustments. Historical experiences too are forgotten in the face of national interest. The existence of conflict among the European nations, despite their cultural links and the development, and continuance of strong US Japanese friendship and relations bear ample proof that cultural and historical factors have to have combination with other factors before influencing the course of Foreign Policy.

India's strategic culture has been shaped by its history, philosophy and traditions. Mahatma Gandhi's philosophy of non-violence, moral behavior and Satyagraha was rooted in India's moral, ethical and philosophical traditions such as the Vedas, the Ramayana, Mahabharata as well as the teachings of Lord Buddha. Gandhiji's own experiences in South Africa contributed to his understanding that India's freedom was linked to that of other Asian and African colonies. In turn, Gandhiji's thinking influenced Jawaharlal Nehru. Therefore, it is not surprising that the defining characteristics of India's foreign policy in the first few decades after Independence were non-alignment, anti-colonialism, anti-racialism, non-violence, disarmament, and peacemaking.

5. Social Structure:

The structure and nature of the society for which the foreign policy operates is also an important element. The nature of social groups and the degree of conflict and harmony that characterize their mutual relations are determined by the social structure. A society characterized by strong internal conflict and strife acts as a source of weakness for the foreign policy.

A society of united, enlightened and disciplined people with a high degree of group harmony is always a source of strength. The democratization of the process of policy-making in recent times has increased the importance of social structure as an element of foreign policy. The linkages between the domestic and international environments have tended to strengthen the role of this element.

6. Government Structure:

The organization and structure of government i.e. the organizational agencies which handle the foreign policy-making and implementation is another important element of foreign policy. The shape of the foreign policy is also determined by the fact as to whether the government agencies handling it are democratically constituted or not.

Whether the authority relations are centralized or decision-making is free and open. The government officials also act as decision makers and this factor always influences the formulation of foreign policy. Foreign policy of a nation has to adapt to the environment. In a centralized and authoritarian system, the foreign policy can remain and often remains isolated from the domestic environment.

The nature of legislature-executive relations is also an influential factor in Foreign Policy decision-making. The harmony between the two, as is there in a parliamentary system, can be a source of strength and lack of harmony between the two can be a source of hindrance for the foreign policy makers. Similarly, the nature of party system, elections and electorate are other influential factors. The continuity in Indian Foreign Policy has been also due to the nature of government-making in India.

7. Internal Situation:

Like the external situational factors, sudden changes, disturbances or disorders that occur within the internal environment of a nation also influence the nature and course of foreign policy. The resignation of President Nixon over the issue of Watergate Scandal considerably limited the foreign policy of USA under President Ford.

The internal opposition to the military regime in Pakistan during 1947-89 was a determinant of Pakistani foreign policy. Similarly, the declaration of emergency in India in 1975 did materially affect the relations of India with other countries particularly the super powers. A change of government is always a source of change in the foreign policy of a state.

The rise of new leadership in China is now an important input of Chinese Foreign Policy. The rise of BJP led Government in India from 2014 acted as a source of some changes in relations with India's neighbors. The internal situation of Pakistan, a military dominated state trying to be a democratic political system has always been a factor of Pakistan's Foreign Policy.

8. Values, Talents, Experiences and Personalities of Leaders:

Since the Foreign Policy of a nation is made and implemented by leaders, statesmen and diplomats, naturally it bears an imprint of their values, talents, experiences and personalities. The ideas, orientations, likings, disliking, attitudes, knowledge, skill and the world-view of the national decision-makers are influential inputs of Foreign Policy. The differences among the leaders are also influential inputs of a foreign policy.

The Indian Foreign Policy till 1964 was often, and rightly so, described as Nehru's Foreign Policy. The support at home and the popularity that PM Nehru enjoyed acted as imputes of foreign policy. Pakistani Foreign Policy, under the influence of the ideas of General Musharraf, has undergone a big change. India's decision to develop nuclear weapons was definitely made under the influence of the ideas and the world- view of BJP leaders, who came to be power holders in 1998. The foreign policy of each nation is influenced by the personalities of its leaders. The change in leadership often produces a change in the foreign policy of a nation. The rise of strong leaders like Narendra Modi and Donald Trump has shaped the foreign policy of their nations in recent past.

However, this does not mean that this factor is an independent determinant of Foreign Policy. Leaders are always guided by the dictates and demands of national interest. Each leader is committed to the securing of national interests of the nation.

9. Political Accountability:

In the words of Rosenau, *"the degree to which public officials are accountable to the citizenry, either through elections, party competitions, legislative oversight, or other means, can have important consequences for the timing and contents of the plans that are made and the activates undertaken in foreign affairs."*

A political system which is both responsive to and responsible before the people, works in a different environment than the political system which is a closed system i.e., a system which is neither open nor accountable to the people. As such foreign policy of an open political system is more responsive to public opinion and public demands than the foreign policy of a closed political system.

The difference between the foreign policies of democratic and totalitarian/ authoritarian states is always largely due to his factor.

10. Ideology:

Foreign Policy is a set of principles and a strategic plan of action adopted by a nation to fulfill the goals of national interest. It has always an ideological content. For securing support for its goal as well as for criticizing the foreign policy goals of other nations, it needs and adopts an ideology or some ideological principles.

The ideology of communism remained an important factor of the foreign policies of communist nations during 1945-90. Anti- Communism and Pro-Liberal Democracy ideologies have always influenced the shape and course of foreign policies of non-communist Western nations. Ideological conflict remained determining factor in the cold war policies (1945-90) of both the super powers.

The drive in favor of democratization, decentralization and liberalization in the socialist states of Europe, the new states of Central Asia, Russia and Mongolia has given a new direction to international relations of post-1990 period. Similarly, ideological commitments have been a source of affinity in the foreign policies of Islamic nations.

11. Public Opinion:

Public Opinion, national as well as international is another important input of Foreign Policy. Decision-makers of each nation have to accept and give due place to the opinion of the people they represent as well as to the World Public Opinion. Undoubtedly, the decision-makers as leaders have to lead the public yet they also have to accommodate the demands of public opinion.

The American Senate's refusal to ratify the American membership of the League of Nations, and the opposition of Vietnam War by the Americans and other peoples, had a big impact on the Foreign Policy of the U.S.A.

The real strength behind the objectives of Disarmament, Arms Control and Nuclear Disarmament, Anti- colonialism, Anti-apartheid policies of various nations, has been the World Public Opinion. The rise of several peace and development movements in the World has decidedly acted as a check against foreign policies of war, aggression and destruction. No one is now prepared to talk and act as Hitler and Mussolini did in 1930s.

Hence, as the international world order undergoes significant changes, world and India's foreign policy continues to evolve. The other factors like technology, International power structure, alliances and international treaties and world organizations also play pivotal role in shaping the foreign policy of a country. All the determinants of foreign policy are inter-related and interdependent. They act together or in combination for influencing the making and implementation of a foreign policy. None of these factors can work in isolation and independently. All these determinants have to be analyzed together for understanding the nature and objective of Foreign Policy of each nation.

Chapter Six

War

War is an intense **armed conflict** between states, governments, societies, or paramilitary groups such as mercenaries, insurgents, and militias. It is generally characterized by extreme violence, aggression, destruction, and mortality, using regular or irregular military forces. **Warfare** refers to the common activities and characteristics of types of war, or of wars in general. Total war is warfare that is not restricted to purely legitimate military targets, and can result in massive civilian or other non-combatant suffering and casualties.

The English word *war* derives from the 11th-century Old English words *wyrre* and *werre*, from Old French *werre* (also *guerre* as in modern French), in turn from the Frankish **werra*, ultimately deriving from the Proto-Germanic **werzō* 'mixture, confusion'. The word is related to the Old Saxon *werran*, Old High German *werran*, and the German *verwirren*, meaning "to confuse", "to perplex", and "to bring into confusion".Types of warfare

Asymmetric warfare is a conflict between belligerents of drastically different levels of military capability or size.

Biological warfare, or germ warfare, is the use of weaponized biological toxins or infectious agents such as bacteria, viruses, and fungi.

Chemical warfare involves the use of weaponized chemicals in combat. Poison gas as a chemical weapon was principally used during World War I, and resulted in over a million estimated casualties, including more than 100,000 civilians.

Cold warfare is an intense international rivalry without direct military conflict, but with a sustained threat of it, including high levels of military preparations, expenditures, and development, and may involve active conflicts by indirect means, such as economic warfare, political warfare, covert operations, espionage, cyberwarfare, or proxy wars.

Conventional warfare is declared war between states in which nuclear, biological, or chemical weapons are not used or see limited deployment.

Cyberwarfare involves the actions by a nation-state or international organization to attack and attempt to damage another nation's information system.

Insurgency is a rebellion against authority, when those taking part in the rebellion are not recognized as belligerents (lawful combatants). An insurgency can be fought via counterinsurgency, and may also be opposed by measures to protect the population, and by political and economic actions of various kinds aimed at undermining the insurgents' claims against the incumbent regime.

Information warfare is the application of destructive force on a large scale against information assets and systems, against the computers and networks that support the four critical infrastructures (the power grid, communications, financial, and transportation)

Nuclear warfare is warfare in which nuclear weapons are the primary, or a major, method of achieving capitulation.

Total war is warfare by any means possible, disregarding the laws of war, placing no limits on legitimate military targets, using weapons and tactics resulting in significant civilian casualties, or demanding a war effort requiring significant sacrifices by the friendly civilian population.

Unconventional warfare, the opposite of conventional warfare, is an attempt to achieve military victory through acquiescence, capitulation, or clandestine support for one side of an existing conflict.

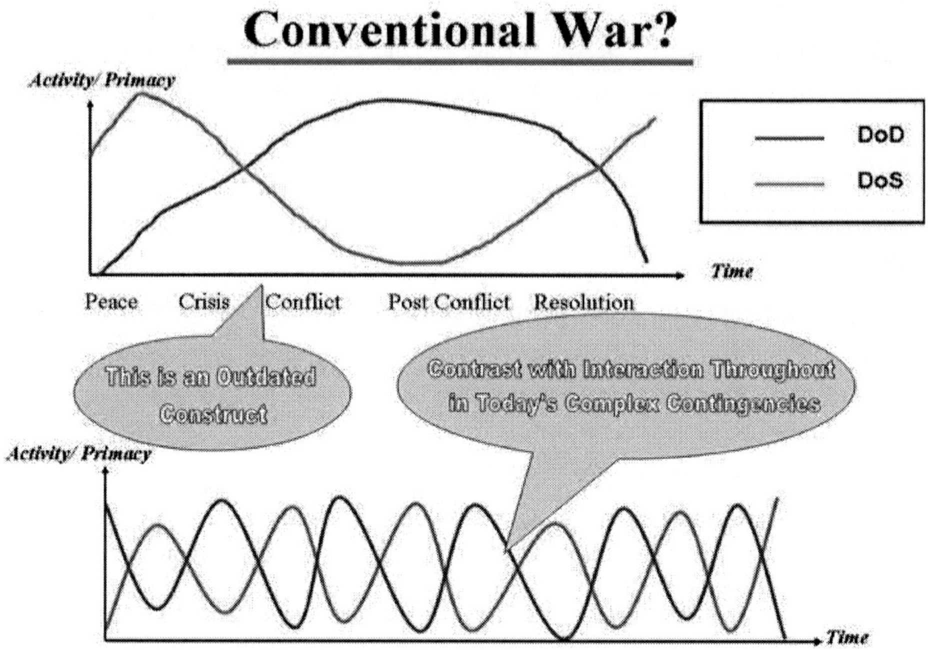

- Ogling, Episodic Conflict
- Conventional war?

Definition

Fried defines war aims as "the desired territorial, economic, military or other benefits expected following successful conclusion of a war".

Classification

Tangible/intangible aims:

Tangible war aims may involve (for example) the acquisition of territory (as in the German goal of Lebensraum in the first half of the 20th century) or the recognition of economic concessions (as in the Anglo-Dutch Wars).

Intangible war aims – like the accumulation of credibility or reputation – may have more tangible expression ("conquest restores prestige, annexation increases power").

Explicit/implicit aims:

- Explicit war aims may involve published policy decisions.

- Implicit war aims can take the form of minutes of discussion, memoranda and instructions.

Positive/negative aims:

- "Positive war aims" cover tangible outcomes.
- "Negative war aims" forestall or prevent undesired outcomes.

War aims can change in the course of conflict and may eventually morph into "peace conditions" – the minimal conditions under which a state may cease to wage a particular war.

Changing Nature of War

The Rise of Cyber and the Changing Nature of War – Grounded Curiosity

Warfare in Contemporary International Order

As discussed above in view of post-Second War developments, there have been significant changes in the nature and type of conflicts. Important of these are given below:

Even a cursory glance at the pattern of contemporary international conflicts would reveal that we are moving into an era where large scale international conflicts or wars are becoming increasingly irrelevant. The utility of war as a rational instrument of state policy to gain political objective is being seriously questioned (Ken Booth, 1991). Territorial disputes do exist and they can be cause of inter-state armed conflicts. For example, India and Pakistan have long standing dispute over Jammu and Kashmir. India and China also have dispute over demarcation of borders. However, the inter-state conflicts in contemporary international order are not resorted for the reasons that generated such conflicts in the past.

Changing nature of war

In the post-World War II international order, there have been a number of developments both at ideological and structural level that have strengthened global norms against war. There have been concerted efforts by the UN and other international agencies toward prevention and management of conflicts. In addition, the imperatives of globalization and resultant interdependence, expansion of mass media, information technology, emphasis on trade and development have created an environment where armed conflicts and wars are not encouraged. There is a growing realization that economic development, trade and commerce, greater democratization and empowerment of common people have created incentives and structures where peaceful resolutions of conflicts are encouraged. Additionally, the evolving and expanding global security governance, despite all its limitations, has been effective in driving down the number of armed conflicts in contemporary international order.

In such a situation, internal conflicts of various types occur: low intensity conflict, insurgency, terrorism, revolutionary war, protracted war, proxy war etc. These are far more common than inter-state war. As Liddle Hart says, "This is the only kind of war that fits the condition of modern age (Quoted in Frank Kitson, 1971, p.16). For external powers, involvement in such conflicts is emerging as the most preferred strategy. While they can be initiated at modest cost, the defending nation has to spend many times more to defend itself and counter it.

Plural democracies, multi-cultural and multi-lingual societies are more prone to such conflicts because these differences can be used as the most potent factors to be exploited to hurt a country, to break its unity, fragment it, create insurgency, terrorism and other social turbulences.

According to Reydams, L., "....by a constant switching of friends and foes and by a breakdown of institutional authorities (such as the military and the police) responsible for ordering and having recourse to the use of force". In this context, acts of war and criminality become indistinguishable and the war drags on with no prospect of peace accord to end it. Such wars, which had already multiplied in the 1980s and 1990s, look set – along with guerrilla-terrorist wars – to determine the course of violence in the twenty-first century in many parts of the world" (Reydams, L '*A la guerre Comme ala guerre*: "Patterns of Armed Conflict, humanitarian law responses and new challenges", *International Review of Red Cross*, vol. 88, no. 864, Dec 2006).

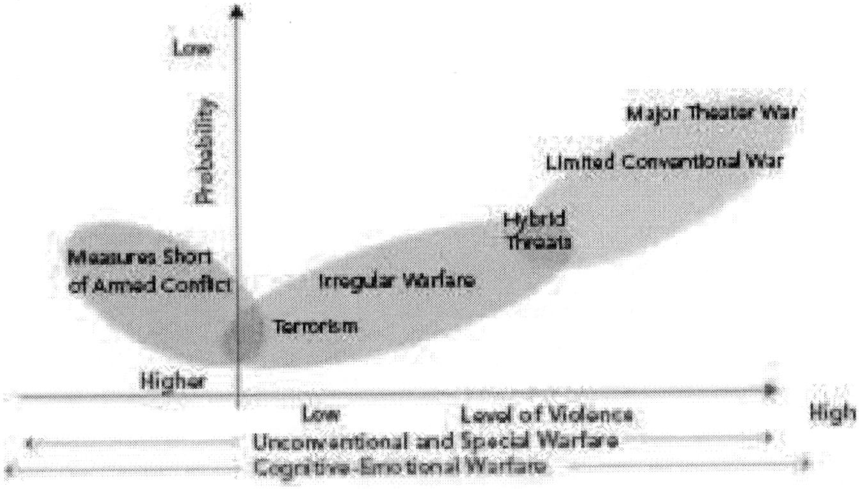

Changing nature of war

Another shift in the pattern of international conflicts has been in terms of regions affected by them. While the first part of the century was dominated by warfare between rich states, most of the contemporary conflicts take place overwhelmingly in the world's underdeveloped and poorest countries. These parts of the world witnessed 98% of all international conflicts since 1945 (Matin Wight, 1966, p. 103). According to K.J. Holsti, out of 164 armed conflicts between 1945 and 1995, all but five were located in the third world (K.J. Holsti, 1996, pp. 22, 210-24). Holsti has excluded anti-colonial wars from this data. If one includes these figures, the concentration of conflicts would appear to be more alarming. Regions most affected by various forms of armed conflicts are parts of West Asia, Africa, and South and Central Asia. Most of these areas are populous and characterized by poor levels of economic development, weak states, inability of institutions of governance to address conflicts in society both in terms of conflict prevention, management and resolution, ethnic polarization and religious extremism.

Hybrid Warfare

One aspect of modern wars seems to distinguish them from conflicts of earlier era, that is, their complex combination of international and internal elements. Modern conflicts are rarely categorized as being purely 'international' or purely 'non-international' in character, but rather a mixture of internal and international conflicts taking place in a globalized context, involving both state and non-state actors. In some cases, the state is battling rebels who wish to take control of the state or secede from it, in others there is conflict over control of natural resources, or is fueled by extremist ideologies or ethnic conflicts. The ongoing conflicts in West Asia, Afghanistan, South Asia and Sub-Saharan Africa are examples of mixed/hybrid warfare. In reality, the modern conflict is often a mixture of all these: territoriality, religious ideologies, economic interests, criminal activities, proxy war, foreign intervention, conflict over resources and ethnic polarization. One aspect that is common in all these conflicts are, however, that the enemies and battlefields are not defined, objectives are often not clear and keep changing and civilian populations become easy target.

A classic example of this hybrid warfare is ongoing conflict in Syria, which witnessed a mixture of internal and international conflict since 2011, in which the Bashar Assad's regime, with support from Russia, Iran and Iran supported Hizbullah fighting against a range of opposition groups, including Al Qaeda affiliate Jabhat-al-Nusra and Islamic State of Iraq and al-Sham (ISIS), both of which have also been target of air strike by US- led coalition forces. This conflict is a classic example of a mixture of opposition against repressive regime, religious extremism, geo-strategic interest of global and regional powers such as US, Russia, Iran, Saudi Arabia and Turkey that have fueled and sustained the conflict. The Syrian conflict has resulted in approximately 2,00,000 deaths, 70,000 of which occurred in 2014, and 3.4 million refugees of which 1.4 million fled to neighboring states and various European countries in 2014.

The conventional military capability of states remains important. But the hybrid conflicts demand additional requirements from conventional armed forces in terms of their capabilities to deal with such conflicts. They are often found lacking in softer skills like cultural awareness, training, language skills, psychological operations, human intelligence and their interface with local population. Other aspects of conventional capability such as air power and missile capabilities play a significant role in conventional conflict. However, to remain relevant and sustainable for contemporary conflict a radical re-assessment in areas of strategy, tactics and intensity becomes necessary. In the absence of a defined battlefield or enemy, innocent civilians often become target and that only helps the rebel forces in consolidating their positions among civilians. The focus, therefore, should be to minimize collateral damage and enable the provision of intimate close air support to ground forces. . Similarly, the maritime capability of states involved in such conflicts in terms of sea denial and sea control remains essential elements to enforce deterrence on the potential adversary. Operational maneuver from the seas and coercive diplomacy will also form important components of capability development.

Information technology and network-centricity have transformed methodologies of warfare. Their impact, however, needs to be pragmatically assessed against realistic battlefield scenarios. Aerospace capability is a potent dimension of land warfare, with a vast applicability in all forms of conflict. Insurgent and terrorist activities have added complex politico-military dynamics to the nature of conflict. The contemporary nature of conflict mandates realistic transformation in the conventional force structure, deployment methodologies, support structures and emerging technologies, to be able to face the multi-spectrum challenges that would emerge in the future.

Sub-Conventional Conflicts and Non-State Actors

In contemporary conflicts, the non-state actors are increasingly becoming lethal, with access to technology and equipment that previously only conventional state forces could afford to. Almost all contemporary conflicts such as in Syria, where great powers are involved primarily to serve their political interest, Lebanon war

(2006), Russia-Georgia conflict (2008), Sri Lanka conflict (2009) and India-Pakistan conflict over Jammu and Kashmir (since 1990s), operation enduring freedom in Afghanistan clearly indicate growing importance of non-state actors.

In almost all the theatres of conflict, the non-state actors have cross border linkage in terms of support structures, sources of finance, state support, arms procurement and safe haven. In many of the countries, internal conflicts are often exacerbated and sustained through these cross-border linkages. For example, India has faced a number of internal armed conflicts right since its independence. Cross-border terrorism in Jammu and Kashmir and other parts of India, multiple insurgencies in the Northeastern region often fueled by demands for secession and ethnic fault lines, Maoist movements in parts of Chhattisgarh, Orissa, Jharkhand, Telangana, Maharashtra and other parts of India. Though internal factors remain important, many of these movements have grown and are sustained due to their cross-border linkage in terms of state support, financial network, arms supply and ideological affinity with similar groups.

Sub-conventional wars are fought for winning the political loyalty of the people and are people-centric. These wars are always protracted and political outcomes are determined by the staying power, reflected in political will and the ability to achieve the desired strategic effect by application of all means. Technology has empowered the individuals and today, even a single terrorist/guerrilla can cause severe damage to adversaries through cyber, financial and kinetic attacks, which earlier only large organizations and states could do. The dynamics of deterrence and escalatory control are more relevant against nation states. Against non-state actors, these capabilities have little effect. However, several diplomatic, informational, military and socio-economic measures can be effectively used in a complementary and comprehensive approach to enforce restraint on the activities of non-state actors.

Religious Extremism and Terrorism

Religious extremism and terrorism has emerged as one of the key patterns of international conflicts. In June 2014, the Islamic State of Iraq and al-Sham announced the establishment of 'caliphate' led by Abu Bakr al-Baghdadi. For the last few years, the group has steadily expanded its presence in Iraq and Syria, filling up the vacuum created by internal instability in the region. The conflict in Syria is linked to that taking place in the Sunni heartland of Iraq, where the ISIS was able to capture a large swathe of territory with resources. The growth of ISIS in

Iraq and Syria resulted in unprecedented brutality resulting in more than 18,000 deaths and two million internally displaced persons. (Armed Conflict Survey, 2015).With US-led coalition air strikes since August 2014 and subsequently by Russia and ground attacks by Iran-supported Shia militia, the ISIS suffered significant damage. But, the ISIS continues to control significant territory and resources. The group has been able to exploit information technology and social media very effectively to put across its views and radicalize a section of youth not only in the region but also in European countries and South Asia. One of the key features in the rise of ISIS is a trend towards localization. According to Alia Brahimi, the Al Qaeda emerged partly due to the globalization of a local conflict in Afghanistan. Religious extremism has also played a substantial role in other parts of West Asia such as Libya, Egypt and Yemen.

The growth of ISIS in Iraq and Syria has brought to the fore not only the threat from religious extremism and radical mobilization but also the use of these elements by state actors to further their own geo-strategic interests. In West Asia, for example, religious extremism was encouraged in the aftermath of US campaign against Iraq, interests of Iran to secure a strategic space in the

region and political interests of Saudi Arabia, Turkey and Russia. The Taliban consolidated their position in Afghanistan and emerged as a threat to regional and international security. The terrorist attack in the US was a direct impact of growth of religious extremism supported by the great powers.

Summary

The meaning, scope and character of international conflicts have evolved over the years to incorporate changes in social, political, economic and technological fields at the level of international system and their constituent units. In the literature of international relations, the concept has been treated as a very complex subject with divergent definitions and perspectives. Historically, inter-state armed conflict or War between or among states has been considered as dominant form of international conflict. However, in contemporary international system, the pattern of conflict is changing. They are different from wars that took place in early 20th century primarily in Europe in terms of tactics employed, weapons used, the objectives to be achieved and nature of parties involved in conflicts. Over a period of time, our understanding of conflicts has expanded to include sub- nationalities, terrorists, insurgents, religious extremism and ethnic interests. This reflects evolution from the first generation of warfare to the fourth generation of warfare. Even a cursory glance at the pattern of contemporary international conflicts would reveal that weare moving into an era where large scale international conflicts or wars are becoming increasingly irrelevant. On the other hand, internal conflicts of various types occur: low intensity conflict, insurgency, terrorism, revolutionary war, protracted war, proxy war etc. These are far more common than inter-state war.

Kargil war

Kargil war

Kargil War or Kargil conflict occurred between May and July 1999 within the Kargil district of Jammu and Kashmir. The war signifies an armed conflict between India and Pakistan.

Kargil Vijay Diwas - 26 July 2021: Kargil Vijay Diwas is observed on 26 July annually to commemorate the sacrifices made by the soldiers in the Kargil War. No doubt the war represents an example of high altitude warfare in mountainous terrain and constitutes significant logistical problems for the counter sides. In the war, 'Operation Vijay' was launched by the Indian Army to recapture the Indian territories from Pakistani intruders in the Kargil-Drass sector in 1999.

'Operation Vijay' an Indian Army mission achieved ultimate success for India and the Air Force called the mission 'Operation Safed Sagar'.

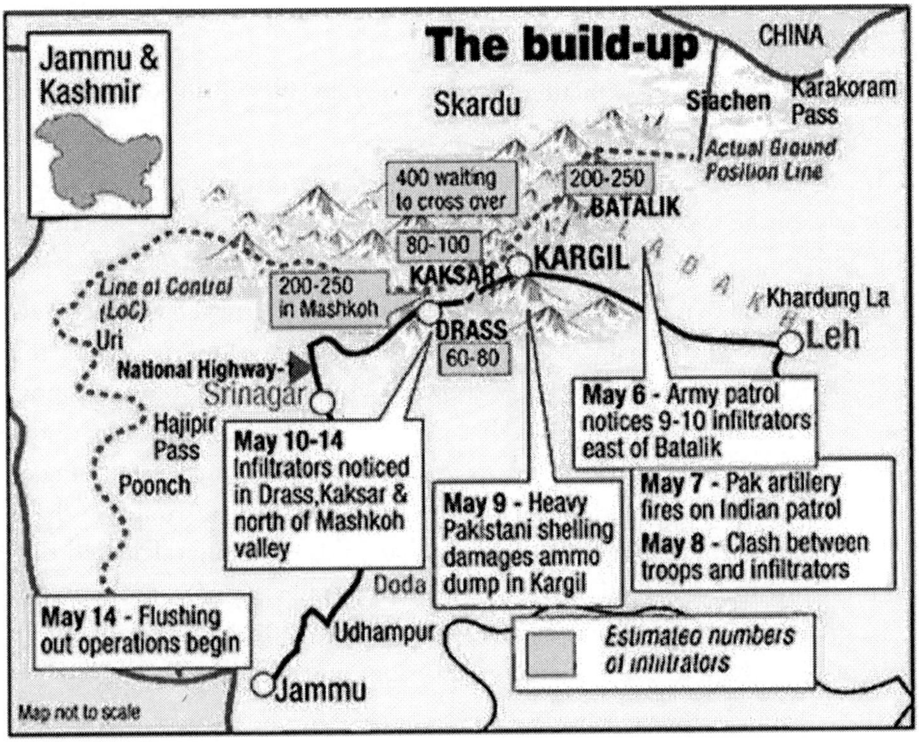

Map of Kargil war

Kargil War 1999: Conflict

The Kargil War took place in 1999 between 8 May, when Pakistani forces and Kashmiri militants were detected at top of the Kargil ridges. It is believed that Pakistan was planning for the operation as early as the autumn of 1998.

There were three major phases in the Kargil War: First, in the Indian-controlled section of Kashmir, Pakistan captured various strategic high points. Second, India responded by first capturing strategic transportation routes and third military pushing Pakistani forces back across the Line of Control.

Occupation by Pakistan

After February Lahore Summit 1999 that took place between Pakistani Prime Minister Nawaz Sharif and the Indian Prime Minister Atal Bihari Vajpayee, the Pakistani effort to take Kargil occurred. It was believed that this conference has de-escalated the tensions that had existed since May 1998. The main objective behind the operation was to help in internationalizing the issue of Kashmir and for which global attention had been flagging for some time. It is said that the plan of intrusion was the brainchild of Pakistani's Chief of Army Staff Gen Pervez Musharraf and Lt. Gen Mohammed Aziz, the Chief of General Staff. Only an 'in principle' concurrence they obtained, without any specifics, from Nawaz Sharif, the Pakistani Prime Minister.

The main objective of the Pakistani military for carrying out the intrusions was to rely on the exploitation of the large gaps that exist in the defenses in the sector both on the Indian and Pakistani sides of the Line of Control (LoC).

Let us tell you that the terrain over there was extremely rugged with very few tracks leading from the main roads towards the LoC. And during, winter the area is covered with snow due to heavy snowfall which makes movement almost impossible. The only mountain pass that was connecting the Kargil area to the Kashmir Valley, Zoji La, basically opens by the end of May or the beginning of June. Therefore, moving reinforcements by surface via Srinagar would not have been possible till then. One more thing is that Pakistan Army calculated that even if the intrusions were discovered by the Indian's in early May, as they were, the action of the Indian Army would be slow and limited which provides more time and allow them to consolidate the intrusions more effectively.

Therefore, in early May only Zoji La was opened for the induction of troops. If the action of intruding were effective then it would allow Pakistani troops to secure some dominating heights from where the Srinagar-Leh National Highway 1A might be prohibited at a variety of places. And the intrusions would draw in and tie down the Indian Army reserves. Also, the intrusions have provided Pakistan control over substantial tracts of strategic acreage across the LoC, thereby allowing Islamabad to negotiate from a strong position. And they decisively alter the status of the LoC.

Apart from keeping the plan top secret, the Pakistan Army also undertook certain steps to take care of a component of surprise and maximize deception. No new administrative bases for the intrusions were to be created, instead, they were to be catered for from those already within the existing defenses. Along the ridgelines, there were the logistic lines of communication and therefore the mullahs were far away from the tracks, positions of the Indian Army troops were already in position.

After the finalization, the plan was put into action towards the end of April. The main groups were broken into a number of smaller subgroups of 30 to 40 each for carrying out multiple intrusions along the ridgelines and occupy dominating heights.

The Pakistani army was hoping and trying to gain the upper hand in Kashmir and plunging the Indian subcontinent in brief and limited war and raising the specter of nuclear war.

Indian Army detected intruders

Intruders are detected by Indian Army Patrols atop Kargil ridges during the period 8-15 May, 1999. The infiltration pattern clearly entrenched the participation of trained Mujahideen and Pakistani Army regulars in these operations in areas east of Batalik and north of Dras.

In general areas of Kargil and Dras, Pakistan resorted to artillery firing from across the border. Some operations were launched by the Indian army which succeeded in cutting off the infiltrators in the Drass sector. Also, the infiltrators were pushed back in the Batalik sector.

On the heights, the intruders were both professional soldiers and mercenaries including the 3rd, 4th, 5th, 6th, and 12th battalions of the Pakistan Army's Northern Light Infantry (NLI). Among them, there were the members of Pakistan's Special Services Group (SSG) and several Mujaheddin. Initially, it was estimated that there were about 500 to 1000 intruders were there occupying the heights but later it was estimated that the actual strength may have been around 5000. The intrusion area extended in an area of 160 Km. In fact, the Army of Pakistan had set up a complex logistical network so that the intruders across the LoC would be well supplied from the bases in POK. Intruders were well armed with AK 47 and 56 mortars, artillery, anti-aircraft guns, and Stinger missiles.

What are the new pension rules for Armed Forces Personnel in India?

Now, let us have a look at the Indian Army Operations

The intrusions were detected by the Indian Army between 3 May-12 May. And from 15 May-25 May, 1999, military operations were planned, to their attack locations troops moved, artillery and other equipment were also moved in and the equipment that was necessary is purchased also. In **May, 1999**, an operation was launched by the Indian Army named **'Operation Vijay'**. Now, the Indian troops moved towards the occupied Pakistani positions with air cover provided by aircraft and helicopters.

The Indian Army Operation Vijay of 1999 was a joint Infantry-Artillery endeavor to evict regular Pakistani soldiers of the Northern Light Infantry (NLI) who had intruded across the LoC into Indian territory and had engrossed un-held mountain peaks at high-altitude and ridgelines. Soon it became clear that only massive and sustain firepower could destroy the intruders' sangars. Therefore, a unique saga in the history of the employment of Artillery firepower in battle began.

On 13 June, 1999, the first major ridgeline to fall was **Tololing in the Drass sub-sector** which was captured after several weeks of fighting. The attacks were lead up to sustained fire assaults from over one hundred Artillery guns, mortars, and rocket launchers. Thousands of shells, bombs, and rocket warheads wreaked havoc and prevented the enemy from interfering with the assault. In the direct firing were the 155 mm Bofors medium guns and 105 mm Indian field guns that destroyed all visible enemy sangars and forced them to abandon various positions.

Tololing complex capture paved the way for successive assaults to be launched on the Tiger Hill complex from various directions. On 4-5 July, 1999, Tiger Hill was re-captured and **Point 4875.** To the west of Tiger Hill was another dominating feature of Tiger Hill and on 7 July, 1999, Mashkoh Valley was recaptured. Point 4875 was re-named as "Gun Hill" in honour of the astounding performance of the Gunners in the Drass and Mashkoh sub-sectors.

Do you know around 12,000 rounds of high explosives rained down on Tiger Hill and caused large scale devastation and death? In the direct fighting 122mm Grad multi-barrel rocket launchers (MBRLs) were employed.

The terrain in the **Batalik Sector** was much tougher and the enemy was far more strongly entrenched. Almost a month was taken by the containment battle. Artillery observation posts (OPs) were instituted on dominating heights and sustained Artillery fire was brought down on the enemy continuously by day and night allowing them no rest. On 21 June, 1999, **point 5203** was recaptured and on 6 July, 1999, Khalubar was also recaptured. Within the next few weeks, further attacks were pressed against the remaining Pakistani posts in the Batalik sub-sector. Once again, Artillery played a crucial role in destroying the enemy's battalion and logistics infrastructure.

It is said that during the Kargil conflict the Indian Artillery fired over 250,000 shells, bombs, and rockets? Daily from 300 guns mortars and MBRLs approximately 5,000 Artillery shells, mortar bombs, and rockets were fired. It is also said that such type of high rates of fire over long periods had not been witnessed anywhere in the world since the Second World War.

Now let us have a look at Air Operations

Ground troops were supported by the Air Force from 11 May to 25 May and tried to contain the threat, judge the positions of the enemy dispositions, and carried out several preparatory actions. On 26 May, the entry of the Air Force into combat action represented an exemplar shift in the nature and prognosis of the conflict. Do you know that in Air Force **Operation Safed Sagar,** Air Force carried out about 5000 sorties of all types over 50-odd days of operations?

Before Kargil, the Western Air Command conducted the three-week-long exercise Trishul. During Trishul, the Indian Air Force flew 5,000 sorties with 300 aircraft using around 35,000 personnel and engaged targets at high elevations in the Himalayas. It was claimed by IAF that they have flown around 550 sorties in Kargil, though just about 80 were on or close to the target.

The threat of shoulder-fired missiles was ubiquitous and there was no doubt about this. Pakistani Stinger damaged an IAF Canberra recce aircraft possibly from across the LoC. Operation, second and third day, the IAF lost one MiG-21 fighter and one Mi-17 helicopter to shoulder-fired missiles by the enemy. Also, one MiG-27 was lost on the second day due to engine failure just after the pilot had carried out successful attacks on one of the enemy's supply dumps. These events went to reinforce the tactics of the IAF in carrying out attacks from outside the Stinger SAM envelope and avoid the use of helicopters for attack purposes. Under relatively benign conditions attack helicopters have a certain utility in operations but are extremely at risk in an intense battlefield. Let us tell you that the enemy had fired more than 100 shoulder-fired SAMs against IAF aircraft which one side indicates the strength of the enemy air defences in the area but on the other side shows the success of the IAF tactics, mainly after the first three days of the war as not a single aircraft then received even a scratch.

In the Kargil area, the terrain is around 16,000 to 18,000 feet above sea level. And it was required by the aircraft to fly at about 20,000 feet. At these heights, the density of the air is 30% less than at sea level.

This resulted in the reduction in weight that can be carried and also reduces the ability to manoeuvre as the radius of a turn is more than what is at lower levels. The turn's largest radius reduces the mobility in the restricted width of the valley. The performance of the engine also deteriorates due to the lesser mass of the air which is going into the jet engine of the fighter or helicopter. The trajectory of weapons was also gets affected by the non-standard air density. Hence, the firing may not be accurate. The targets are relatively small in the mountains, they spread out and are also difficult in spotting visually mainly by pilots in high-speed jets.

India's 6 Gallantry Awards: Facts at a Glance

Srinagar and Avantipur were the Indian airfields nearest to Kargil. Also, Adampur near Jalandhar was also close enough to support air operations. Therefore, **IAF operated from these three bases.** For ground attack, the planes used were namely MiG-2Is, MiG-23s, MiG-27s, Jaguars, and the Mirage-2000. Mainly, for air interception with a secondary role of ground attack, MiG-21 was built. Therefore, it was capable of operating in restricted spaces that were important in the Kargil terrain.

To attack the targets on the ground, MiG-23s and 27s were optimised. They can carry a load of 4 tonnes each and could be a mix of weapons including cannon, rocket pods, free-fall, and retarded bombs, and smart weapons. It also has a computerised bombsight that enables accurate weapon delivery. These planes were ideal to use at such types of terrain.

Flight **Lt. Nachiketa** was flowing MiG-27 on May 27 and while attacking a target in the Batalik sector, developed engine trouble and he had to bail out. To locate the downed pilot, **Sqn Ldr Ajay Ahuja** in a MiG-21, went out and so in this process, he was hit by a Pakistani surface to surface air missile (SAM). He came out safely but his body had gun-wounds was returned subsequently. For electronic warfare, reconnaissance and ground attack, the state-of-the-art Mirage-2000s were used.

With pinpoint accuracy, this fighter delivers its weapons. Also carried free-fall bombs and laser-guided bombs with deadly effects. In fact, due to this weapon, sizeable devastation was caused to the Pakistani bunkers on the ridges at Tiger Hill and Muntho Dhalo. On Muntho Dhalo in the Mirage attack, it is said that Pakistani troops suffered around 180 casualties.

To engage the Pakistani targets in the valleys and on ridges, the slower helicopter gunship became an important requirement. Also, Mi-17 was modified to carry 4 rocket pods with air-to-ground rockets and proved effective in engaging Pakistani bunkers and troops.

While attacking Point 5140 on 28 May in the Tololing sector, one helicopter and its crew were lost to a counter heat-seeking missile.

One thing here to be noted is that there were restrictions for the Air Force of not crossing the Line of Control (LoC) to the Pakistan side. Otherwise, the Indian Air Force would have destroyed or would get the liberty to destroy the supply lines of Pakistani and also splinter the logistic bases across the LoC. However, these attacks were done on Pakistani facilities on the Indian side of the Line of Control. Supply lines, logistic bases, and enemy strong points were smashed. As a result, the Indian Army pursued its operations at a faster rate and with fewer losses.

In **Operation Vijay,** it is estimated that approximately 700 intruders were killed by air action alone. The Indian Air Force has intercepted a variety of enemy wireless transmissions that reveal the effectiveness of IAF attacks.

Therefore, we can say that in the recent past no war has been won without control of the air space in which operations are conducted.

Monetary Allowance for the Gallantry Award Winners of India

Now at the end, let us have a look at the Naval Operations.

As Indian Air Force and The Army prepared themselves for the battle on the heights of Kargil and the Indian Navy began to draw out its plan. The Indian aim was that all efforts must be made to deter Pakistan from escalating the conflict into a full-scale war. From 20 May on wards, therefore, the Indian Navy was put on a full alert, a few days prior to the launch of the Indian retaliatory offensive. Naval and Coast Guard aircraft were placed on endless surveillance and therefore the units are ready for meeting any challenge at sea.

Now the time came to put pressure on Pakistan and it was necessary that the right message went down to the masterminds in that country. From Visakhapatnam, strike elements from the Eastern Fleet were sailed on the East Coast to take part in a major naval exercise called 'SUMMEREX' in the North Atlantic Sea. This was envisaged as the largest ever-amassing of naval ships in the region. This message was driven home and in a defensive mood, Pakistan

Navy directed all its units to keep clear of Indian Naval ships. The exercise was shifted closer to the Makran Coast, Pakistan moved all its major combatants out of Karachi. It also shifted its focus to protect its oil trade from the Gulf in the prospect of attacks by Indian ships.

As the retaliation from the Indian Army and the Air Force gathered momentum and defeat of Pakistan seemed a close possibility then naval focus now shifted to the Gulf of Oman. In the North Arabian Sea various rapid reaction missile-carrying units and ships from the fleet were deployed for carrying missile firing, anti-submarine, and electronic warfare exercises. The Navy also readied itself for implementing a blockade of the Pakistani ports, should the necessity arise. Also further, the Naval forces moved to the western sea-board from the Andaman group of islands.

Under **'Operation Talwar',** the 'Eastern Fleet' joined the 'Western Naval Fleet' and blocked the Arabian Sea routes of Pakistan. The blockade was so powerful that was created by the Indian Navy that the former Prime Minister Nawaz Sharif disclosed that Pakistan was left with just six days of fuel (POL) to sustain itself if a full-fledged war had broken out. This is how the Indian Navy played a pivotal role and helped the Indian Army and Air Force during the Kargil War.

Chapter Seven

Challenges to National Security/Cross Border Trrorism

India continues to face many complex threats and challenges to its national security, a few of which are predictable and well-defined.

Background

- Over the years, we have entered into an era of complex and uncertain threats and challenges, due to dynamic changes in the geo-politico-economic landscape and revolutionary changes in technology.
- These threats include traditional, non-traditional, cyber, information, space, chemical, biological, radiological, nuclear and propaganda.
- In order to ascertain the preparedness of our defence forces, it would be prudent to analyse it both from threat and capability-centric points of view.

Security threats and challenges:

- **Dichotomy of thought:** The thought process of **uniformed personnel and civilian research scholars** towards national security challenges is **completely different.**
- **Uniformed personnel:** They perceive national security challenges as **well-defined external or internal threats** or the **challenges of hybrid warfare** in the future and mostly **ignore non-traditional threats.**
- **Civilian Research scholars:** They have thought-provoking perceptions towards security challenges like:
- **Lack of education among masses** leading to the election of non-suitable leaders having no vision on national security;
- The triangle formed by the **huge youth population, unemployment among the youth and threat to food security** is a deadly recipe detrimental to national security;
- Lack of social cohesion and harmony, dilution in the integrity of institutions, the polarisation of people along the lines of religion, caste and region, and non-inclusive growth pose a potent threat and challenge to national security.

External Threats and Challenges:

- Two neighbours of India—**China and Pakistan**—are not just the **principal source** of its external security threats, but are **also nuclear-armed states who share a deep friendship.**
- The **territorial disputes and external threats** on our sub-continent are a result of its **unique geostrategic location, its neighbourhood, its history and the Partition.**
- Security of India's long and porous coastline, offshore islands, exclusive economic Zone and sea lines of communications in the Indian Ocean require a high level of surveillance, situational awareness, rapid response capability, and synergy between all enforcement agencies to provide effective maritime security.
- Detailed examination of the economic and security implications of CPEC (China Pakistan Economic Corridor), Belt and Road Initiative (BRI), and the 21st-century Maritime silk road on India and the region is required.

Internal Threats and Challenges:

- **Huge diversity** in geographical regions, ethnicity, religions, and languages **coupled with** social discrimination, inequality in human development indices (HDI), lack of inclusive growth, the polarisation of population-based on religion and caste, and mass unemployment among the youth **makes India vulnerable to internal armed conflicts.**
- The aim of the armed conflicts like **Naga insurgency, Bodoland army,** , in India is primarily to capture political power or seek separation or secession or greater autonomy. We have been more successful in **conflict-management and not conflict-resolution.**
- Internal security is a function of political morality, responsiveness of the governance system, integrity of institutions, social cohesion, the status of the economy, wealth distribution in the population, and social justice. India is suffering **from dysfunctional institutions,** which further add to the problems in the internal security environment.
- **Pakistan** has continued to indulge in **proxy-war-cum-cross-border-terrorism** in J&K with a view to destabilising India, which poses a serious threat to **India's internal security.**

Dynamics of Limited Conflict

- Considering the geo-political-economic-strategic environment with nuclear-armed states, the probability **of a total war appears less likely.**
- However, given our unresolved border disputes with our neighbours, history of our earlier conflicts, and the continued proxy war-cum-cross-border terrorism from Pakistan, **the probability of limited conflicts or border skirmishes, with irregular, information and asymmetric threats would always remain high.**
- Such conflicts would have the potential to **spill over to a larger area/ region.**
- **Economic Cost of Violence** refers to the **direct and indirect costs** incurred in preventing, containing, and dealing with the consequences of violence. The **economic cost of violence to India has been 9% of its GDP.**

Way forward

- **Build an effective military deterrence**
- India needs to progressively improve its military capabilities in **conventional as well as non-conventional war-fighting mechanisms,** soft power and demonstrated power.
- Military deterrence needs to be backed by **comprehensive national power**: political will, strong economy, social cohesion, vibrant industrial base, supportive public information system, and strong technology and innovation culture.

Integration and Jointness

- The future conflicts would be short, intense, multi-dimensional and hybrid in nature and straddle land, sea, air, space, and cyber and information domains.
- Therefore, we will not have the luxury of delayed decision-making, delayed mobilisation and delayed application of forces.
- **Integrated organisations** would certainly help us become effective operationally, with the ability to ensure synergistic application of all available resources for that operation in the very limited window of opportunity.

Defence Industry and Capability

- There is a need to holistically and pragmatically review the existing system of defence production in India, with a **greater focus to boost indigenous manufacturing to achieve self-reliance with quality products.**
- To produce state-of-the-art weapon systems in India, **innovation** has to be accorded with a very high priority and **private sector participation needs to be enhanced**, with substantial **investment in R&D** to revolutionise our industry.

Border Management Strategy

- The aim of border management strategy should be to effectively maintain the territorial integrity of the borders and to take care of the multifaceted threats and challenges along each border.
- Besides utilising technology to manage borders (smart management), there is a need to have clarity in responsibility, command and control, authority and accountability for each border, more importantly, the borders under dispute.
- **Cyber and Space Domains:** While looking at the offensive aspects of cyber-warfare, it is important to first take actions to protect our networks from cyber-attacks. The militarization of space is yet another dimension that needs to be explored for military purposes.

Conclusion

India has to use all instruments of its national power—political, economic, diplomatic, military, social, technological, psychological, cultural—in a coordinated manner to address its security concerns. This can happen only if we put an end to turf wars between different elements of national power, and look at the national security with a national outlook.

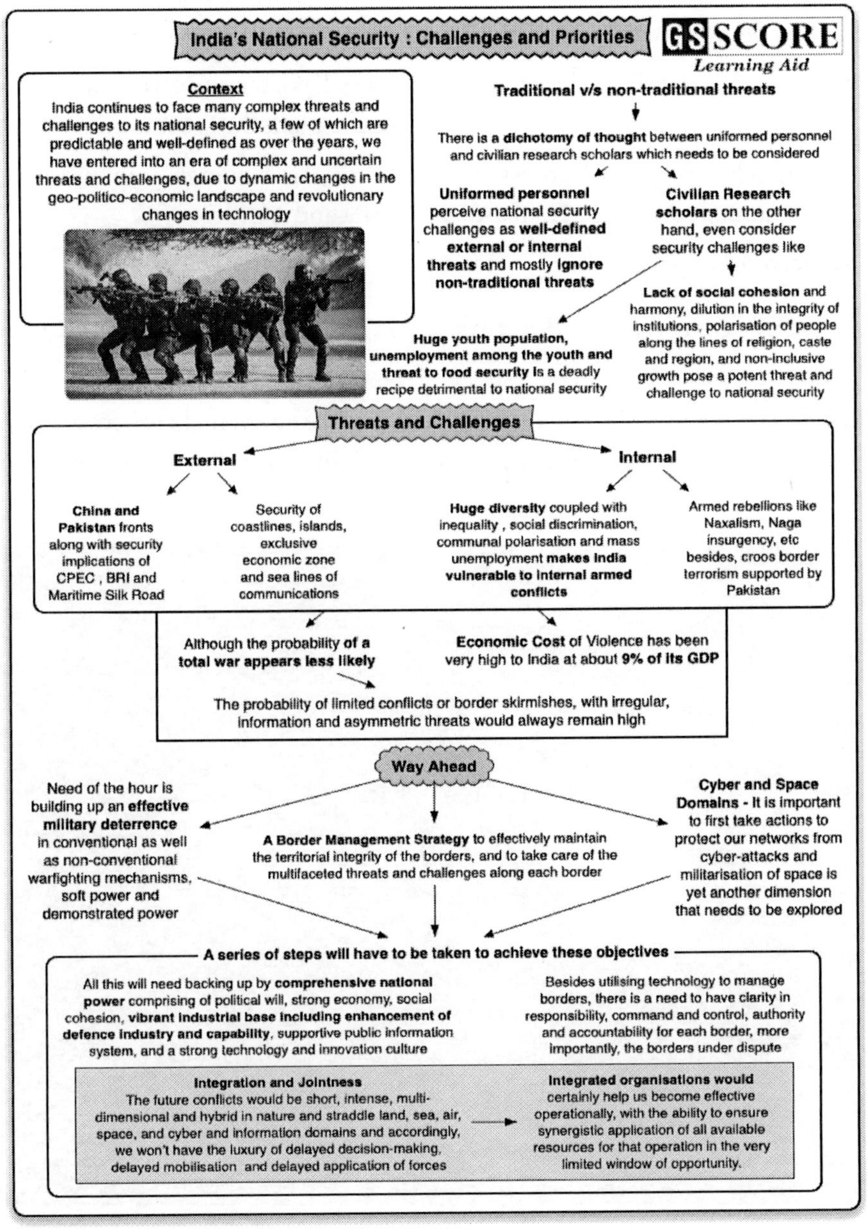

Cross Border Terrorism

Indian Border

- India has 15,106.7 kms of land border and a coastline of 7,516.6 kms including island territories.

- Out of the total 29 states of India except for six states (Madhya Pradesh, Chhattisgarh, Jharkhand, Telangana, Delhi and Haryana), rest all states have either maritime boundary or land border with other nations.
- India has land borders with countries: Pakistan, Afghanistan (PoK), China, Nepal, Bhutan, Myanmar and Bangladesh.
- India has maritime borders with seven countries: Bangladesh, Indonesia, Myanmar, Pakistan, Thailand, Sri Lanka and Maldives.

Modern trend of cross border terrorism:

India warns of cross-border terror via cyberspace, calls for global action

Raising an alarm about the emergence of cyberspace as a vehicle for cross-border terrorism by nations and terror organisations, India has called for international action.

Raising an alarm about the emergence of cyberspace as a vehicle for cross-border terrorism by nations and terror organisations, India has called for international action to achieve a framework for global cybersecurity.

Outlining the dangers to international peace emanating from cyberspace,

India's Foreign Secretary Harsh Vardhan told the Security Council on June 30,2021: "We need to adopt a collaborative rules-based approach in cyberspace and work towards ensuring its openness, stability and security."

UN's High Representative for Disarmament Affairs, Izumi Nakamitsu also warned of the risks from cyberattacks and said that situations could develop that "can encourage states to adopt offensive postures for the hostile use of these technologies".

Because of this risk and the potential for "criminal groups and others" to create global destabilisation, she said that the Security Council should get involved in ensuring cybersecurity.

Vardhan said: "The borderless nature of cyberspace, and more importantly anonymity of actors involved, has challenged the traditionally accepted concepts of sovereignty, jurisdiction and privacy.

"As a victim of terrorism, India has always underlined the need for member states to address and tackle the implications of terrorist exploitation of the cyber domain more strategically."

Some countries "are leveraging their expertise in cyberspace to achieve their political and security-related objectives and indulge in contemporary forms of cross-border terrorism", he said.

He added that cyber tools were being used to "compromise state securityaż through attacks on critical national infrastructure, including health and energy facilities and to "disrupt social harmony through radicalisation".

Terrorists have used social media to plan and execute terror attacks and for "virulent propaganda" to incite hatred and violence, recruit youth and raise funds, he said.

Vardhan warned of the dangers from malware that can "create potential flashpoints between states".

"It is in the interest of the international community to ensure that all actors abide by their international obligations and commitments and not indulge in practices that could have potentially disruptive effects on global supply chains and trade in ICT (Information Communication Technology) product.

"There are widespread concerns that state and non-state actors are introducing vulnerabilities and harmful hidden functions, including through backdoor channels, into ICT networks and products.

"The Open-Ended Working Group (OEWG) on developments in ICT (OEWG) should be leveraged to find further common ground and improve upon the already agreed cyber norms and rules," he said.

The OEWG, set up by the General Assembly in 2018, submitted its final report this March.

It did not recommend specific rules or regulations for adoption, but outlined areas of consensus and suggested further consultations.

Vardhan spoke of the positive potential of ICT citing the role of the Co-WIN platform in India's vaccination drive against coronavirus. He said that India was sharing it with partner countries.

The contrast between totalitarian countries like China, which he did not name, that have closed their cyberspace to outside influences and open societies like India came up in his speech when Vardhan spoke of the vulnerabilities of nations that allow external cyber access.

While committing India to "an open, secure, free, accessible and stable cyberspace environment", he pointed out that "open societies have been particularly vulnerable to cyber-attacks and disinformation campaigns".

The dangers outlined by Vardhan are widely manifest around the world.

In view of the dangers from ICT equipment being compromised with spyware, India has banned the use of some Chinese-made products.

There has been a proliferation of malware introduced into even computer systems used by the Pentagon.

Systems used in the US for petroleum distribution and for beef supply, as well as local governments, have been hit by cybercriminals to extort ransomware.

Washington has said that they operated from Russia.

Hospitals and health systems in the US and the UK have also been victims of cybercrime.

US Permanent Representative Linda Thomas-Greenfield said that countries should act against cybercriminals operating in their territories.

"Let me be clear: when a state is notified of harmful activity emanating from its own territory, it must take reasonable steps to address it. Given the transnational nature of cyberspace, this cooperation is essential," she said.

Estonia's Prime Minister Kaja Kallas, who presided over the meeting said: "Existing international law applies in cyberspace, with states accountable for any acts that contravene their obligations."

Cross-Border Terrorism

Why in News?

- On 14 February 2019, suicide bombing attack on a CRPF convoy in the Pulwama district of Jammu and Kashmir has killed 40 security personnel.
- Pakistan based terrorist group Jaish-e-Mohammad has claimed the responsibility for the attack.
- Cross-border terrorism remains a core concern for India. According to parliamentary report 323 infiltration bids have been made by terrorists from across the border in 2018.

What is Cross-Border Terrorism?

- The term 'cross-border' implies a movement or an activity across a border between the two countries.
- Cross-Border Terrorism is a form in which soil of one country is used to create terror in bordering countries.
- As a grey zone conflict, it is an undeclared war and considered to be highest form of strategy to bleed a nation for prolonged period by small efforts.

Cross-Border Terrorism in India

- During last 15 years thousands of civilians have lost their lives in acts of terrorism, apart from thousands of defence, paramilitary and police personnel who have sacrificed their lives in the line of duty.
- Infiltration and smuggling of narcotics, arms and weapons across the borders have been matters of constant and unmitigated anxiety to all concerned agencies manning the borders.

Indo-Pakistan Border

- Indo-Pakistan Border (3,323 Km) runs along the states of Gujarat, Rajasthan, Punjab and J&K. Direct accessibility of the borders and some technological developments enabling quick passage of information and transfer of funds has changed the focus and tenor of border security.

- Cross-Border Terrorism from Pakistan has exacerbated due to non-recognition of boundaries by its terrorist groups and their success in acquiring legitimacy due to religious or ethnic identity.
- Inadequate Cooperation from Pakistan has made the management of border further difficult for India.

Indo-Bangladesh Border

- The Indo-Bangladesh Border (4,096 Km) passes through West Bengal, Assam, Meghalaya, Tripura and Mizoram.
- The entire stretch consists of plains, riverine belts, hills & jungles which make illegal migration very easy.
- Illegal Migration across this border poses serious security threats and acts as a fertile ground for organisations like the Inter Services Intelligence of Pakistan to penetrate and expand their activities.
- Also, poor law and order situation at the border, has led to smuggling of arms and drugs. Supply of arms help in sustaining any conflict.

Indo-China Border

- India shares a long land border with China (3,488 Km) in the Indian states of Jammu & Kashmir, Himachal Pradesh, Uttarakhand, Sikkim and Arunachal Pradesh.
- Although this border remains relatively aloof from illegal migrations, this border remains a cause of constant vigil for Indian forces.
- India has a longstanding border dispute with China running back to British era in Aksai Chin and Arunachal Pradesh.

Indo-Nepal Border

- India-Nepal Border (1,751 Km) is an open border in the sense that people of both the countries can cross it from any point, despite the existence of border check posts at several locations.
- Anti-India organizations use this border to plant their people in the territory of India.

- Also, smuggling of gold, small arms, drugs and fake currency helps terrorists in executing an attack.

Indo-Bhutan Border

- This border (699 km) passes through states of Assam, Arunachal Pradesh, West Bengal and Sikkim.
- Illicit establishment of camps by militant outfits in the dense jungles of south-east Bhutan helps insurgents from India in executing anti-India activities.

Indo-Myanmar Border

- The northeast states of Arunachal Pradesh, Nagaland, Manipur and Mizoram share the border with Myanmar (1,643).
- Some of the insurgents groups like the National Socialist Council of Nagaland (NSCN) and ULFA operate from Myanmar, which threatens the security of India as well as Myanmar.

Cross-Border Terrorism through Maritime Borders

- Not only contiguous Border States with land borders are vulnerable to the cross border terrorism but **coastal areas are equally vulnerable.**
- Long coastline of the country remains comparatively unguarded. The presence of the Coast Guard is minimal.
- In 26/11 attack in terrorists came from the western coast through boats.

Steps Taken by India

- Government of India has created National Investigation Agency (NIA) in 2008 after Mumbai attacks which acts as a federal agency to combat terror.
- Multi Agency Centre (MAC) revamped after 26/11 attacks, acts as a multi-agency intelligence coordination mechanism for counter terrorism.
- Combating Financing of Terrorism Cell (CFT- Cell) is also created to deal with the policy matters on combating terrorist financing and Fake Indian Currency.
- India is also a member of FATF (Financial Action Task Force) whose aim

is to establish international standards for combating money laundering and terrorist financing.

- Recently FATF puts Pakistan on 'grey-list' over global terror finance.
- The government has created observation posts, Border fencing, flood lighting, deployment of modern and hi-tech surveillance equipment to prevent increased immigration.
- Comprehensive Integrated Border Management System (CIBMS) has replaced manual surveillance/patrolling of the international borders by electronic surveillance to enhance detection and interception capabilities.
- India has been supportive of all efforts, particularly in the UN to combat terrorism and has played a leading role in shaping international opinion and urging the international community to prioritize the fight against terror.
- India since 1996 is trying to push a global intergovernmental convention i.e. Comprehensive Convention on International Terrorism (CCIT) to tackle terrorism. It can provide a legal framework to enhance prosecution and extradition of terrorists.
- Continuous dialogues with neighbouring countries have been initiated from time to time for motivating them for a strict action against terrorists breeding in their respective territories.

Way Forward

- There is a need to reassess our policies on number of issues pertaining to the management of India's international borders such as intelligence apparatus, internal security and border management.
- Technical solutions are necessary to augment and complement the traditional methods of border guarding.
- They not only enhance the surveillance and detection capabilities of the border guarding forces but also improve the impact of the border guarding personnel against infiltration and trans-border crimes.
- India should move in the direction of specialisation of military to fight cross-border terrorism.

- Military should also look at alternative means to strike at the terror camps across the LoC and LAC through mechanisms like Precision Engagement Capability.
- A judicious mix of properly trained manpower and affordable and tested technology is likely to yield better results.

War against terrorism is a low intensity conflict or localized war and cannot be waged without the full and unstinted support of the society and can be lost easily if the morale and resolve of the society to fight against terrorism falters.

The Prevention of Terrorism Act, 2002

- It defines terrorist activity as one which intents to threaten the unity, integrity, security or sovereignty of India or strike terror in the minds of people.
- It can either be created through explosive or lethal weapons or any other substance of hazardous nature to cause death of or injuries to any person and destruction of any property.
- It is a systematic use of violence against civilians for intimidating a population or government for political, religious, or ideological goals.
- Cross Border Terrorism includes unconventional tactics like cyber attacks, political warfare, perception war, sponsorship of armed proxy fighters etc.

Chapter Eight

India-China stand-off: A comparison of the military and air defence prowess

With the standoff at the Ladakh border turning ugly between India and China, here is a military and air power comparison.

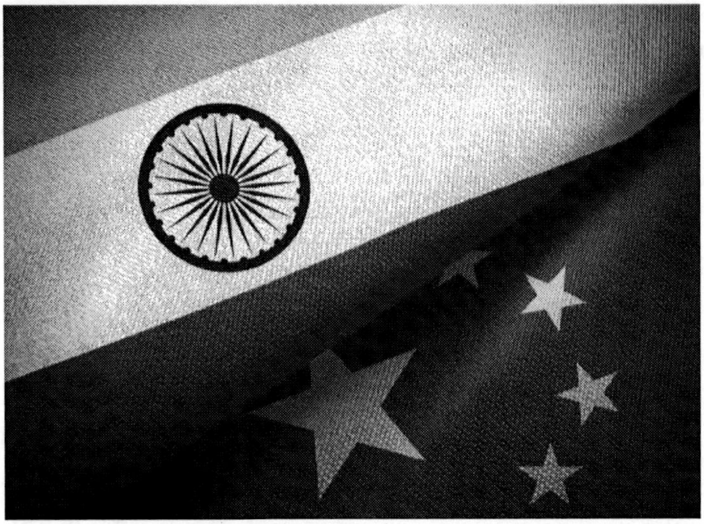

The border between India and China has been volatile in the best of times and over the past few weeks, things have only taken an uglier turn. In eastern Ladakh, a skirmish between the troops broke out as India accused China of violating the unresolved frontier and challenging and obstructing the Indian patrol party.

Defence Minister Rajnath Singh and National Security Advisor Ajit Doval are monitoring the situation and India has made its position clear – it will continue to "defend its interests resolutely" and continue to build infrastructure close to the boundary inside Indian territory.

The Indian Army has moved its battalions of three Infantry Divisions, based in Leh, forward but the country is also looking for a quick diplomatic resolution.

Significantly, Chinese President Xi Jinping also asked the People's Liberation Army to scale up battle preparedness during the parliamentary session being held in Beijing.

Despite the escalation in tensions, a physical outbreak of war is a highly unlikely scenario in contemporary times, with both countries having reached a tacit understanding that more emphasis is needed in securing their economies than wasting resources in combat. This point is even more pertinent when the COVID -19 pandemic has gripped the world and countries are battling hard to contain it.

Nevertheless, an academic exercise in military comparison can be done.

China and India – A military comparison

China has over 2 million troops employed in active military service compared to 1.3 million on the Indian side. Its defence budget is four times at USD 225 billion compared to that of India, which is approximately USD 55 billion.

China's tank strength stands at a stupendous 13,000 plus compared to India's 4,100 plus. And its armoured fighting vehicles are at a staggering 40,000; India pales into insignificance with just over 2,800. Similarly, it has ten times the rocket projectors at 2050 versus India's 266.

INDIA & CHINA- MILITARY COMPARISON

SUBJECTS	INDIA	CHINA
TOTAL MILITARY PERSONNEL	3,462,500	2,693,000
DEFENCE BUDGET (USD)	$ 55.2 BN	$ 224 BN
TOTAL AIRCRAFT	2,082	3,187
HELICOPTERS	692	1,004
FIGHTERS/INTERCEPTORS	520	1,222
ATTACK AIRCRAFT/HELICOPTERS	694/17	1,564/281
TANK STRENGHT	4,184	13,050
ARMORED FIGHTING VEHICLES	2,815	40,000
TOTAL NAVAL ASSETS	295	714
SUBMARINES	16	76

SOURCE: WWW.GLOBALFIREPOWER.COM

As far as prowess at the sea is concerned, China has a total of 714 naval assets compared to 295 of India, with 76 submarines versus 16 owned by India. Our north-eastern neighbor also has three times the number of destroyers at 33 compared with 11 owned by us.

China has managed to produce and deploy a wide range of ballistic missiles, ranging from short-range missiles to Intercontinental Ballistic Missiles (ICBMs). India's Defense Research and Development Organization (DRDO) has also been conducting trials of Prithvi-1 (150 km-range) and Prithvi-2 (250 km-range) ballistic missiles, which have been inducted into the armed forces.

Chinese Launch Pads and Air Prowess

China has 3,000 plus total aircraft compared to over 2,000 in the Indian fleet, but importantly, it has two times the number of fighters and interceptors. It also has 507 serviceable airports compared to 346 in India.

Since the 1990s, China modernized its air force at a rapid rate. In 1990s, it had 5,000 aircraft but most of the aircraft were obsolete like the Soviet MIG 19s and MIG 21s. China is now upgrading its fleet into new generation aircraft.

Can China deploy its entire air force on the India-China front? The answer is "no" as per Group Capt (Retd) Ravinder S Chhatwal, former Senior Fellow Centre for Air Power Studies, New Delhi, and author of the book 'The Chinese Air Threat: Understanding the Reality'.

He says, "To launch any air campaign, fighter aircraft have to be deployed close to the border, roughly about 200 km to 300 km from the border of your enemy. Against India, China will have to deploy its fighter aircraft in Tibet and adjacent airfields in Xinjiang. China has 2,100 combat aircraft but most of them are deployed on its eastern seaboard. They cannot deploy all of them against India because of limited number of airfields in Tibet."

He further adds, "Now Tibet, unfortunately for them and fortunately for us, is a high-altitude plateau with mountainous terrain. They have just about five main airfields in Tibet (Kongka Dzong, Hoping, Pangta, Linzhi and Gargunsa) and another two in Xinjiang (Hotan and Kashgar). They are developing three more airfields in Tibet which are likely to be ready by 2022."

"Now, the second point is that to carry out sustained fighter aircraft operations, airfields have to be mutually supporting. By mutually supporting, I mean, that if you take off from an airfield there should be another airfield nearby within 100 or 200 km, so that in case of requirement for diversion etc., you have an alternative airfield....

In the northern Xinjiang sector's two airfields Hotan and Kashgar - the distance between them is 450 km while the distance between Hotan and Gargunsa is 550 kms. Hotan to Korla, the distance is 750 km so they are not mutually supportive. In western Tibet, there is only one airfield, Gargunsa. If Gargunsa is bombed by the Indian Air Force, there will be a gap of 1,500 km between Hotan and nearest airfield Hoping."

Group Capt (Retd) Chhatwal concludes by making a pertinent point: "There is another limitation which they have. In the airfield, when you park aircraft for fighter operations, they have to be in blast protected shelters - concrete shelters. China doesn't have any blast protected shelters at any of the airfields. After Doklam they have realised their mistake and have now started building these in Kongka Dzong (Lhasa) airfield."

Doklam Stand-Off

Photograph of Indian soldiers on Doklam Plateau taken by Chinese soldiers – Annotations by the Chinese Foreign Ministry showing Chinese claims

The **2017 China India border standoff** or **Doklam standoff** refers to the military border standoff between the Indian Armed Forces and the People's Liberation Army of China over Chinese construction of a road in Doklam near a trijunction border area, known as Donglang, or Donglang Caochang (meaning Donglang pasture or grazing field), in Chinese. On 16 June 2017 Chinese troops with construction vehicles and road-building equipment began extending an existing road southward in Doklam, a territory which is claimed by both China as well as India's ally Bhutan. On 18 June 2017, as part of **Operation Juniper**, about 270 Indian troops armed with weapons and two bulldozers crossed the Sikkim border into Doklam to stop the Chinese troops from constructing the road. On 28 August, both India and China announced that they had withdrawn all their troops from the face-off site in Doklam.

Background

Location of Doklam and border of Bhutan on OpenStreetMap; Sikkim to the west and Chumbi Valley to the north Doklam is an area disputed between

China and Bhutan located near their tri-junction with India. Unlike China and Bhutan, India does not claim Doklam but supports Bhutan's claim.

China's claim on Doklam is based on the 1890 Convention of Calcutta between China and Britain, which states in Article I:

The boundary of Sikkim and Tibet shall be the crest of the mountain range separating the waters flowing into the Sikkim Teesta and its affluents from the waters flowing into the Tibetan Mochu and northwards into other Rivers of Tibet. The line commences at Mount Gipmochi on the Bhutan frontier, and follows the above-mentioned water-parting to the point where it meets Nipal territory.

China asserts that by this convention, the starting point of the Sikkim-Tibet border is "Mount Gipmochi on the Bhutan frontier" and that this clearly defines the tri-junction point. As per Chinese claims, Doklam is located in the Xigaze area of Tibet, bordering the state of Sikkim. However Bhutan was not a party to the convention.

In 1949, Bhutan signed a treaty with India giving allowance to India to guide its diplomatic and defense affairs. In 2007, the treaty was superseded by a new Friendship Treaty that replaced the provision that made it mandatory for Bhutan to take India's guidance on foreign policy, provided broader sovereignty but also stated in its Article 2:

In keeping with the abiding ties of close friendship and cooperation between Bhutan and India, the Government of the Kingdom of Bhutan and the

Government of the Republic of India shall cooperate closely with each other on issues relating to their national interests.

From 1958, Chinese maps started showing large parts of Bhutanese territory as part of China. Localized tensions arose in the 1960s but in the 1970s negotiations between China and Bhutan, with India sometimes playing a supporting role, failed to create a consensus on the status of the Doklam plateau. Bhutan and China have held 24 rounds of boundary talks since they began in 1984, with notable agreements reached in 1988 and 1998, the latter also prohibiting the use of force and encouraging both parties to strictly adhere to peaceful means.

In the early 2000s, China built a road up the Sinchela pass (in undisputed territory) and then over the plateau (in disputed territory), leading up to the

Doka La pass, until reaching within 68 metres distance to the Indian border post on the Sikkim border. Here, they constructed a turn-around facilitating vehicles to turn back. This road has been in existence at least since 2005. It is the southward extension of this road that sparked the 2017 standoff.

Timeline

On 16 June 2017, Chinese troops with construction vehicles and road-building equipment began extending an existing road southward on the Doklam plateau.

On 18 June 2017, around 270 Indian troops, with weapons and two bulldozers, entered Doklam to stop the Chinese troops from constructing the road.

On 29 June 2017, Bhutan protested to China against the construction of a road in the disputed territory. According to the Bhutanese government, China attempted to extend a road that previously terminated at Doka La towards the Bhutan Army camp at Zornpelri near the Jampheri Ridge 2 km to the south; that ridge, viewed as the border by China but as wholly within Bhutan by both Bhutan and India, extends eastward approaching India's highly-strategic Siliguri Corridor. The Bhutanese border was reportedly put on high alert and border security was tightened as a result of the growing tensions.

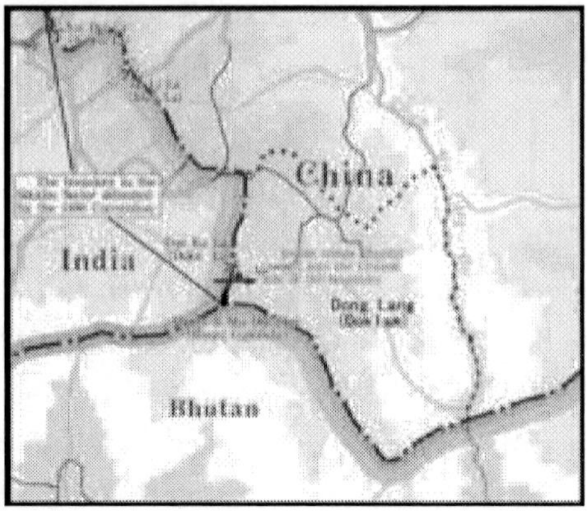

"Sketch Map of the Site of the Indian Troops' Trespass" – Translated Map published by the Chinese Foreign Ministry on 2 August 2017 showing Chinese claims

On the same day, China Foreign Ministry released a map depicting Doklam as part of China. Using the map as illustration, China's Spokesperson Lu Kang read Article I of the 1890 Convention of Calcutta and asserted that it proved that the Donglang (Doklam) area, a territory North East of Gipmochi as shown on the map, belongs to China.

On 30 June, Ministry of External Affairs of India released the statement entitled *Recent Developments in Doklam Area* stating its official position. It charges China of changing status quo in violation of a 2012 understanding between the two governments regarding finalizing the tri-junction boundary points and causing security concerns, widely understood as at its strategic Siliguri Corridor. It says that "Indian personnel" at Doka La coordinated with Bhutan and "approached the Chinese construction party and urged them to desist from changing the status quo."

On 30 June, answering a question about Bhutan's protest, China's Spokesperson Lu Kang made the following statement about Doklam's history after asserting that the area where the construction activities are underway is totally under the jurisdiction of China because it is completely located on the Chinese side of the China-Bhutan traditional customary line:

Before the 1960s, if border inhabitants of Bhutan wanted to herd in Doklam, they needed the consent of the Chinese side and had to pay the grass tax to China. Nowadays the Xi Zang Tibet Archives still retain some receipts of the grass tax.

On 3 July 2017, China Foreign Ministry Spokesperson Geng Shuang stated that former Indian prime minister Jawaharlal Nehru accepted the 1890 Britain–China treaty:

On September 26 of the same year, when writing back to Premier Zhou Enlai, Prime Minister Nehru unequivocally stated "the boundary between Sikkim and Xi Zang, China was defined by the 1890 Convention. This boundary was demarcated in 1895. There is no dispute over the boundary between Sikkim and Xi Zang (Tibet), China".

Indian media reported that Nehru's 26 September 1959 letter to Zhou, cited by China, was in fact a point-by-point refutation of the claims made by the Zhou on 8 September 1959. In the letter, which was accessed by Indian press albeit not published in its entirety, Nehru wrote:

This Convention of 1890 also defined the boundary between Sikkim and Tibet; and the boundary was later, in 1895, demarcated. There is thus no dispute regarding the boundary of Sikkim with the Tibet region.

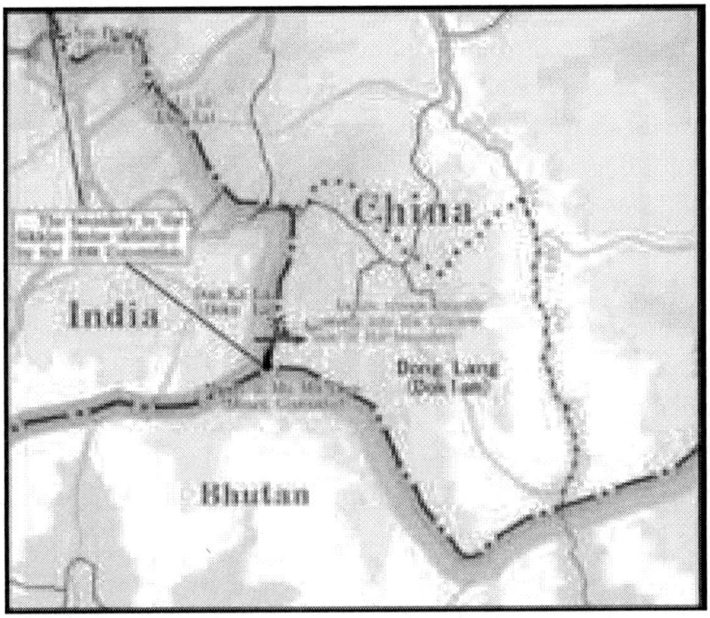

Sketch Map of the Site of the Indian Troops' Trespass" – Translated Map published by the Chinese Foreign Ministry on 2 August 2017 showing Chinese claims

China Foreign Ministry Spokesperson Geng Shuang replied to India media's question about disputed tri-junction with the following comment:

The so-called tri-junction, as the name suggests, is a point. It is not a line, much less an area. India misinterprets tri-junction point as an area, from ulterior motives. This time, the trespassing point of Indian army, is on the Sikkim-China border, which is 2000 metres away from the tri-junction point, Mount Gipmochi, by the 1890 Treaty.

On 5 July 2017, the Chinese government said that it had for the past 24 months a basic consensus with Bhutan that Doklam belongs to China, and there was no dispute between the two countries.

On 19 July 2017, China renewed its call for India to withdraw its troops from Doklam.

On 24 July 2017, Chinese Foreign Minister Wang Yi told reporters that it is very clear who is right and who is wrong in the standoff in Doklam, and that even senior Indian officials have publicly said that Chinese troops have not intruded into Indian territory. "In other words, India admitted that it has entered Chinese territory. The solution to this issue is simple, which is that they behave themselves and withdraw," Wang said.

On 2 August 2017, the Chinese foreign ministry released a 15-page official position statement *The Facts and China's Position Concerning the Indian Border Troops' Crossing of the China-India Boundary in the Sikkim Sector into the Chinese Territory*. According to this document, there were still over 40 Indian troops and one bulldozer in Doklam (Donglang) region. Beijing accused India of using Bhutan as "a pretext" to interfere and impede the boundary talks between China and Bhutan. The report referred to India's "trespassing" into Doklam as a violation of the territorial sovereignty of China as well as a challenge to the sovereignty and independence of Bhutan. China says in the 15-page document that it notified India regarding its plan to construct road "in advance in full reflection of China's goodwill".

On 3 August 2017, China charged with four reasons that "India is certainly not for peace" though it always puts peace on its lips.

On 4 August 2017, The Ministry of External Affairs of India refused to confirm or deny when asked why, if India received notification from China in advance on its plan to construct road, it had not used diplomatic channels before sending its troops across the border since it was asking for diplomatic solution.

On 8 August 2017, Chinese diplomat Wang Wenli claimed that Bhutan had conveyed to China through diplomatic channels that the area of the standoff is not its territory, saying, "After the incident, the Bhutanese made it very clear to us that the place where the trespassing happened is not Bhutan's territory." On the next day, the Bhutanese government denied this, saying over the phone "Our position on the border issue of Doklam is very clear" and referring to the governments 29 June statement.

On 15 August 2017, several Indian and Chinese soldiers were alleged to have been injured after a melee broke out between them when a group of Chinese soldiers were alleged to have attempted to infiltrate across the border near Pangong Lake into Indian controlled territory in Ladakh. An Indian intelligence officer said the confrontation occurred after Indian soldiers intercepted a Chinese patrol that veered into Indian-held territory after losing its way apparently due to bad weather.

On 16 August 2017, the state run news agency released a segment of its show "The Spark" on Twitter racially attacking India, the video named the "Seven Sins of India" portrayed a stereotypical Indian with a turban and beard and a typical Indian accent, the segment spoke of Indians having "thick skin" and "pretending to sleep" on the matter of the border standoff between the two countries. The video went on to claim India was physically threatening Bhutan, and compared India to a "robber who breaks into a house and does not leave". The content of the video were factually incorrect. The video has received strong backlash on Twitter as well as from the international media.

On 9 October 2017 China announced that it was ready to maintain peace at frontiers with India reacting to Indian Defence Minister Nirmala Sitharaman's visit to Nathu La.

Disengagement

On 28 August 2017, India and China announced that they had agreed to pull their troops back from the face-off in Doklam. By the end of the day, it was reported that the withdrawal was completed.

The Indian troops withdrew back to their original positions at their outpost at Doka La, located in a militarily advantageous position on the Bhutanese border, less than 500 meters away down the ridge slope.[49][50] *The Times of India*, citing a source, reported: "Our soldiers sit on the top, hold the ridge and can swiftly intervene, as they pro-actively did in mid-June, if the People's Liberation Army once again tries to unilaterally change the status quo by constructing a road near the Sikkim-Bhutan-Tibet tri-junction."[49]

Ministry of External Affairs (MEA) of India released a press statement stating that India and China had mutually agreed to disengage. It said that India and China had maintained diplomatic communication in recent weeks and that India was able to convey its "concerns and interests". In Beijing, the foreign ministry spokeswoman said that the Chinese forces on site have verified that the Indian troops pulled out, and implied that Chinese troop numbers would be reduced. She said that the Chinese troops would continue to patrol the area, to garrison it and to exercise "sovereign rights". However, she made no mention of road-building activities. The statement from the Chinese Foreign Ministry spokesman, as *The Diplomat* reported, "offered Beijing a face-saving way out of the impasse."[50] Indian MEA issued a second statement later in the day that both the sides have withdrawn "under verification". The Indian news channel NDTV reported that, by the end of the day, Chinese road-building equipment was removed from the face-off site. Some experts warned that one shouldn't be overly optimistic as another standoff is entirely possible.[47][48]

The Washington Post commented that it was not clear if China had offered any concessions in return for the Indian withdrawal, such as agreeing to halt road construction. It said that the deal allowed both sides to save face. However China was continuing to be "cagey" in its official remarks.[47][51] *Al Jazeera* said that China was not giving up its historical claims and it expected India to respect its "historical borders".[52] Scholar Taylor Fravel pointed out that there are plenty of options available to China to garrison the area other than extending the road.[53]

On 29 August, Bhutan welcomed the disengagement and hoped that it would lead to the maintenance of peace and tranquility as well as status quo along the borders.[54]

On 5 September, Prime Minister Narendra Modi and President Xi Jinping held hour-long discussions on the sidelines of the BRICS summit. They agreed on a "forward-looking" approach and vowed to make efforts to ensure that situations like the Doklam standoff do not recur. They reaffirmed that maintaining peace and tranquility in the border areas was essential for the relations between the two countries.[55]

On 7 September, some media reports claimed that both nation's troops still were patrolling the area at the face-off site, simply having moved 150 meters back from their previous position.[56]

Bhutanese reaction

After issuing a press statement on 29 June, the Bhutanese government and media maintained a studious silence. *The Bhutanese* clarified that the territory on which China was building a road was "Bhutanese territory" that was being claimed by China, and it is part of the ongoing border negotiations. It also defended the policy of silence followed by the Bhutanese government, saying "Bhutan does not want India and China to go to war, and it is avoiding doing anything that can heat up an already heated situation." However, *ENODO Global*, a risk management firm, having done a study of social media interactions in Bhutan, recommended that the government should "proactively engage" with citizens and avoid a disconnect between leaders and populations. ENODO found considerable anxiety among the populace regarding the risk of war between India and China, and the possibility of annexation by China similar to that of Tibet in 1951. It found a strengthening of Bhutanese resolve, identity and nationalism, not wanting to be "pushovers".

The New York Times said that it encountered more people concerned about India's actions than China's. It found expressions of sovereignty and concern that an escalation of the border conflict would hurt trade and diplomatic relations with China. Scholar Rudra Chaudhuri, having toured the country, noted that Doklam is not as important an issue for the Bhutanese as it might have been ten years ago. Rather the Bhutanese view a border settlement with China as the top priority for the country. While he noticed terms such as "pro-Chinese" and "anti-Indian" often used, he says that what they mean is not well-understood.

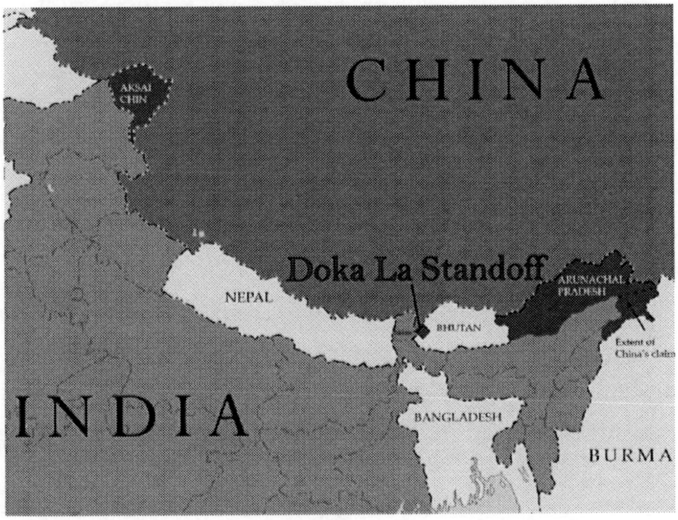

Chapter Nine

Indian Arm Forces

The **Indian Armed Forces** are the military forces of the Republic of India. It consists of three professional uniformed services: the Indian Army, Indian Navy, and Indian Air Force. Additionally, the Indian Armed Forces are supported by the Indian Coast Guard and paramilitary organizations (Assam Rifles, and Special Frontier Force) and various inter-service commands and institutions such as the Strategic Forces Command, the Andaman and Nicobar Command and the Integrated Defense Staff. The President of India is the Supreme Commander of the Indian Armed Forces. The Indian Armed Forces are under the management of the Ministry of Defense (MoD) of the Government of India. With strength of over 1.4 million active personnel, it is the world's second-largest military force and has the world's largest volunteer army. It also has the third-largest defense budget in the world. As per 2015 Credit Suisse report, the Indian Armed Forces is the world's fifth-most powerful military, whereas the 2020 Global Firepower report lists it as the fourth most-powerful military.

It is important to note that the Central Armed Police Forces, which are referred to as 'Paramilitary Forces' are not armed forces. As such they are headed by civilian officers from the Indian Police Service and are under the control of the Ministry of Home Affairs, not the Ministry of Defense. These are central police organizations.

The Indian armed forces have been engaged in a number of major military operations, including: the Indo-Pakistani wars of 1947, 1965 and 1971, the Portuguese-Indian War, the Sino-Indian War, the 1967 Chola incident, the 1987 Sino-Indian skirmish, the Kargil War, and the Siachen conflict among others.

India honors its armed forces and military personnel annually on Armed Forces Flag Day, 7 December. Since 1962, the IAF has maintained close military relations with Russia, including cooperative development of programs such as the Fifth Generation Fighter Aircraft (FGFA) and the Multirole Transport Aircraft (MTA). Armed with the nuclear triad, the Indian armed forces are steadily undergoing modernization, with investments in areas such as futuristic soldier systems and missile defense systems.

The Department of Defense Production of the Ministry of Defense is responsible for the indigenous production of equipment used by the Indian Armed Forces. It comprises the 41 Indian Ordnance Factories under the control of the Ordnance Factories Board, and eight Defense PSUs namely: HAL, BEL, BEML, BDL, MDL, GSL, GRSE and Midhani. India remains one of the largest importer of defense equipment with Russia, Israel, France and the United States being the top foreign suppliers of military equipment. The Government of India has launched a Make in India initiative to indigenize manufacturing and reduce dependence on imports, including defense imports and procurement.

Republic of India (1950 to present)

Upon India becoming a sovereign republic on 26 January 1950, some of the last vestiges of British rule – such as rank badges, imperial crowns, British ensigns and "Royal" monikers – were dropped and replaced with the Indian tricolor and the Lion Capital of Asoka. On 1 April 1951, the remaining units of Imperial Service Troops of the former princely states were integrated with the regular Indian Army, though only a percentage of the former princely states forces were found capable enough to be retained in active service. While India had become a republic, British officers seconded from the British Armed Forces continued to hold senior positions in the Indian Armed Forces into the early 1960s. On 1 April 1954, Air Marshal Subroto Mukherjee became the first Indian Commander-in-Chief of the Indian Air Force. Effective from 1 April 1955, a Parliamentary Act, the *Commanders-In-Chiefs (Change in Designation) Act*, re-designated the office of Commander-in-Chief as the Chief of Staff of each branch. Not until 1958 would the last British chief of staff that of the Indian Navy, be succeeded by an Indian. On 22 April of that year, Vice Admiral Ram Dass Katari became the first Indian Chief of Naval Staff. The Chiefs of Staff of the Indian Air Force and the Indian Navy were upgraded to four-star rank on par with the Chief of Army Staff in 1966 and 1968, respectively.

In 1961 tensions rose between India and Portugal over the Portuguese-occupied territory of Goa, which India claimed for itself. After Portuguese police cracked down violently on a peaceful, unarmed demonstration for union with India, the Indian government decided to invade and initiated Operation Vijay. A lopsided air, sea, and ground campaign resulted in the speedy surrender of Portuguese forces. Within 36 hours, 451 years of Portuguese colonial rule ended, and Goa was annexed by India.

Pakistan's Lt. Gen. A. A. K. Niazi signing the instrument of surrender in Dhaka on 16 Dec' 1971, in the presence of India's Lt. Gen. Aurora. Standing behind them are officers of India's Army, Navy and Air Force. The 1971 War directly involved participation of all three arms of Indian Armed Forces.

India fought four major wars with its neighbour Pakistan in 1947, 1965, 1971 and 1999, and with China in 1962. Indian victory over Pakistan in the 1971 war, helped create the free country of Bangladesh. In the late 1970s and early 1980s, Pakistan began organizing tourist expeditions to the Siachen Glacier, disputed territory with India. Irked by this development, in April 1984 India initiated the successful Operation Meghdoot during which it gained control over all of the 70-kilometre (41-mile)-long Siachen Glacier, and all of its tributary glaciers, as well as the three main passes of the Saltoro Ridge immediately west of the glacier—Sia La, Bilafond La, and Gyong La. According to *TIME* magazine, India gained more than 1,000 square miles (3,000 km) of territory as a result of its military operations in Siachen. In 1987 and in 1989 Pakistan to re-take the glacier but was unsuccessful. The conflict ended with Indian Victory. There has been a ceasefire since 2003.

The Indian Peace Keeping Force (IPKF) carried out a mission in northern and eastern Sri Lanka in 1987–1990 to disarm the Tamil Tigers under the terms of the Indo-Sri Lanka Accord. It was a difficult battle for the Indian Army, which was not trained for an unconventional war. After losing approximately 1,200 personnel and several T-72 tanks, India ultimately abandoned the mission in consultation with the Sri Lankan government. In what was labelled as Operation Pawan, the Indian Air Force flew about 70,000 sorties to and within Sri Lanka.

The beginning of the 21st century saw a reorientation for India on the global stage from a regional role in the subcontinent to a major role in the Indian Ocean region stretching from the Gulf of Aden to the Malacca Strait. India's sphere of influence needs to encompass not just the South Asian Sub-continent, but also the northern Indian Ocean area, from the eastern seaboard of Africa in the west, to the Malacca Straits in the east, and must include Iran, Afghanistan, the Central Asian Republics (CARs), China and Myanmar. India's credibility, as a regional power will be contingent on institutional stability, economic development and military strength, including nuclear deterrence. The long stretches of disputed borders with China and Pakistan, and sizeable areas under their occupation, continue to be major irritants, in spite of the peace processes under-way with both countries.

Current

Overview

The headquarters of the Indian Armed Forces is in New Delhi, the capital city of India. The President of India serves as the formal Supreme Commander of the Indian Armed Forces, while actual control lies with the executive headed by the Prime Minister of India. The Ministry of Defence (MoD) is the ministry charged with the responsibilities of countering insurgency and ensuring external security of India. General Manoj Mukund Naravane is the Chief of the Army Staff (COAS), Admiral Karambir Singh is the Chief of the Naval Staff (CNS) and Air Chief Marshal Rakesh Kumar Singh Bhadauria is the Chief of the Air Staff (CAS).

The Indian armed force are split into different groups based on their region of operation. The Indian Army is divided administratively into seven tactical commands, each under the control of different Lieutenant Generals. The Indian Air Force is divided into five operational and two functional commands. Each command is headed by an air officer commanding-in-chief with the rank of air marshal. The Indian Navy operates three commands. Each command is headed by a flag officer commanding-in-chief with the rank of vice admiral. There are two joint commands whose head can belong to any of the three services. These are the Strategic Forces Command and the Andaman and Nicobar Command. The lack of an overall military commander has helped keep the Indian Armed Forces under civilian control, and has prevented the rise of military dictatorships unlike in neighboring Pakistan.

South Block in New Delhi is the headquarters of the Ministry of Defence.

The Armed Forces have four main tasks;

- To assert the territorial integrity of India.
- To defend the country if attacked by a foreign nation.
- To support the civil community in case of disasters (e.g. flooding).
- To participate in United Nations peacekeeping operations in consonance with India's commitment to the United Nations Charter.

The code of conduct of the Indian military is detailed in a semi-official book called *Customs and Etiquette in the Services*, written by retired Major General Ravi Arora, which details how Indian personnel are expected to conduct themselves generally. Arora is an executive editor of the *Indian Military Review*.

The major deployments of the Indian army constitute the border regions of India, particularly Jammu and Kashmir, Ladakh, and Northeast India, to engage in counter-insurgency and anti-terrorist operations. The major commitments of the Indian Navy constitute patrol missions, anti-piracy operations off the coast of Somalia, the 'Singapore Indian Maritime Bilateral Exercise' with the Republic of Singapore Navy in the Straits of Malacca, maintaining a military presence in Southeast Asias waters, and joint exercises with other countries, such as: Brasil,

South Africa, the United States and Japan, France (Varuna naval exercises), the People's Republic of China, the Russian Navy (INDRA naval exercises), and others.

Top ten military expenditures in US$ Bn. in 2014, according to the International Institute for Strategic Studies.

Between April 2015 and March 2016, India allocated $40 billion to Defense Services, $10 billion to Defense (Civil Estimates) and another $10 billion to the Home Ministry for Paramilitary and CAPF forces – a total allocation for defense and security of about $60 billion for the financial year 2015–16. In 2016–17, the contribution to the Home Ministry has been increased from $10 billion to $11.5 billion.

Contemporary criticism of the Indian military have drawn attention to several issues, such as lack of political reform, obsolete equipment, lack of adequate ammunition, and inadequate research and development due to over-reliance on foreign imports. In addition, the lack of a 'strategic culture' among the political class in India is claimed to have hindered the effectiveness of the Indian military. Critics believe these issues hobble the progress and modernization of the military. However, analysis by the Central Intelligence Agency indicates that India is projected to have the fourth most capable concentration of power by 2015. According to a report published by the US Congress, India is the developing world's leading arms purchaser. It is investing ₹ 99.7 billion (US$1.4 billion) to build a dedicated and secure optical fibre cable (OFC) network for exclusive use of the Army, Navy and Air Force. This will be one of the world's largest closed user group (CUG) networks.

Personnel

During 2010, the Indian Armed Forces had a reported strength of 1.4 million active personnel and 2.1 million reserve personnel. In addition, there were approximately 1.3 million paramilitary personnel, making it one of the world's largest military forces. A total of 1,567,390 ex- servicemen are registered with the Indian Army, the majority of them hailing from: Uttar Pradesh (271,928), Punjab (191,702), Haryana (165,702), Maharashtra (143,951), Kerala

(127,920), Tamil Nadu (103,156), Rajasthan (100,592) and Himachal Pradesh

(78,321). Many of them are re-employed in various Central government sectors. Prior to 1992, women served in auxiliary services. Since then, women have been granted the right to serve as officers in the military and starting 2015, women fighter jet combat pilots were also inducted. As of 2014, the percentage of the women in the army was 3%, in the navy was 2.8% and in the air force was 8.5%.

The highest wartime gallantry award given by the Military of India is the Param Vir Chakra (PVC), followed by the Maha Vir Chakra (MVC) and the Vir Chakra (VrC). Its peacetime equivalent is the Ashoka Chakra Award. The highest decoration for meritorious service is the Param Vishisht Seva Medal.

Branches

Picture showing equivalent ranks and insignia of Indian Armed Forces

Indian Armed Forces				
	Active	Reserve	Governing Body	Area
Indian Army	1,237,117	960,000	Ministry of Defence (India)	
Indian Navy	67,228	55,000	Ministry of Defence (India)	
Indian Air Force	139,576	140,000	Ministry of Defence (India)	
	1,443,921	1,155,000		
Paramilitary Forces				

	Active	Reserve	Governing Body	Area
Indian Coast Guard	11,000		Ministry of Defence (India)	
Assam Rifles	66,000		Ministry of Home Affairs (India)	
Special Frontier Force	10,000		Ministry of Home Affairs (India)	
	87,000	N.A.		
Central Armed Police Forces and Others				
Border Security Force	257,363		Ministry of Home Affairs (India)	Indo-Pak Border, Indo-Bangladesh, others
Central Industrial Security Force	144,418		Ministry of Home Affairs (India)	Industries, PSUs
Central Reserve Police Force	313,678		Ministry of Home Affairs (India)	
Indo-Tibetan Border Police	89,432		Ministry of Home Affairs (India)	India-China Border
National Security Guard	12,000		Ministry of Home Affairs (India)	
Sashastra Seema Bal	76,337		Ministry of Home Affairs (India)	Indo-Nepal Border and Indo-Bhutan Border
Railway Protection Force	70,000		Ministry of Railways (India)	Indian Railways
National Disaster Response Force	13,000		Ministry of Home Affairs (India)	Area prone to Disaster in India
Defence Security Corps	31,000			
Special Protection Group	3,000		Cabinet Secretariat of India	Cabinet Secretariat of India
State Armed Police Forces	450,000		State Govt.	Respective States
Civil Defence		500,000		
Home Guard		441,800		
	1,403,700	987,800		

Recruitment and Training

The National Defence Academy (NDA) at Pune. NDA serves as the joint services academy for the army, the navy and the air force.

The vast majority of soldiers in Indian Army are enlisted personnel, called by the Army as Soldier, general duty. These soldiers are recruited at different recruitment rallies across the country. At the rally Army recruiters look at candidates from surrounding districts and examine their fitness for the Army. Candidates for Soldier, general duty must have Class 10 Leaving Certificate and in the range of 17 to 21 years. The Army also does online applications to appear at recruitment rallies. Requirements for technical roles, like nurses, artillery, Missile Defense have more stringent educational requirements. The least restrictive job in Army is House Keeper and Cleaner, for which candidates only have to be 8th pass.

At the rally, prospective soldiers are evaluated for Height, Weight, vision and hearing, and physical fitness. Fitness tests include a 1.6 km Run, Pull Ups, jumping a 9 Feet ditch, and doing a zig zag balance test. After recruitment rally, accepted candidates go to Basic Training.

The Indian Armed Forces have set up numerous military academies across India for training personnel. Military schools, Sainik Schools, and the Rashtriya Indian Military College were founded to broaden the recruitment base of the Defence Forces. The three branches of the Indian Armed Forces jointly operate several institutions such as: the National Defence Academy (NDA), the Defence Services Staff College (DSSC), the National Defence College (NDC) and the College of Defence Management (CDM) for training its officers. The Armed Forces Medical College (AFMC) at Pune is responsible for providing the entire pool of medical staff to the Armed Forces by giving them in-service training.

Officer recruitment is through many military-related academies. Besides the tri-service National Defence Academy, Pune, the three services have their own training institutes for this purpose. These include: the Indian Military Academy, Dehradun, Indian Naval Academy, Ezhimala, Air Force Academy, Hyderabad, Officers Training Academy at Chennai and Gaya. Other notable institutions are the Army War College, at Mhow, Madhya Pradesh, the High Altitude Warfare School (HAWS), at Gulmarg, Jammu and Kashmir, the Counter Insurgency and Jungle Warfare School (CIJW), in Vairengte, Mizoram, and the College of Military Engineering (CME), in Pune. After being commissioned, officers are posted and deputed, and are at the helm of affairs not only inside India but also abroad. Officers are appointed and removed only by the President of India.

Overseas bases and relations

Farkhor Air Base is a military air base located near the town of Farkhor in Tajikistan, 130 kilometres (81 mi) southeast of the capital Dushanbe. It is operated by the Indian Air Force in collaboration with the Tajikistan Air Force. Farkhor is India's first and only military base outside its territory. There was an unconfirmed report of India building some assets at Ayni Air Base in Tajikistan although the Tajik government has denied this. However, India had deployed its Army and Border Roads Organisation personnel to upgrade Ayni airbase by extending its runway, constructing an air-traffic control tower and perimeter fencing around the base. India provided medium-lift choppers to Tajikistan and a dedicated hospital there as part of efforts to build on the strategic ties between the two countries against the backdrop of US-led troops pulling out from Afghanistan in 2014. India is also helping with the development of Chah Bahar Seaport in southeastern Iran, which is speculated to be done to secure India's Maritime assets and also as a gateway to Afghanistan & Central Asia. However, India and Israel also have a very strong defence relationship.

Contingent from the Indian Armed Forces at the Moscow Victory Day Parade, 2015

In the 1950 Indo-Nepal Treaty of Peace and Friendship, India took on the obligation to actively assist Nepal in national defence and military preparedness, and both nations agreed not to tolerate threats to each other's security. In 1958, the then-Indian Prime Minister Jawaharlal Nehru visited Bhutan and reiterated India's support for Bhutan's independence and later declared in the Indian Parliament that any aggression against Bhutan would be seen as aggression against India. India started the process to bring the island country Maldives into India's security grid. India is also one of three countries with whom Japan has a security pact, the others being Australia and the United States. India and Russia maintain strong military co-operation. India has defence pacts with the US focusing on areas including security, joint training, joint development and manufacture of defence equipment and technology. In 1951, India and Burma signed a Treaty of Friendship in New Delhi. Article II of the treaty stipulates that "There shall be everlasting peace and unalterable friendship between the two States who shall ever strive to strengthen and develop further the cordial relations existing between the peoples of the two countries." India had signed a pact to develop ports in Myanmar and various bilateral issues, including economic co-operation, connectivity, security and energy. India has a "comprehensive strategic partnership" with UAE. India has maritime security arrangements in place with Oman and Qatar. In 2008, a landmark defence pact was signed, under which India committed its military assets to protect "Qatar from external threats". On 9 June 2012, the JIMEX 2012 naval exercise took place off the coast of Tamil Nadu in India to Tokyo in Japan. This was the first ever bilateral maritime exercise between the two nations in a long time, reflecting their similar interests, especially those involving spontaneous regional security against common external aggressors. The Indian Navy has berthing rights in Oman and Vietnam.

As part of its two-decade-old Look East policy, India has substantially stepped up military engagement with East Asian and ASEAN nations. Although never explicitly stated, ASEAN and East Asian nations want New Delhi to be a counterweight to increasing Chinese footprints in the region. Philippines, Thailand, Indonesia and, particularly, Vietnam and Myanmar have time and again pressed India to help them both in terms of military training and weapons supply. Myanmar's Navy Chief, Vice Admiral Thura Thet Swe during his four-day visit to India in late July 2012 held wide-ranging consultations with top officials from the Indian Ministry of Defence. Apart from increasing the number of training slots of Myanmar officers in Indian military training establishments, India has agreed to build at least four Offshore Patrol Vehicles (OPV) in Indian Shipyards to be used by Myanmar's navy. For more than a decade now, India has assisted Vietnam in beefing up its naval and air capabilities. For instance, India has repaired and upgraded more than 100 MiG 21 planes of the Vietnam People's Air Force and supplied them with enhanced avionics and radar systems.

Indian Air Force pilots have also been training their Vietnamese counterparts. In a first, India has offered a $100-million credit line to Vietnam to purchase military equipment. A bilateral agreement for the use of facilities in India by the Singapore Air Force and Army was signed in October 2007 and August 2008 respectively and has been extended up to 2017. Singapore is the only country to which India is offering such facilities.

Indian Army

Indian Army's Arjun Mark 1 Alpha tank

The Indian Army is a voluntary service, the military draft having never been imposed in India. It is one of the largest standing armies (and the largest standing volunteer army) in the world, with 1,237,000 active troops and 800,000 reserve troops. The force is headed by the Chief of Army Staff of the Indian Army, General Manoj Mukund Naravane. The highest rank in the Indian Army is Field Marshal, but it is a largely ceremonial rank and appointments are made by the President of India, on the advice of the Union Cabinet of Ministers, only in exceptional circumstances. (See Field Marshal (India)). Late Field Marshal

S.H.F.J. Manekshaw and the late Field Marshal Kodandera Madappa Cariappa are the only two officers who have attained this rank.

The army has rich combat experience in diverse terrains, due to India's varied geography, and also has a distinguished history of serving in United Nations peacekeeping operations. Initially, the army's main objective was to defend the nation's frontiers. However, over the years, the army has also taken up the responsibility of providing internal security, especially in insurgent-hit Kashmir and the north-east. The Indian Army has seen military action during the First Kashmir War, Operation Polo, the Sino-Indian War, the Second Kashmir War, the Indo-Pakistani War of 1971, the Sri Lankan Civil War and the Kargil War. It has dedicated one brigade of troops to the UN's standby arrangements. Through its large, sustained troop commitments India has been praised for taking part in difficult operations for prolonged periods. The Indian Army has participated in several UN peacekeeping operations including those in: Cyprus, Lebanon, the Democratic Republic of the Congo, Angola, Cambodia, Vietnam, Namibia,

El Salvador, Liberia, Mozambique and Somalia. The army also provided a paramedical unit to facilitate the withdrawal of the sick and wounded in the Korean War.

Doctrine, corps, field force

Indian Army Pinaka multi barrel rocket launcher

The current combat doctrine of the Indian Army is based on effectively utilising holding formations and strike formations. In the case of an attack, the holding formations would contain the enemy, and strike formations would counter-attack to neutralise enemy forces. In the case of an Indian attack, the holding formations would pin enemy forces down whilst the strike formations attack at a point of India's choosing. The Indian Army is large enough to devote several corps to the strike role. The army is also looking at enhancing its special forces capabilities. With the role of India increasing, and the need to protect India's interests on far-off shores becoming important, the Indian Army and Indian Navy are jointly planning to set up a marine brigade.

The Army's field force comprises thirteen corps, three armoured divisions, four Reorganised Army Plains Infantry Divisions (RAPID), eighteen infantry divisions and ten mountain divisions, a number of independent brigades, and requisite combat support and service support formations and units. Among the thirteen, three are "strike" corps – Mathura (I Corps), Ambala (II Corps) and Bhopal (XXI Corps). The main combat and combat support units are 62 armoured regiments, and over 350 infantry battalions and 300 artillery regiments (including two surface-to-surface missile (SSM) units). Amongst major armaments and equipment, there are nearly 4000 main battle tanks, 2000 armoured personnel carriers, 4300 artillery pieces and 200 light helicopters.

Mountain Strike Corps

India is raising a new mountain strike corps to strengthen its defence along its disputed border with China in the high reaches of the Himalayas. However, the entire XVII Corps, with its headquarters at Panagarh in West Bengal, will only be fully raised with 90,274 troops at a cost of 646.7 Billion Indian Rupees by 2018–2019 (circa US$7.3 Billion at 2018 rates). With units spread across the 4,057 kilometres (2,521 mi) Line of Actual Control (LAC) from Ladakh to Arunachal Pradesh, the corps will have two high-altitude infantry divisions (59 Div at Panagarh and 72 Div at Pathankot) with their integral units, two independent infantry brigades, two armoured brigades and the like. It will include 30 new infantry battalions and two Para-Special Forces battalions. In other words, it will have "rapid reaction force" capability to launch a counter-offensive into Tibet Autonomous Region (TAR) in the event of any Chinese attack.

Army Aviation Corps

Indian Army's HAL Dhruv helicopter

The Army Aviation Corps is another vital part of the Indian Army formed on 1 November 1986. The army aviation pilots are drawn from other combat arms, including artillery officers, to form a composite third dimensional force for an integrated battle. IAF operates and flies attack Helicopters like the Mil Mi-25/Mi-35 which are owned and administered by the Indian Air Force, but under the operational control of the Army and play a major role to support the armoured columns and infantry. Apart from the attack role, helicopters like the HAL Chetak, HAL Cheetah, and HAL Dhruv provide logistical support for the Indian Army in remote and inaccessible areas, especially the Siachen Glacier. To equip Army Aviation Corps, procurement process for 197 light utility helicopters (LUH) is ongoing, of which 64 will be inducted in the Army Aviation to replace the Cheetak and Cheetah Helicopters. HAL has obtained a firm order to deliver 114 HAL Light Combat Helicopters to the Indian Army.

Modernisation

Mechanised forces

Indian Army's tanks and infantry vehicles during an exercise.

India is re-organising its mechanised forces to achieve strategic mobility and high-volume firepower for rapid thrusts into enemy territory. At present, the Indian army has severe deficiencies in its artillery (particularly self-propelled guns) and ammunition stocks, not to mention the inability of some of its modern tanks to operate in the heat and dust of the desert regions around the international border. India proposes to progressively induct as many as 248 Arjun MBT and to develop and induct the Arjun MK-II variant, 1,657 Russian-origin T-90S main-battle tanks, apart from the ongoing upgrade of its T-72 fleet. Arjun MK- II trials had already begun in August 2013. The improved features of the MK-II version of Arjun are night vision capabilities with a thermal imaging system for detecting all kinds of missiles, Explosive Reactive Armour (ERA), mine ploughs, the ability to fire anti-tank missiles with its 120 mm main gun, an Advanced Air Defence gun capable of shooting down helicopters with a 360-degree coverage, Automatic Target Tracking (ATT) lending a greater accuracy when it comes to moving targets and superior Laser Warning and Control systems. The Indian

Army will upgrade its entire Boyevaya Mashina Pekhoty-2 (BMP-2)/2K infantry combat vehicle (ICV) fleet to enhance their ability to address operational requirements. Upgrades include integration of the latest generation fire control system, twin missile launchers and commander's thermal imaging panoramic sights, anti- tank guided missiles, as well as automatic grenade launchers.

Artillery

Under the Field Artillery Rationalisation Plan, the army plans to procure 3000 to 4000 pieces of artillery at a cost of US$3 billion. This includes purchasing 1580 towed, 814 mounted, 180 self-propelled wheeled, 100 self-propelled tracked and 145 ultra-light 155 mm/52 calibre artillery guns. After three years of searching and negotiations, India ordered M777 155 mm howitzers from USA in September 2013.

To lend greater firepower support to the Mechanized infantry, DRDO has developed the Pinaka multiple rocket launcher. The system has a maximum range of 39–40 kilometres (24–25 mi) and can fire a salvo of 12 HE rockets in 44 seconds, neutralising a target area of 3.9 square kilometres (1.5 sq mi). The system is mounted on a Tatra truck for mobility. Pinaka saw service during the Kargil War, where it was successful in neutralising enemy positions on the mountain tops. It has since been inducted into the Indian Army in large numbers.

Infantry

Indian Army personnel from White Knight crop ,2021

The Indian Army has also embarked on an infantry modernisation programme known as Futuristic **In**fantry **S**oldier **As** a **S**ystem (F-INSAS). The infantry soldiers will be equipped with modular weapon systems that will have multiple functions. The core systems include bullet proof helmet and visor. The bullet proof helmet is an integrated assembly equipped with helmet mounted

flashlight, thermal sensors and night vision device, miniature computer with audio headsets. The personal clothing of the soldier of the future would be lightweight with a bullet-proof jacket. The futuristic jacket would be waterproof, yet it would be able to breathe. The new attire will enable the troops to carry extra loads and resist the impact of nuclear, chemical and biological warfare. The new uniform will have vests with sensors to monitor the soldier's health parameters and to provide quick medical relief. The weapons sub-system is built around a multi-calibre individual weapon system with the fourth calibre attached to a grenade launcher. These include a 5.56 mm, a 7.62 mm and a new 6.8 mm under development for the first time in India.

In November 2013, the Indian Army moved a step closer to the battlefield of the future, where command networks know the precise location of every soldier and weapon, with whom generals can exchange reports, photos, data and verbal and written communications. Army headquarters called in 14 Indian companies and issued them an expression of interest (EoI) for developing a Battlefield Management System (BMS). The BMS will integrate combat units – armoured, artillery and infantry regiments, infantry battalions, helicopter flights, etc. – into a digital network that will link together all components of the future battlefield. While precise costs are still unclear, vendors competing for the contract say the army expects to pay about Rs 40,000 crore for developing and manufacturing the BMS. However, in 2015, the Indian Army decided to replace the F-INSAS program in favour of two separate projects. The new program will have two components: one arming the modern infantry soldier with the best available assault rifle, carbines and personal equipment such as the helmet and bulletproof vests, the second part is the Battlefield Management Systems (BMS).

People's Liberation Army

The **People's Liberation Army (PLA)** is the regular armed forces of the People's Republic of China (PRC) and the armed wing of the PRC's founding and ruling political party, the Chinese Communist Party (CCP). Besides the Central Military Commission (CMC) and several minor units directly under it, the PLA has five major service branches: the Ground Force (PLAGF), Navy (PLAN), Air Force (PLAAF), Rocket Force (PLARF), and the Strategic Support Force (PLASSF). A majority of military units around the country are assigned to one of five theater commands by geographical location. The PLA is the world's largest military force and constitutes the second largest defense budget in the world. It is also one of the fastest modernizing militaries in the world, and has been termed as a potential military superpower, with significant regional defense and rising global power projection capabilities. Per *Business Insider* in 2018, the PLA is the world's second-most powerful military.

PRC law explicitly affirms the leadership of the party over the armed forces of China and designates the CMC as the nationwide military command of the People's Republic of China. The Party CMC operates under the name of the State CMC for legal and governmental functions and as the ceremonial Ministry of National Defense (MoD) for diplomatic functions. The PLA is obliged to follow the principle of the Communist Party's absolute civilian control of the military under the doctrine of "the party commands the gun" -taken from a speech given by Mao Zedong during an emergency meeting of top party leadership on the 7th of August 1927 at the beginning of the Chinese civil war. In this sense, the PLA is not a national army of the type of traditional Western nation states, but a political army or the armed branch of the CCP itself since its allegiance is to the party itself and not the state or any constitution. Its commander-in-chief is the Chairman of the Central Military Commission (customarily also the General Secretary of the Chinese Communist Party). Since 1949, China has used nine different military strategies, which the PLA calls "strategic guidelines". The most important came in 1956, 1980, and 1993. In times of national emergency, the People's Armed Police (PAP) and the China Militia act as a reserve and support element for the PLAGF.

Politically, the PLA is represented in the National People's Congress with 294 deputies, all of them are CCP members

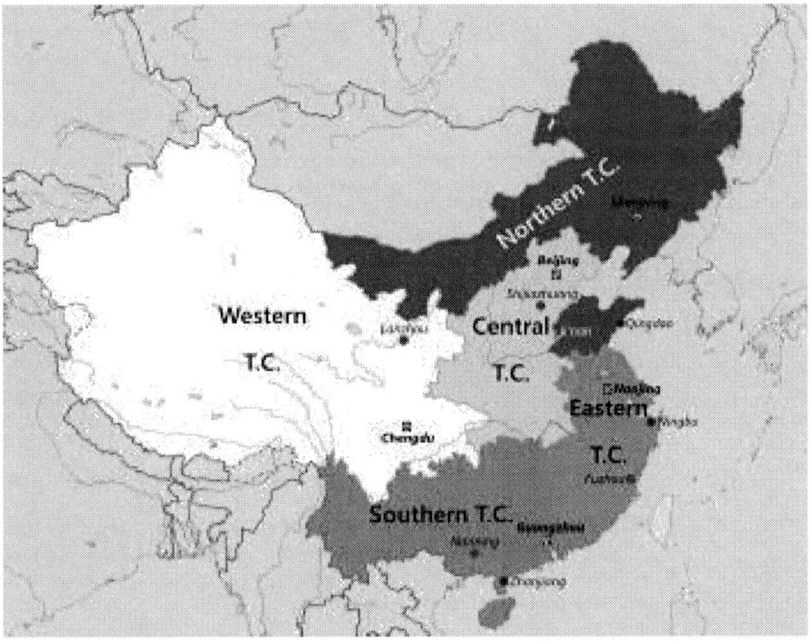

The five theater commands of the PLA

Until 2016, China's territory was divided into seven military regions, but they were reorganized into five theater commands in early 2016. This reflects a change in their concept of operations from primarily ground-oriented to mobile and coordinated movement of all services. The five new theatre commands are:

- Eastern Theater Command
- Western Theater Command
- Northern Theater Command

- Southern Theater Command
- Central Theater Command

The PLA garrisons in Hong Kong and Macau both come under the Southern Theater Command.

The military reforms have also introduced a major change in the areas of responsibilities. Rather than separately commanding their own troops, service branches are now primarily responsible for administrative tasks (like equipping and maintaining the troops). It is the theater commands now that have the command authority. This should, in theory, facilitate the implementation of joint operations across all service branches.

Coordination with civilian national security groups such as the Ministry of Foreign Affairs is achieved primarily by the

Service Branches

The PLA encompasses five main service branches: the Ground Force, the Navy, the Air Force, the Rocket Force, and the Strategic Support Force. Following the 200,000 troop reduction announced in 2003, the total strength of the PLA has been reduced from 2.5 million to just under 2.3 million. Further reforms will see an additional 300,000 personnel reduction from its current strength of 2.28 million personnel. The reductions will come mainly from non-combat ground forces, which will allow more funds to be diverted to naval, air, and strategic missile forces. This shows China's shift from ground force prioritisation to emphasising air and naval power with high-tech equipment for offensive roles over disputed coastal territories.

In recent years, the PLA has paid close attention to the performance of US forces in Afghanistan and Iraq. As well as learning from the success of the US military in network-centric warfare, joint operations, C4ISR, and hi-tech weaponry, the PLA is also studying unconventional tactics that could be used to exploit the vulnerabilities of a more technologically advanced enemy. This has been reflected in the two parallel guidelines for the PLA ground forces development. While speeding up the process of introducing new technology into the force and retiring the older equipment, the PLA has also placed an emphasis on asymmetric warfare, including exploring new methods of using existing equipment to defeat a technologically superior enemy.

In addition to the four main service branches, the PLA is supported by two paramilitary organisations: the People's Armed Police (including the China Coast Guard (CCG)) and the Militia (including the maritime militia).

A Type 99A main battle tank in service with the PLAGF

Ground Force (PLAGF)

A Type 99A main battle tank in service with the PLAGF

The PLA ground force or PLAGF is estimated to have a ground force composing of 975,000 personnel, approximately half of the PLA's total manpower of around 2 million. The ground forces are divided among the five theatre commands as named above. In times of crisis, the ground Force is reinforced by numerous reserve and paramilitary units. The PLAGF reserve component is composed of 510,000 personnel divided into 30 infantry and 12 anti-aircraft artillery (AAA) divisions. In recent years two amphibious mechanised divisions were also established in Nanjing and Guangzhou military regions. At least 40 percent of PLA divisions and brigades are now mechanised or armoured, twice the percentage before 2015.

While much of the PLA Ground Force was being reduced over the past few years, technology-intensive elements such as special operations forces (SOF), army aviation, surface-to-air missiles (SAMs), and electronic warfare units have all experienced rapid expansion. The latest operational doctrine of the PLA ground forces highlights the importance of information technology, electronic and information warfare, and long-range precision strikes in future warfare. The older generation telephone/radio-based command, control, and communications (C3) systems are being replaced by an integrated battlefield information networks featuring local/wide-area networks (LAN/WAN), satellite communications, unmanned aerial vehicle (UAV)-based surveillance and reconnaissance systems, and mobile command and control centres.

On 1 January 2016, as part of military reforms, China created for the first time a separate headquarters for the ground forces. China's ground forces have never had their own headquarters until now. Previously, the People's Liberation Army's Four General Departments served as the de facto army headquarters, functioning together as the equivalent of a joint staff, to which the navy, air force and the newly renamed Rocket Force would report. The Commander of the PLA Ground Force is Han Weiguo. The Political Commissar is Liu Lei.

PLAN destroyer conducting maritime interdiction operations at RIMPAC 2016

Navy (PLAN)

PLAN destroyer conducting maritime interdiction operations at RIMPAC 2016

Until the early 1990s, the navy performed a subordinate role to the PLA ground force (PLAGF). Since then it has undergone rapid modernisation. The 250,000 strong People's Liberation Army Navy (PLAN) is organised into three major fleets: the North Sea Fleet headquartered at Qingdao, the East Sea Fleet headquartered at Ningbo, and the South Sea Fleet headquartered in Zhanjiang. Each fleet consists of a number of surface ship, submarine, naval air force, coastal defence, and marine units.

The navy includes a 25,000 strong Marine Corps (organised into seven brigades), a 26,000 strong Naval Aviation Force operating several hundred attack helicopters and fixed-wing aircraft. As part of its overall programme of naval modernisation, the PLAN is in the stage of developing a blue water navy. In November 2012, then Party General Secretary Hu Jintao reported to the Chinese Communist Party 18th National Congress his desire to "enhance our capacity for exploiting marine resource and build China into a strong maritime power".

Chengdu J-20 5th generation stealth fighter

Air Force (PLAAF)

Chengdu J-20 5th generation stealth fighter

The 395,000 strong People's Liberation Army Air Force (PLAAF) is organised into five Theater Command Air Forces (TCAF) and 24 air divisions. The largest operational units within the Aviation Corps is the air division, which has 2 to 3 aviation regiments, each with 20 to 36 aircraft. The surface-to-air missile (SAM) Corps is organised into SAM divisions and brigades. There are also three airborne divisions manned by the PLAAF. J-XX and XXJ are names applied by Western intelligence agencies to describe programs by the People's Republic of China to develop one or more fifth-generation fighter aircraft.

DF-21Ds at the 2015 Victory Parade

Rocket Force (PLARF)

DF-21Ds at the 2015 Victory Parade

The People's Liberation Army Rocket Force (PLARF) is the main strategic missile force of the PLA and consists of at least 120,000 personnel. It controls China's nuclear and conventional strategic missiles. China's total nuclear arsenal size is estimated to be between 100 and 400 thermonuclear warheads

Strategic Support Force (PLASSF)

Founded on 31 December 2015 as part of the first wave of reforms of the PLA, the People's Liberation Army Strategic Support Force or PLASSF was established as the newest and latest branch of the PLA. Personnel numbers are estimated at 175,000. Initial announcements regarding the Strategic Support Force did not provide much detail, but Yang Yujun of the Chinese Ministry of Defense described it as an integration of all current combat support forces including but limited to: space, cyber, electronic and intelligence branches. Additionally, commentators have speculated that the new service branch will include high-tech operations forces such as space, cyberspace and electronic warfare operations units, independent of other branches of the military. Yin Zhuo, rear admiral of the People's Liberation Army Navy and member of the eleventh Chinese People's Political Consultative Conference (CPPCC) said that "the major mission of the PLA Strategic Support Force is the provision of support to the combat operations so that the PLA can gain regional advantages in the aerospace, space, network and electromagnetic space warfare and ensure integrated operations in the conduction of US joint warfare style operations."

Military Intelligence

Joint Staff Department

The Joint Staff Department carries out staff and operational functions for the PLA and had major responsibility for implementing military modernisation plans. Headed by chief of general staff, the department serves as the headquarters for the entire PLA and contained directorates for the five armed services: Ground Forces, Air Force, Navy, Rocket Forces and Support Forces. The Joint Staff Department included functionally organised subdepartments for operations, training, intelligence, mobilisation, surveying, communications and politics, the departments for artillery, armoured units, quartermaster units and joint forces engineering units were later dissolved, with the former two forming now part of the Ground Forces, the engineering formations now split amongst the service branches and the quartermaster formations today form part of the Joint Logistics Forces.

Navy Headquarters controls the North Sea Fleet, East Sea Fleet, and South Sea Fleet. Air Force Headquarters generally exercised control through the commanders of the five theater commands. Nuclear forces were directly subordinate to the Joint Staff Department through the Rocket Forces commander and political commissar. Conventional main, regional, and militia units were controlled administratively by the theater commanders, but the Joint Staff Department in Beijing could assume direct operational control of any main-force unit at will. Thus, broadly speaking, the Joint Staff Department exercises operational control of the main forces, and the theater commanders controlled as always the regional forces and, indirectly, the militia. The post of principal intelligence official in the top leadership of the Chinese military has been taken up by a number of people of several generations, from Li Kenong in the 1950s to Xiong Guangkai in the late 1990s; and their public capacity has always been assistant to the deputy chief of staff or assistant to the chief of staff.

Ever since the CCP officially established the system of "theater commands" for its army in the 2010s as a successor to the "major military regions" policy of the 1950s, the intelligence agencies inside the Army have, after going through several major evolutions, developed into the present three major military intelligence setups:

1. The central level is composed of the Second and Third Departments under the Joint Staff Headquarters and the Liaison Department under the Political Work Department.
2. At the Theater Command level intelligence activities consist of the Second Bureau established at the same level as the Operation

Department under the headquarters, and the Liaison Department established under the Political Work Department.

3. The third system includes a number of communications stations directly established in the garrison areas of all the theater commands by the Third Department of the Joint Staff Headquarters.

The Second Bureau under the headquarters and the Liaison Department under the Political Work Departments of the theater commands are only subjected to the "professional leadership" of their "counterpart" units under the Central Military Commission (CMC) and are still considered the direct subordinate units of the major military region organizationally. Those entities whose names include the word "institute", all research institutes under the charge of the Second and the Third Departments of the Joint Staff Headquarters, including other research organs inside the Army, are at least of the establishment size of the full regimental level. Among the deputy commanders of a major Theater command in China, there is always one who is assigned to take charge of intelligence work, and the intelligence agencies under his charge are directly affiliated to the headquarters and the political department of the corresponding theater command.

The Conference on Strengthening Intelligence Work held from 3 September 1996 – 18 September 1996 at the Xishan Command Center of the Ministry of State Security and the General Staff Department. Chi Haotian delivered a report entitled "Strengthen Intelligence Work in a New International Environment To Serve the Cause of Socialist Construction." The report emphasised the need to strengthen the following four aspects of intelligence work:

Efforts must be made to strengthen understanding of the special nature and role of intelligence work, as well as understanding of the close relationship between strengthening intelligence work on the one hand, and of the Four Modernizations of the motherland, the reunification of the motherland, and opposition to hegemony and power politics on the other.

The United States and the West have all along been engaged in infiltration, intervention, sabotage, and intelligence gathering against China on the political, economic, military, and ideological fronts. The response must strengthen the struggle against their infiltration, intervention, sabotage, and intelligence gathering.

Consolidating intelligence departments and training a new generation of intelligence personnel who are politically reliable, honest and upright in their ways, and capable of mastering professional skills, the art of struggle, and advanced technologies.

Strengthening the work of organising intelligence in two international industrial, commercial, and financial ports—Hong Kong and Macau.

Although the four aspects emphasised by Chi Haotian appeared to be defensive measures, they were in fact both defensive and offensive in nature.

Second Department

The Second Department of the Joint Staff Headquarters is responsible for collecting military intelligence. Activities include military attachés at Chinese embassies abroad, clandestine special agents sent to foreign countries to collect military information, and the analysis of information publicly published in foreign countries. This section of the PLA Joint Staff Headquarters act in similar capacity to its civilian counterpart the Ministry of State Security.

The Second Department oversees military human intelligence (HUMINT) collection, widely exploits open source (OSINT) materials, fuses HUMINT, signals intelligence (SIGINT), and imagery intelligence data, and disseminates finished intelligence products to the CMC and other consumers. Preliminary fusion is carried out by the Second Department's Analysis Bureau which mans the National Watch Center, the focal pointfor national-level indications and warning. In-depth analysis is carried out by regional bureaus. Although traditionally the Second Department of the Joint Staff Department was responsible for military intelligence, it is beginning to increasingly focus on scientific and technological intelligence in the military field, following the example of Russian agencies in stepping up the work of collecting scientific and technological information.

The research institute under the Second Department of the Joint Staff Headquarters is publicly known as the Institute for International Strategic Studies; its internal classified publication "Foreign Military Trends" is published every 10 days and transmitted to units at the division level.

The PLA Institute of International Relations at Nanjing comes under the Second Department of the Joint Staff Department and is responsible for training military attachés, assistant military attachés and associate military attachés as well as secret agents to be posted abroad. It also supplies officers to the military intelligence sections of various military regions and group armies. The institute was formed from the PLA "793" Foreign Language Institute, which moved from

Zhangjiakou after the Cultural Revolution and split into two institutions at Luoyang and Nanjing.

The Institute of International Relations was known in the 1950s as the School for Foreign Language Cadres of the Central Military Commission (CMC), with the current name being used since 1964. The training of intelligence personnel is one of several activities at the institute. While all graduates of the Moscow Institute of International Relations were employed by the KGB, only some graduates of the Beijing Institute of International Relations are employed by the Ministry of State Security. The former Institute of International Relations, since been renamed the Foreign Affairs College, is under the administration of the Ministry of Foreign Affairs and is not involved in secret intelligence work. The former Central Military Commission (CMC) foreign language school had foreign faculty members who were either Communist Party sympathizers or were members of foreign communist parties. But the present Institute of International Relations does not hire foreign teachers, to avoid the danger that its students might be recognised when sent abroad as clandestine agents.

Those engaged in professional work in military academies under the Second Department of the Joint Staff Headquarters usually have a chance to go abroad, either for advanced studies or as military officers working in the military attaché's office of Chinese embassies in foreign countries. People working in the military attaché's office of embassies are usually engaged in collecting military information under the cover of "military diplomacy". As long as they refrain from directly subversive activities, they are considered as well-behaved "military diplomats".

Some bureaus under the Second Department which are responsible for espionage in different regions, of which the First Bureau is responsible for collecting information in the Special Administrative Regions of Hong Kong and Macau, and also in Taiwan. Agents are dispatched by the Second Department to companies and other local corporations to gain cover.

The "Autumn Orchid" intelligence group assigned to Hong Kong and Macau in the mid-1980s mostly operated in the mass media, political, industrial, commercial, and religious circles, as well as in universities and colleges. The "Autumn Orchid" intelligence group was mainly responsible for the following three tasks:

- Finding out and keeping abreast of the political leanings of officials of the Hong Kong and Macau governments, as well as their views on major issues, through social contact with them and through information provided by them.

- Keeping abreast of the developments of foreign governments' political organs in Hong Kong, as well as of foreign financial, industrial, and commercial organisations.
- Finding out and having a good grasp of the local media's sources of information on political, military, economic, and other developments on the mainland, and deliberately releasing false political or military information to the media to test the outside response.

The "Autumn Orchid" intelligence group was awarded a Citation for Merit, Second Class, in December 1994. It was further awarded another Citation for Merit, Second Class, in 1997. Its current status is not publicly known. During the 2008 Chinese New Year celebration CCTV held for Chinese diplomatic establishments, the head of the Second Department of the Joint Headquarters was revealed for the first time to the public: the current head was Major General Yang Hui.

Third Department

The Third Department of the Joint Staff Department is responsible for monitoring the telecommunications of foreign armies and producing finished intelligence based on the military information collected.

The communications stations established by the Third Department of the Joint Staff Headquarters are not subject to the jurisdiction of the provincial military district and the major theater command of where they are based. The communications stations are entirely the agencies of the Third Department of the Joint Staff Headquarters which have no affiliations to the provincial military district and the military region of where they are based. The personnel composition, budgets, and establishment of these communications stations are entirely under the jurisdiction of the Third Department of the General PLA General Staff Headquarters, and are not related at all with local troops.

China maintains the most extensive SIGINT network of all the countries in the Asia-Pacific region. As of the late 1990s, SIGINT systems included several dozen ground stations, half a dozen ships, truck-mounted systems, and airborne systems. Third Department headquarters is in the vicinity of the GSD First Department (Operations Department), AMS, and NDU complex in the hills northwest of the Summer Palace. As of the late 1990s, the Third Department was allegedly manned by approximately 20,000 personnel, with most of their linguists trained at the Luoyang Institute of Foreign Languages.

Ever since the 1950s, the Second and Third Departments of the Joint Staff Headquarters have established a number of institutions of secondary and higher learning for bringing up "special talents." The PLA Foreign Language Institute at Luoyang comes under the Third Department of the Joint Staff Department and is responsible for training foreign language officers for the monitoring of foreign military intelligence. The institute was formed from the PLA "793" Foreign Language Institute, which moved from Zhangjiakou after the Cultural Revolution and split into two institutions at Luoyang and Nanjing.

Though the distribution order they received upon graduation indicated the "Joint Staff Headquarters", many of the graduates of these schools found themselves being sent to all parts of the country, including remote and uninhabited backward mountain areas. The reason is that the monitoring and control stations under the Third Department of the PLA General Staff Headquarters are scattered in every corner of the country.

The communications stations located in the Shenzhen base of the PLA Hong Kong Garrison started their work long ago. In normal times, these two communications stations report directly to the Central Military Commission (CMC) and the Joint Staff Headquarters. Units responsible for co-ordination are the communications stations established in the garrison provinces of the military regions by the Third Department of the PLA General Staff Headquarters.

By taking direct command of military communications stations based in all parts of the country, the CCP Central Military Commission (CMC) and the Joint Staff Headquarters can not only ensure a successful interception of enemy radio communications, but can also make sure that none of the wire or wireless communications and contacts among major military regions can escape the detection of these communications stations, thus effectively attaining the goal of imposing a direct supervision and control over all the theater commands, all provincial military districts, and all group armies.

Monitoring stations

China's main SIGINT effort is in the Third Department of the Joint Staff Department of the Central Military Commission (CMC), with additional capabilities, primarily domestic, in the Ministry of State Security (MSS).

SIGINT stations, therefore, are scattered through the country, for domestic as well as international interception. Prof. Desmond Ball, of the Australian National University, described the largest stations as the main Technical Department SIGINT net control station on the northwest outskirts of Beijing, and the large complex near Lake Kinghathu in the extreme northeast corner of China.

As opposed to other major powers, China focuses its SIGINT activities on its region rather than the world. Ball wrote, in the eighties, that China had several dozen SIGINT stations aimed at the Soviet Union, Japan, Taiwan, Southeast Asia and India, as well as internally. Of the stations apparently targeting Russia, there are sites at Jilemutu and Jixi in the northeast, and at Erlian and Hami near the Mongolian border. Two Russian-facing sites in Xinjiang, at Qitai and Korla may be operated jointly with resources from the US CIA's Office of SIGINT Operations, probably focused on missile and space activity. Other stations aimed at South and Southeast Asia are on a net controlled by Chengdu, Sichuan. There is a large facility at Dayi, and, according to Ball, "numerous" small posts along the Indian border. Other significant facilities are located near Shenyang, near Jinan and in Nanjing and Shanghai. Additional stations are in the Fujian and Guangdong military districts opposite Taiwan.

On Hainan Island, near Vietnam, there is a naval SIGINT facility that monitors the South China sea, and a ground station targeting US and Russian satellites. China also has ship and aircraft platforms in this area, under the South Sea Fleet headquarters at Zhanjiang immediately north of the island. Targeting here seems to have an ELINT as well as COMINT flavor. There are also truck-mounted mobile ground systems, as well as ship, aircraft, and limited satellite capability. There are at least 10 intelligence-gathering auxiliary vessels.

As of the late nineties, the Chinese did not appear to be trying to monitor the United States Pacific Command to the same extent as does Russia. In future, this had depended, in part, on the status of Taiwan.

Fourth Department

The Fourth Department (ECM and Radar) of the Joint Staff Headquarters Department has the electronic intelligence (ELINT) portfolio within the PLA's SIGINT apparatus. This department is responsible for electronic countermeasures, requiring them to collect and maintain data bases on electronic signals. 25 ELINT receivers are the responsibility of the Southwest Institute of Electronic Equipment (SWIEE). Among the wide range of SWIEE ELINT products is a new KZ900 airborne ELINT pod. The GSD 54th Research Institute supports the ECM Department in development of digital ELINT signal processors to analyse parameters of radar pulses.

Special forces

A PLA Navy Special Operations Forces marine during a maritime operations exercise in RIMPAC 2014.

China's special ground force is called PLASF (People's Liberation Army Special Operations Forces). Typical units include consist of highly trained soldiers, a team commander, assistant commander, sniper, spotter, machine-gun support, bomber, and a pair of assault groups. China's counter terrorism unit members are drawn from the public security apparatus rather than the military. The name of such units change frequently. As of 2020, it is known as the Immediate Action Unit (IAU).

China has reportedly developed a force capable of carrying out long-range airborne operations, long-range reconnaissance, and amphibious operations. Formed in China's Guangzhou military region and known by the nickname "South Blade", the force supposedly receives army, air force, and naval training, including flight training, and is equipped with "hundreds of high-tech devices", including global-positioning satellite systems. All force members officers are military staff college graduates, and 60 percent are said to have university degrees. Soldiers are reported to be cross-trained in various specialties, and training encompassing a wide range of operating environments. It is far from clear whether this unit is considered operational by the Chinese. It is also not clear how such a force would be employed. Among the missions stated missions include: "responding to contingencies in various regions" and "cooperating with other services in attacks on islands". According to the limited reporting, the organisation appears to be in a phase of testing and development and may constitute an experimental unit. While no size for the force has been revealed, there have been Chinese media claims that "over 4,000 soldiers of the force are all-weather and versatile fighters and parachutists who can fly airplanes and drive terrain vehicles and amphibious boats".

Other branches

- The Third Department and the Navy co-operate on shipborne intelligence collection platforms.
- PLAAF Sixth Research Institute: Air Force SIGINT collection is managed by the PLAAF Sixth Research Institute in Beijing.

Weapons and equipment

According to the United States Defense Department, China is developing kinetic-energy weapons, high-powered lasers, high-powered microwave weapons, particle-beam weapons, and electromagnetic pulse weapons with its increase of military fundings.

The PLA has said of reports that its modernisation is dependent on sales of advanced technology from American allies, senior leadership have stated "Some have politicized China's normal commercial cooperation with foreign countries, damaging our reputation." These contributions include advanced European diesel engines for Chinese warships, military helicopter designs from Eurocopter, French anti-submarine sonars and helicopters, Australian technology for the Houbei class missile boat, and Israeli supplied American missile, laser and aircraft technology.

According to the Stockholm International Peace Research Institute's data, China became the world's third largest exporter of major arms in 2010–14, an increase of 143 percent from the period 2005–2009. SIPRI also calculated that China surpassed Russia to become the world's second largest arms exporter by 2020. China's share of global arms exports hence increased from 3 to 5 percent. China supplied major arms to 35 states in 2010–14. A significant percentage (just over 68 percent) of Chinese exports went to three countries: Pakistan, Bangladesh and Myanmar. China also exported major arms to 18 African states. Examples of China's increasing global presence as an arms supplier in 2010–14 included deals with Venezuela for armoured vehicles and transport and trainer aircraft, with Algeria for three frigates, with Indonesia for the supply of hundreds of anti-ship missiles and with Nigeria for the supply of a number of unmanned combat aerial vehicles. Following rapid advances in its arms industry, China has become less dependent on arms imports, which decreased by 42 percent between 2005–2009 and 2010–14. Russia accounted for 61 percent of Chinese arms imports, followed by France with 16 percent and Ukraine with 13 per cent. Helicopters formed a major part of Russian and French deliveries, with the French designs produced under licence in China. Over the years, China has struggled to design and produce effective engines for combat and transport vehicles. It continued to import large numbers of engines from Russia and Ukraine in 2010–14 for indigenously designed combat, advanced trainer and transport aircraft, and for naval ships. It also produced British-, French- and German-designed engines for combat aircraft, naval ships and armoured vehicles, mostly as part of agreements that have been in place for decades.

Cyberwarfare

There is a belief in the Western military doctrines that the PLA have already begun engaging countries using cyber-warfare. There has been a significant increase in the number of presumed Chinese military initiated cyber events from 1999 to the present day.

Cyberwarfare has gained recognition as a valuable technique because it is an asymmetric technique that is a part of Chinese Information Operations. As is written by two PLAGF Colonels, Qiao Liang and Wang Xiangsui in the book 'Unrestricted Warfare', "Methods that are not characterised by the use of the force of arms, nor by the use of military power, nor even by the presence of casualties and bloodshed, are just as likely to facilitate the successful realisation of the war's goals, if not more so.

While China has long been suspected of cyber spying, on 24 May 2011 the PLA announced the existence of having 'cyber capabilities'.

In February 2013, the media named "Comment Crew" as a hacker military faction for China's People's Liberation Army. In May 2014, a Federal Grand Jury in the United States indicted five Unit 61398 officers on criminal charges related to cyber attacks on private companies based in the United States after alleged investigations by the FBI who exposed their identities in collaboration with US intelligence agencies such as the CIA.

In February 2020, the United States government indicted members of China's People's Liberation Army for the 2017 Equifax data breach, which involved hacking into Equifax and plundering sensitive data as part of a massive heist that also included stealing trade secrets, though the Chinese Communist Party denied these claims.

Nuclear capabilities

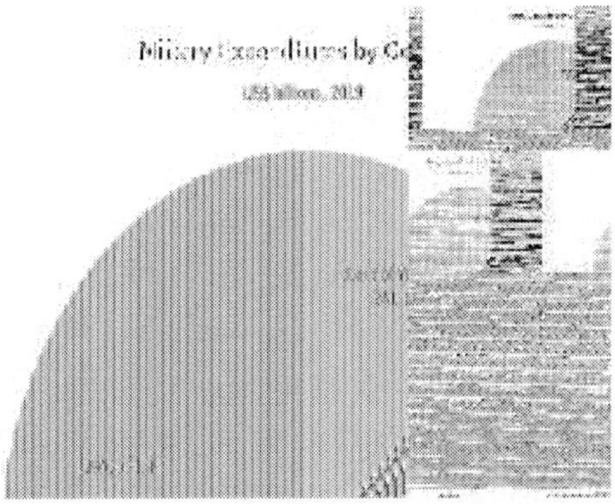

Range of medium and intercontinental ballistic missiles (2006)

In 1955, China decided to proceed with a nuclear weapons program. The decision was made after the United States threatened the use of nuclear weapons against China should it take action against Quemoy and Matsu, coupled with the lack of interest of the Soviet Union for using its nuclear weapons in defence of China.

After their first nuclear test (China claims minimal Soviet assistance before 1960) on 16 October 1964, China was the first state to pledge no-first-use of nuclear weapons. On 1 July 1966, the Second Artillery Corps, as named by Premier Zhou Enlai, was formed. In 1967, China tested a fully functional hydrogen bomb, only 32 months after China had made its first fission device.

China thus produced the shortest fission-to-fusion development known in history.

China became a major international arms exporter during the 1980s. Beijing joined the Middle East arms control talks, which began in July 1991 to establish global guidelines for conventional arms transfers, and later announced that it would no longer participate because of the US decision to sell 150 F-16A/B aircraft to Taiwan on 2 September 1992.

It joined the International Atomic Energy Agency (IAEA) in 1984 and pledged to abstain from further atmospheric testing of nuclear weapons in 1986. China acceded to the nuclear Non-Proliferation Treaty (NPT) in 1992 and supported its indefinite and unconditional extension in 1995. Nuclear weapons tests by China ceased in 1996, when it signed the Comprehensive Test Ban Treaty and agreed to seek an international ban on the production of fissile nuclear weapons material.

In 1996, China committed to provide assistance to unsafeguarded nuclear facilities. China attended the May 1997 meeting of the NPT Exporters (Zangger) Committee as an observer and became a full member in October 1997. The Zangger Committee is a group which meets to list items that should be subject to IAEA inspections if exported by countries, which have, as China has, signed the Non-Proliferation Treaty. In September 1997, China issued detailed nuclear export control regulations. China began implementing regulations establishing controls over nuclear-related dual-use items in 1998. China also has decided not to engage in new nuclear co-operation with Iran (even under safeguards), and will complete existing co-operation, which is not of proliferation concern, within a relatively short period. Based on significant, tangible progress with China on nuclear nonproliferation, President Clinton in 1998 took steps to bring into force the 1985 US–China Agreement on Peaceful Nuclear Cooperation.

Beijing has deployed a modest ballistic missile force, including land and sea-based intermediate-range and intercontinental ballistic missiles (ICBMs). It was estimated in 2007 that China has about 100–160 liquid fuelled ICBMs capable of striking the United States with approximately 100–150 IRBMs able to strike Russia or Eastern Europe, as well as several hundred tactical SRBMs with ranges between 300 and 600 km. Currently, the Chinese nuclear stockpile is estimated to be between 50 and 75 land and sea based ICBMs.

China's nuclear program follows a doctrine of minimal deterrence, which involves having the minimum force needed to deter an aggressor from launching a first strike. The current efforts of China appear to be aimed at maintaining a survivable nuclear force by, for example, using solid-fuelled ICBMs in silos rather than liquid-fuelled missiles. China's 2006 published deterrence policy states that they will "uphold the principles of counterattack in self-defense and limited development of nuclear weapons", but "has never entered, and will never enter into a nuclear arms race with any country". It goes on to describe that China will never undertake a first strike, or use nuclear weapons against a non-nuclear state or zone. US strategists, however, suggest that the Chinese position may be ambiguous, and nuclear weapons may be used both to deter conventional strikes/invasions on the Chinese mainland, or as an international political tool – limiting the extent to which other nations can coerce China politically, an inherent, often inadvertent phenomenon in international relations as regards any state with nuclear capabilities.

Space

The PLA has deployed a number of space-based systems for military purposes, including the imagery intelligence satellite systems like the ZiYan series, and the militarily designated JianBing series, synthetic aperture satellites (SAR) such as JianBing-5, BeiDou satellite navigation network, and secured communication satellites with FENGHUO-1.

The PLA is responsible for the Chinese space program. To date, all the participants have been selected from members of the PLA Air Force. China became the third country in the world to have sent a man into space by its own means with the flight of Yang Liwei aboard the Shenzhou 5 spacecraft on 15 October 2003 and the flight of Fei Junlong and Nie Haisheng aboard Shenzhou 6 on 12 October 2005 and Zhai Zhigang, Liu Boming, and Jing Haipeng aboard Shenzhou 7 on 25 September 2008.

The PLA started the development of an anti-ballistic and anti-satellite system in the 1960s, code named Project 640, including ground-based lasers and anti-satellite missiles. On 11 January 2007, China conducted a successful test of an anti-satellite missile, with an SC-19 class KKV. Its anti ballistic missile test was also successful.

The PLA has tested two types of hypersonic space vehicles, the Shenglong Spaceplane and a new one built by Chengdu Aircraft Corporation. Only a few pictures have appeared since it was revealed in late 2007. Earlier, images of the

High-enthalpy Shock Waves Laboratory wind tunnel of the CAS Key Laboratory of high-temperature gas dynamics (LHD) were published in the Chinese media. Tests with speeds up to Mach 20 were reached around 2001.

Pakistan Army

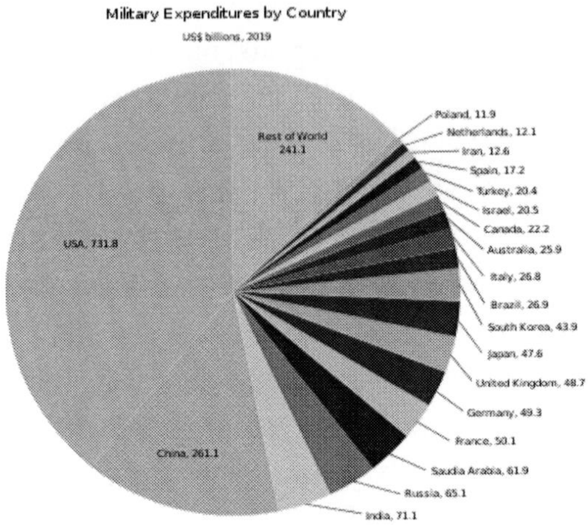

The **Pakistan Army** is the land service branch of the Pakistan Armed Forces. The roots of its modern existence trace back to the British Indian Army that ceased to exist following the partition of the Indian subcontinent, resulting in the parliamentary act that established the sovereign state of Pakistan (as the dominion of Pakistan) from the United Kingdom on 14 August 1947. According to statistics provided by the International Institute for Strategic Studies (IISS) in 2020, the Pakistan Army has approximately 560,000 active-duty personnel, supported by the Army Reserve and National Guard. Pakistani citizens can enlist for voluntary military service upon reaching 16 years of age, but cannot be deployed for combat until age 18 in accordance with the constitution of Pakistan.

The Pakistan Army's primary objective and constitutional mission is to ensure the national security and national unity of Pakistan by defending it against external aggression or the threat of war. It can also be requisitioned by the federal government to respond to internal threats by enforcing security to keep the peace within its land borders. During events of national and international calamities and emergencies, it conducts humanitarian rescue operations at home and is an active participant in peacekeeping missions mandated by the United Nations—most notably playing a major role in rescuing trapped American soldiers who had requested for a quick reaction force during Operation Gothic Serpent in Somalia. Troops from the Pakistan Army also had a relatively strong presence as part of a larger UN and NATO coalition during the Bosnian War and larger Yugoslav Wars.

The Pakistan Army, a major component of the Pakistani military alongside the Pakistan Navy and Pakistan Air Force, is a volunteer force that has seen extensive combat during three major wars with neighbouring India, several border skirmishes on its porous border with Afghanistan as well as a long-running insurgency in Balochistan which it has been combatting alongside Iranian security forces since 1948. Since the 1960s, elements of the army have been repeatedly deployed to act in an advisory capacity in the Arab states during the events of the Arab–Israeli wars as well as to aid the United States-led coalition against Iraq in the First Gulf War. Other notable military operations during the global war on terrorism in the 21st century included: *Zarb-e-Azb*, *Black Thunderstorm*, and *Rah-e-Nijat*.

In violation of its constitutional mandate, it has repeatedly overthrown elected civilian governments overreaching its protected constitutional mandate to "act in the aid of civilian federal governments when called upon to do so". The army has been involved in enforcing martial law against the federal government with the claim of restoring law and order in the country by dismissing the legislative branch and parliament on multiple occasions in past decades—while maintaining a wider commercial, foreign and political interest in the country. This has led it facing allegations of acting as state within a state.

Division of British Indian Army and the first war with India (1947–52)

The Pakistan Army has a regimental system but is operationally and geographically divided into command zones, with its most basic fields being the various corps. The constitution of Pakistan mandates the role of the president of Pakistan as the civilian commander-in-chief of the Pakistani military. The Pakistan Army is commanded by the Chief of Army Staff, who is by statute a four-star ranking general and a senior member of the Joint Chiefs of Staff Committee appointed by the prime minister and subsequently affirmed by the president. As of January 2021, the current Chief of Army Staff is General Qamar Javed Bajwa, who was appointed to the position on 29 November 2016.

The 6th Frontier Force Regiment of the British Indian Army in the fronts of World War II in Italy in 1943–44

The Pakistan Army came into its modern birth from the division of the British Indian Army that ceased to exist as a result of the partition of India that resulted in the creation of Pakistan on 14 August 1947. Before even the partition took place, there were plans ahead of dividing the British Indian Army into different parts based on the religious and ethnic influence on the areas of India.

On 30 June 1947, the War Department of the British administration in India began planning the dividing of the ~400,000 men strong British Indian Army, but that only begin few weeks before the partition of India that resulted in violent religious violence in India. The Armed Forces Reconstitution Committee (AFRC) under the chairmanship of British Field Marshal Sir Claude Auchinleck had devised the formula to divide the military assets between India and Pakistan with ratio of 2:1, respectively.

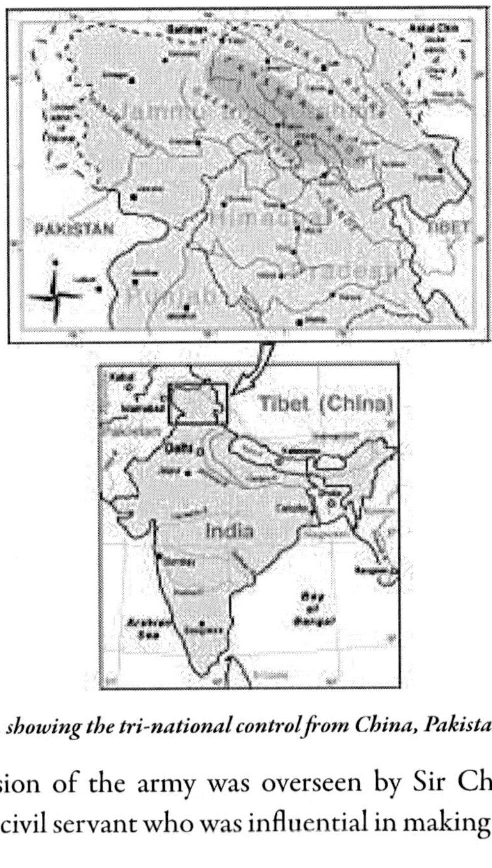

The Map of Kashmir, showing the tri-national control from China, Pakistan, and India, ca. 2005

A major division of the army was overseen by Sir Chandulal Madhavlal Trivedi, an Indian civil servant who was influential in making sure that ~260,000 men would be transferred into forming the Indian Army whilst the remaining balance going to Pakistan after the independence act was enacted by the United Kingdom on the night of 14/15 August 1947.

Command and control at all levels of the new army was extremely difficult, as Pakistan had received six armoured, eight artillery and eight infantry regiments compared to the twelve armoured, forty artillery and twenty-one infantry regiments that went to India. In total, the size of the new army was about ~150,000 men strong. To fill the vacancy in the command positions of the new army, around 13,500 military officers from the British Army had to be employed in the Pakistan Army, which was quite a large number, under the command of Lieutenant-General Frank Messervy, the first commander-in-chief of the Pakistan Army.

Eminent fears of India's seizing the control over the state of Kashmir, the armed tribes and the irregular militia scouts entered in the Muslim-majorityvalley of Kashmir to oppose the rule of Hari Singh, a Hindu and the ruling Maharaja of Kashmir, in October 1947. Attempting to maintain his control over the princely state, Hari Singh deployed his troops to check on the tribal advances but his troops failed to halt the advancing tribes towards the valley. Eventually, Hari Singh appealed to Louis Mountbatten, the Governor-General of India, requesting for the deployment of the Indian Armed Forces but Indian government maintained that the troops could be committed if Hari Singh acceded to India. Hari Singh eventually agreed to concede to the Indian government terms which eventually led to the deployment of the Indian Army in Kashmir– this agreement, however, was contested by Pakistan since the agreement did not include the consent of the Kashmiri people. Sporadic fighting between militia and Indian Army broke out, and units of the Pakistan Army under Maj-Gen. Akbar Khan, eventually joined the militia in their fight against the Indian Army.

Although, it was Lieutenant-General Sir Frank Messervy who opposed the tribal invasion in a cabinet meeting with Prime Minister Liaquat Ali Khan in 1947, later leaving the command of the army in 1947, in a view of that British officers in the Indian and Pakistan Army would be fighting with each other in the war front. It was Lt-Gen. Douglas Gracey who reportedly disobeyed the direct orders from Muhammad Ali Jinnah, the Governor-General of Pakistan, for the deployment of the army units and ultimately issued standing orders that refrained the units of Pakistan Army to further participate in the conflict.

By 1948, when it became imperative in Pakistan that India was about to mount a large-scale operation against Pakistan, Gen. Gracey did not object to the deployment of the army units in the conflict against the Indian Army.

This earlier insubordination of Gen. Gracey eventually forced India and Pakistan to reach a compromise through the United Nation's intervention, with Pakistan controlling the Western Kashmir and India controlling the Eastern Kashmir.

20th Century: Cold war and conflict performances

Reorganization under the United States Army (1952–58)

General Ayub Khan arriving to take over command of the Pakistan Army at the Army GHQ in Rawalpindi, Punjab in Pakistan on 17 January 1951[34]

At the time of the partition of British India, British Field Marshal (United Kingdom) Sir Claude Auchinleck favored the transfer of the infantry divisions to the Pakistan Army including the 7th, 8th and 9th. In 1948, the British army officers in the Pakistan Army established and raised the 10th, 12th, and the 14th infantry divisions— with the 14th being established in East Bengal. In 1950, the 15th Infantry Division was raised with the help from the United States Army, followed by the establishment of the 15th Lancers in Sialkot. Dependence on the United States grew furthermore by the Pakistan Army despite it had worrisome concerns to the country's politicians. Between 1950–54, Pakistan Army raised six more armoured regiments under the U.S. Army's guidance: including, 4th Cavalry, 12th Cavalry, 15th Lancers, and 20th Lancers.

After the incident involving Gracey's disobedience, there was a strong belief that a native commander of the Pakistan army should be appointed, which resulted in the Government of Pakistan rejecting the British Army Board's replacement of Gen. Gracey upon his replacement, in 1951. Eventually, Prime Minister Liaquat Ali Khan approved the promotion paper of Maj-Gen. Iftikhar Khan as the first native commander-in-chief, a graduate of the Imperial Defence

College in England, but died in an aviation accident en route to Pakistan from the United Kingdom.

After the death of Maj-Gen. Iftikhar, there were four senior major-generals in the army in the race of promotion but the most junior, Maj-Gen. Ayub Khan, whose name was not included in the promotion list was elevated to the promotion that resulted in a lobbying provided by Iskandar Mirza, the Defense Secretary in Ali Khan administration. A tradition of appointment based on favoritism and qualification that is still in practice by the civilian Prime Ministers in Pakistan. Ayub was promoted to the acting rank of full general to command the army as his predecessors Frank Messervy and Douglas Gracey were performing the duty of commander-in-chief of the Pakistan Army in the acting rank of general, the neighbouring country India's first commanders-in-chief were same in this context.

The department of the army under General Ayub Khan steered the army's needs towards heavy focus and dependence towards the imported hardware acquired from the United States, in spite of acquiring it from the domestic industry, under the Military Assistance Advisory Group attached to Pakistan in 1954–56. In 1953, the 6th Infantry Division was raised and disbanded the 6th Division in 1956 followed by the disbandment of the 9th Infantry Division as the American assistance was available only for one armored and six infantry divisions. During this time, an army combat brigade team was readily made available by Gen. Ayub Khan to deploy to support the American Army's fighting troops in the Korean war.

Working as cabinet minister in Bogra administration, Gen. Ayub's impartiality was greatly questioned by country's politicians and drove Pakistan's defence policy towards the dependence on the United States when the country becoming the party of the CENTO and the SEATO, the U.S. active measures against the expansion of the global communism.

In 1956, the 1st Armored Division in Multan was established, followed by the Special Forces in Cherat under the supervision of the U.S Army's Special Forces. Under Gen. Ayub's control, the army had eradicated the British influence but invited the American expansion and had reorganized the East Bengal Regiment in East Bengal, the Frontier Force Regiment in Northern Pakistan, Kashmir Regiment in Kashmir, and Frontier Corps in the Western Pakistan. The order of precedence change from Navy–Army–Air Force to Army–Navy-

Air Force, with army being the most senior service branch in the structure of the Pakistani military.

In 1957, the I Corps was established and headquarter was located in Punjab. Between 1956–58, the schools of infantry and tactics, artillery, ordnance, armoured, medical, engineering, services, aviation, and several other schools and training centers were established with or without U.S. participation.

Military takeovers in Pakistan and second war with India (1958–1969)

The protest march in East Pakistan in 1954. The martial law was imposed through the army in East by Prime Minister Mohammad Ali Bogra to control the law and order situation.[:75][47]

As early as 1953, the Pakistan Army became involved in national politics in a view of restoring the law and order situation when Governor-General Malik Ghulam, with approval from Prime Minister Khawaja Nazimuddin, dismissed the popularly-mandated state government of Chief Minister Mumtaz Daultana in Punjab in Pakistan, and declared martial law under Lt-Gen. Azam Khan and Col. Rahimuddin Khan who successfully quelled the religious agitation in Lahore. In 1954, the Pakistan Army's Military Intelligence Corps reportedly sent the intelligence report indicating the rise of communism in East Pakistan during the legislative election held in East-Bengal. Within two months of the elections, Prime Minister Mohammad Ali Bogra, with approval from Governor-General Malik Ghulam, dismissed another popularly-mandated state government of Chief Minister Fazlul Huq in East Bengal in Pakistan, and declared governor's rule under Iskandar Mirza who relied in the Pakistan Army to manage the control and security of the East Bengal at all levels of command. With General

Ayub Khan becoming the Defense Minister under Ministry of Talents led by Prime Minister Bogra, the involvement of the army in the national politics grew further with the implementation of the controversial One Unit program, abolishing the status of Four Provinces, despite the strong protests by the public and the West Pakistan's politicians. Major defense funding and spending was solely focused towards Ayub's army department and the air force department led by Air Marshal Asghar Khan, giving less priority to the national needs for the Navy.

The Pakistan Army's troops hoisting the Pakistan Flag in Rajasthan in India in 1965

From 1954–58, Ayub Khan was made subjected with receiving multiple service extensions by the civilian Prime Ministers first receiving in 1954 that extended his commission to last till 1958.

The Pakistan Army under Ayub Khan had been less supportive towards the implementation of the first set of Constitution of Pakistan that had established the civilian control of the military, and the army went on to completely endorse and support the first martial law in the country imposed by President Iskander Mirza– the army later took control of the power from President Mirza in mere two weeks and installed Ayub Khan as the second President. The subsequent change of command resulted in Gen. Musa Khan becoming the army commander with Ayub Khan promoting himself as controversial rank of field marshal. In 1969, the Supreme Court reversed its decision and overturned its convictions that called for validation of martial law in 1958.

The army held the referendum and tightly control the political situation through the intelligence agencies, and banned the political activities in the country.

The public society in Pakistan rallying in support of the Pakistan Army in 1965

From 1961 to 1962, military aid continued to Pakistan from the United States and they established the 25th Cavalry, followed by the 24th Cavalry, 22nd, and 23rd Cavalry. In 1960–61, the Army Special Forces was reportedly involved in taking over the control of the administration of Dir from the Nawab of Dir in Chitral in North-West Frontier Province over the concerns of Afghan meddling in the region. In 1964–65, the border fighting and tensions flared with the Indian Army with a serious incident taking place near the Rann of Kutch, followed by the failed covert action to take control of the Indian-side of Kashmir resulted in a massive retaliation by the Indian Army on 5 August 1965. On the night of 6 September 1965, India opened the front against Pakistan when the Indian Army's mechanized corps charged forwards taking over the control of the Pakistan-side of Punjab, almost reaching Lahore. At the time of the conflict in 1965, Pakistan's armory and mechanized units' hardware was imported from the United States including the M4 Sherman, M24 Chaffee, M36 Jackson, and the M47 and M48 Patton tanks, equipped with 90 mm guns. In contrast, the Indian Army's armor had outdated in technology with Korean war-usage American M4 Sherman and World War II manufactured British Centurion Tank, fitted with the French-made CN-75 guns.

In spite of Pakistan enjoying the numerical advantage in tanks and artillery, as well as better equipment overall, the Indian Army successfully penetrated the defences of Pakistan's borderline and successfully conquered around 360 to 500 square kilometres (140 to 190 square miles) of Pakistani Punjab territory on the outskirts of Lahore. A major tank battle took place in Chawinda, at which the newly established 1st Armoured Division was able to halt the Indian invasion. Eventually, the Indian invasion of Pakistan came to halt when the Indian Army concluded the battle near Burki. With diplomatic efforts and involvement by the Soviet Union to bring two nation to end the war, the Ayub administration reached a compromise with Shastri ministry in India when both governments signed and ratified the Tashkent Declaration. According to the Library of Congress Country Studies conducted by the Federal Research Division of the United States:

The war was militarily inconclusive; each side held prisoners and some territory belonging to the other. Losses were relatively heavy—on the Pakistani side, twenty aircraft, 200 tanks, and 3,800 troops. Pakistan's army had been able to withstand Indian pressure, but a continuation of the fighting would only have led to further losses and ultimate defeat for Pakistan. Most Pakistanis, schooled in the belief of their own martial prowess, refused to accept the possibility of their country's military defeat by "Hindu India" and were, instead, quick to blame their failure to attain their military aims on what they considered to be the ineptitude of Ayub Khan and his government.

At the time of ceasefire declared, per neutral sources, Indian casualties stood at 3,000 whilst the Pakistani casualties were 3800. Pakistan lost between 200-300 tanks during the conflict and India lost approximately 150-190 tanks.

However, most neutral assessments agree that India had the upper hand over Pakistan when ceasefire was declared, but the propaganda in Pakistan about the war continued in favor of Pakistan Army. The war was not rationally analysed in Pakistan with most of the blame being heaped on the leadership and little importance given to intelligence failures that persisted until the debacle of the third war with India in 1971. The Indian Army's action was restricted to Punjab region of both sides with Indian Army mainly in fertile Sialkot, Lahore and Kashmir sectors, while Pakistani land gains were primarily in southern deserts opposite Sindh and in the Chumb sector near Kashmir in the north.

With the United States' arms embargo on Pakistan over the issue of the war, the army instead turned to the Soviet Union and China for hardware acquisition, and correctly assessed that a lack of infantry played a major role in the failure of Pakistani armour to translate its convincing material and technical superiority into a major operational or strategic success against the Indian Army. Ultimately, the army's high command established the 9th, 16th, and 17th infantry divisions in 1966–68. In 1966, the IV Corps was formed and its headquarter was established, and permanently stationed in Lahore, Punjab in Pakistan.

The army remained involved in the nation's civic affairs, and ultimately imposed the second martial law in 1969 when the writ of the constitution was abrogated by then-army commander, Gen. Yahya Khan, who took control of the nation's civic affairs after the resignation of President Ayub Khan, resulted in a massive labor strikes instigated by the Pakistan Peoples Party in West and Awami League in East Pakistan.

In a lawsuit settled by the Supreme Court of Pakistan, the legality of the martial law was deemed questionable as the Supreme Court settled the suit by retroactively invalidated the martial law that suspended the Constitution and notably ruled that Yahya Khan's assumption of power was "illegal usurpation". In light of the Supreme Court's judgement, the army held the publicly televised conference when President Yahya Khan announced to hold the nationwide general elections in 1969–70.

Suppression, civil conflict in East Pakistan and Indian invasion (1969– 1971)

In 1969, President Yahya Khan decided to make administrative changes in the army by appointing the Gen. Abdul Hamid Khan as the Army Chief of Staff (ACOS) of the Pakistan Army, who centralized the chain of command in Rawalpindi in a headquarters known as "High Command". From 1967–69, a series of major military exercises was conducted by infantry units on East Pakistan's border with India. In 1970, the Pakistan army's military mission in Jordan was reportedly involved in tackling and curbing down the Palestinian infiltration in Jordan. In June 1971, the enlistment in the army had allowed the Army GHQ in Rawalpindi to raise and established the 18th infantry division, stationed in Hyderabad, Sindh, for the defence of 900 kilometres (560 mi) from Rahimyar Khan to Rann of Kutch, and reestationed the 23rd infantry division for defending the Chhamb-Dewa Sector.

In 1971, the II Corps was established and headquartered in Multan, driven towards defending the mass incursion from the Indian Army. In December 1971, the 33rd infantry division was established from the army reserves of the II Corps, followed by raising the 37th Infantry Division. The Pakistan Army reportedly helped the Pakistan Navy to toward establishing the amphibious branch, the Pakistan Marines, whose battalion was airlifted to East Pakistan along with the 9th Infantry Division. The other battalions of marines were stationed with the army troops in the skirts of Punjab to support the defence in the events of the war with India.

The intervention in East Pakistan further grew when the Operation Searchlight resulted in the overtaking of the government buildings, communication centers, and restricting the politicians opposed to military rule. Within a month, Pakistani national security strategists realized their failure of implementing the plan which had not anticipated civil resistance in East, and the real nature of Indian strategy behind their support of the resistance.

The Yahya administration is widely accused of permitting the army to commit the war crimes against the civilians in East and curbing civil liberties and human rights in Pakistan. The Eastern Command under Lt-Gen. A. A. K. Niazi, who had area responsibility of the defending the Eastern Front and had the responsibility to protect, was leveled with accusations of escalating the political violence in the East by the serving military officers, politicians, and journalists in Pakistan. Since the general elections in 1970, the army had detained several key politicians, journalists, peace activists, student unionists, and other members of civil society while curbing the freedoms of movement and speech in Pakistan. In East Pakistan, the unified Eastern Military Command under Lt-Gen. A.A.K. Niazi, began its engagement with the armed militia that had the direct terror support from India in April 1971, and eventually fought against the Indian Army in December 1971. The army, together with marines, launched ground offensives on both fronts but the Indian Army successfully held its ground and initiated well-coordinated ground operations on both fronts, initially capturing 15,010 square kilometres (5,795 sq mi) of Pakistan's territory; this land gained by India in Azad Kashmir, Punjab and Sindh sectors.

Responding to the ultimatum issued on 16 December 1971 by the Indian Army in East, Lt-Gen. Niazi agreed to concede defeat and move towards signing the documented surrender with the Indian Army which effectively and unilaterally ended the armed resistance and led the creation of Bangladesh, only after India's official engagement that lasted 13 days. It was reported that the Eastern Command had surrendered ~93,000–97,000 uniform personnel to Indian Army– the largest surrender in a war by any country after the World War

II. Casualties inflicted to army's I Corps, II Corps, and Marines did not sit well with President Yahya Khan who turned over control of the civic government to Zulfikar Ali Bhutto through an executive decree.

Commenting on the defeat, the military observer in the Pakistan Army, Major A.H. Amin, reported that the war strategists in the army had not seriously considered a full-fledged invasion from India until December 1971, because it was presumed that the Indian military would not risk intervention by China or the United States, and the high command failed to realize that the Chinese would be unable to intervene during the winter months of November to December, due to snowbound Himalayan passes, and the Americans had not made any real effort to persuade India against attacking East Pakistan.

Restructuring of armed forces, stability and restoration (1971–1977)

The army officers in the 9th Battalion of the Frontier Force Regiment on 23 March 1974

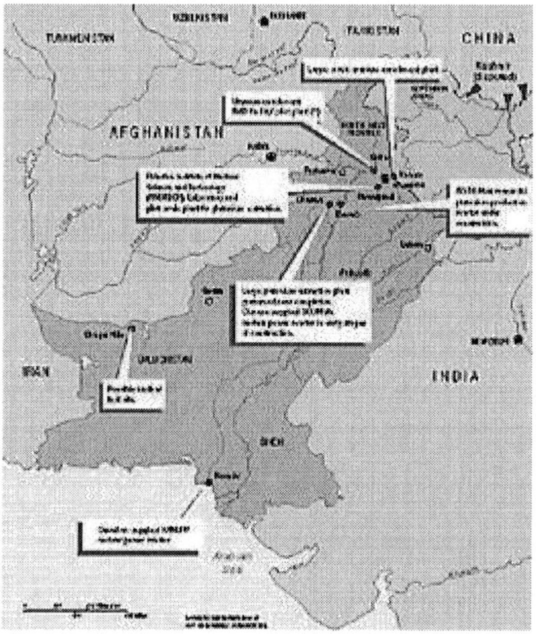

In the 1970s, the Corps of Engineers built many secretive weapon-testing laboratories and sites in the graphite mountain ranges of Pakistan.:[144–145][100] The footage is provided as an example by the CEIP.

In January 1972, the Bhutto administration formed the POW Commission to investigate the numbers of war prisoners held by the Indian Army while requesting the Supreme Court of Pakistan to investigate the causes of the war failure with India in 1971. The Supreme Court formed the famed War Enquiry Commission (WEC) that identified many failures, fractures, and faults within the institution of the department of the army and submitted recommendations to strengthen the armed forces overall. Under the Yahya administration, the army was highly demoralized and there were unconfirmed reports of mutiny by soldiers against the senior army generals at the Corps garrisons and the Army GHQ in Rawalpindi.

Upon returning from the quick visit in the United States in 1971, President Bhutto forcefully dishonorably discharge the commission of seven senior army generals, which he called the "army waderas" (lit. *Warlords*). In 1972, the army leadership under Lt-Gen. Gul Hassan refrained from acting under Bhutto administration's order to tackle the labor strikes in Karachi and to detained the labor union leaders in Karachi, instead advising the federal government to use the Police Department to take the actions.

On 2 March 1972, President Bhutto dismissed the commission of Lt-Gen. Gul Hassan as the army commander, replacing with Lt-Gen. Tikka Khan who was later promoted to four-star rank and appointed as the first Chief of Army Staff (COAS). The army under Bhutto administration was reconstructed in its structure, improving its fighting ability, and reorganized with the establishment of the X Corps in Punjab in 1974, followed by the V Corps in Sindh and XI Corps in the Khyber-Pakhtunkhwa in Pakistan in 1975. The trilateral agreement in India, the Bhutto administration transferred all the war prisoners back to the country but the military struggle to fill in the vacancies and employments due to some suffering from the PTSD and other mental health complications, while others simply did not wanted to serve in the military any longer. Under Bhutto administration, the army engage in self-reliance production and eventually reached to China for establishing the material and metal industries to overcome the material shortage and manufacturing of weapons industry in the country.

In 1973, the Bhutto administration dismissed the state government in Balochistan that resulting in another separatist movement, culminating the series of army actions in largest province of the country that ended in 1977. With the military aid receiving from Iran including the transfer of the Bell AH-1 Cobra to Aviation Corps, the conflict came to end with the Pakistani government offering the general amnesties to separatists in the 1980s. Over the issue of Baloch conflict, the Pakistani military remained engage in Omani civil war in favor of Omani government until the rebels were defeated in 1979. The War Enquiry Commission noted the lack of joint grand strategy between the four-branches of the military during the first, the second, and the third wars with India, recommending the establishment of the Joint Chiefs of Staff Committee to maintain strategic military communication between the inter-services and the federal government, that is to be chaired by the appointed Chairman joint chiefs as the government's principal military adviser. In 1976, the first Chairman joint chiefs was appointed from the army with Gen. Muhammad Shariff taking over the chairmanship, but resigned a year later. In 1975, Prime Minister Zulfikar Ali Bhutto controversially superseded at least seven senior army generals to promote Lt-Gen. Zia-ul-Haq to the four-star rank, appointing him the Chief of Army Staff (COAS) in spite of army recommendations forwarded to the federal government.

In the 1970s, the army's engineering formations, notable the Corps of Engineers, played a crucial role in supporting the clandestine atomic bomb program to reach its parity and feasibility, including the constructions of iron-steel tunnels in the secretive nuclear weapons-testing sites in 1977–78.

PAF and Navy fighter pilots voluntarily served in Arab nations' militaries against Israel in the Yom Kippur War (1973). In the 1973 war one of the PAF pilots, Flt. Lt. Sattar Alvi flying a MiG-21 shot down an Israeli Air Force Mirage and was honoured by the Syrian government.

Middle East operations, peacekeeping missions, and covert actions (1977–1999)

Transferred from Iranian Ground Force in 1973–75, the Pakistan Army acquired additional the AH-1S Cobra attack helicopters from the United States under the Foreign Military Sales to improve the Pakistan's defences in the 1980s.

The political instability increased in the country when the conservative alliance refused to accept the voting turnout in favor of Pakistan Peoples Party (PPP) after the general elections held in 1977. The army, under Gen. Zia-ul-Haq–the army chief, began planning the military takeover of the federal government under Prime Minister Zulfikar Bhutto, eventually leading the coup d'état that suspended the writ of the Constitution amid responding to the call from one of the opposition leader of threatening to call for another civil war. The military interference in civic matters grew further when the martial law was extended for an infinite period despite maintaining that the elections to be held in 90-days prior. At the request from the Saudi monarchy, the Zia administration deployed the company of the special forces to end seizure of the Grand Mosque in Mecca from Islamists.

The army under President Zia weakened due to the army officers were needed in running the affairs of civic government and the controversial military courts that held trials of the communists, dissidents, and the oppositions of Zia's administration. In 1984–85, Pakistan lost the control of her northern glaciers due to the successful expedition and penetration by the Indian Army, and army had to engage in years long difficult battles with Indian Army to regain their areas from the Indian Army. Concerns over the military officers and army personnel needed to counter the further advances by the Indian Army in Northern fronts in 1984, the martial law was lifted following the referendum that approved Zia's presidency and provided a way of holding the general elections in 1985. The military control the under army administration had successfully stabilized the law and order in Balochistan despite the massive illegal immigration from Afghanistan, and issued the general amnesties to separatists and rebels. To address the Afghan containment and security, the army established the XII Corps in 1985 that is permanently headquartered in Quetta, that is designed to provide defence against the infiltration by the Afghan National Army from Afghanistan.

The Pakistan Army's troops, as part of their deployment in Somalia, patrolling off their mission in the Mogadishu in Somalia in 1993[115]

In 1985, the United States approved the military aid package, worth $4.02 billion, to Pakistan when the mujaheddin fighting with the Soviet Union in Afghanistan increased and intensified, with Soviet Army began violating and attacking the insurgents in the tribal areas in Pakistan. In 1986, the tensions with India increased when the Indian Army's standing troops mobilized in combat position in Pakistan's southern frontier with India failing to give notification of exercise to Pakistan prior. In 1987–88, the XXX Corps, headquartered in North of Punjab, and the XXXI Corps, headquartered in South of Punjab, was raised and established to provide defence against the Indian army's mass infiltration.

After the aviation accident that resulted in passing of President Zia in 1988, the army organized the massive military exercise with the Pakistan Air Force to evaluate the technological assessment of the weapon systems and operational readiness. In the 1980s, Pakistan Army remained engage in the affairs of Middle East, first being deployed in Saudi Arabia during the Iran–Iraq War in 1980–1988, and later overseeing operational support measures and combat actions during the Gulf War in 1990–91.

The period from 1991–98 saw the army engaged in professionalism and proved its fighting skills in the Somalian theater (1991–94), Bosnian-Serb War (on Bosnian side from 1994–98), and the other theaters of the Yugoslav Wars, as part of the United Nation's deployment. In 1998, the army's Corps of Engineers played a crucial role in providing the military administration of preparing the atomic weapon-testing in Balochistan when the air force's bombers flown and airlifted the atomic devices. The controversial relief of Gen. Jehangir Karamat by the Sharif administration reportedly disturbed the balance of the civil-military relations with the junior most Lt-Gen. Pervez Musharraf replacing it as chairman joint chiefs and the army chief in 1999.

In May 1999, the army's northern light infantry, the paramilitary unit at that time, slipped into Kargil that resulted in heavy border fighting with the Indian Army, inflicted with heavy casualties on both sides. The ill-devised plan without meaningful consideration of the outcomes of the border war with India, the army under Chairman joint chiefs Gen. Pervez Musharraf (also army chief at that time) failed to its combat performance and suffered with similar outcomes as the previous plan in 1965, with the American military observers in the Pakistan military famously commenting to news channels in Pakistan: Kargil was yet another example of Pakistan's (lack of) grand strategy, repeating the follies of the previous wars with India."

After its commendable performance, the President of Pakistan commissioned the Northern Light Infantry as a regular regiment in the army and its personnel eventually becoming officers and enlisted personnel in the army in 1999.

21st Century: War performances

Religious insurgency and War on terror (2001 – present)

The Pakistan Army's paratroopers watching the Swat Valley from its highest point after the intense battle with Taliban fighters in 2009

In October 1999, the army engaged in another military takeover of the federal government from the Sharif administration when the Army GHQ refused to accept the relief of commission of Gen. Pervez Musharraf over his failure in succeeding the control of Kargil sector from India. This controversial takeover of the federal government was subjected to a lengthy and an expensive lawsuit fought between the lawyers of the department of army and the former Sharif administration at the Supreme Court, with the landmark verdict rendered in 2009 ultimately sided and favored the Sharif administration's arguments as the Justices of the Supreme Court accepted the fact that the army's takeover was in fact a direct violation of the constitution and breach of its given constitutional mandate.

The Pakistan Army's Special Forces (Special Services Groups/SSG) soldiers conducting a tactical training exercise in 2016

Responding to the terror attacks in New York in the United States, the army joined the combat actions in Afghanistan with the United States and simultaneously engage in military standoff with Indian Army in 2001–02. In 2004–06, the military observers from the army were deployed to guide the Sri Lankan army to end the civil war with the Tamil fighters.

To overcome the governance crises in 2004–07, the Musharraf administration appointed several army officers in the civilian institutions with some receiving extensions while others were deployed from their combat service– thus affecting the fighting capabilities and weakening the army. Under Gen. Musharraf 's leadership, the army's capabilities fighting the fanatic Talibans and Afghan Arab fighters in Pakistan further weakened and suffered serious setbacks in gaining control of the tribal belt that fell under the control of the Afghan Arabs and Uzbek fighters. From 2006–09, the army fought the series of bloody battles with the fanatic Afghan Arabs and other foreign fighters including the army action in a Red Mosque in Islamabad to control the religious fanaticism. With the controversial assassination of Baloch politician in 2006, the army had to engage in battles with the Baloch separatists fighting for the Balochistan's autonomy.

In April 2007, the major reorganization of the commands of the army was taken place under Gen. Ahsan S. Hyatt, the vice army chief under Gen. Musharraf, establishing the Southern, Central, and the Northern Commands to "improve the operational efficiency and working of its land forces." With Gen. Musharraf 's resignation and Gen. Ashfaq Parvez Kayani becoming the army chief, the army realigned itself to review its combat policies and withdrew officers in civilian institutions to focus on its primary constitutional mission to protect and responsible in 2009–14. In 2012, there was a serious accident involving the entire battalion from the Northern Light Infantry when the avalanche struck the battalion base in Siachen, entrapping 135 soldiers and including several army officers.

In 2013–16, the homegrown far-right guerrilla war with the Taliban, Afghan Arabs, and the Central Asian fighters took the decisive turn in favor of the army under Sharif administration, eventually gaining the control of the entire country and established the writ of the constitution in the affected lawless regions. As of its current deployment as of 2019, the army remained engage in border fighting with the Indian Army while deploying its combat strike brigade teams in Saudi Arabia in a response of Saudi intervention in Yemen.

Commands

The reorganization of the position standing army in 2008, the Pakistan Army now operates six tactical commands, each commanded by the GOC-in-C, with a holding three-star rank: Lieutenant-General.The each of the six tactical commands directly reports to the office of Chief of Army Staff, operating directly at the Army GHQ.Each command consists of two or more Corps– an army field formation responsible for zone within a command theater.

There are nine active Corps in the Pakistan Army, composing of mixed infantry, mechanized, armored, artillery divisions, while the Air Defense, Aviation, and the Aviation and Special Forces are organized and maintained in the separate level of their commands.

Established and organized in March 2000, the Army Strategic Forces Command is exercise its authority for responsible training in safety, weapons deployments, and activation of the atomic missile systems

nfantry branch

The Honor Guards from the Guides Cavalry Regiment, in traditional Red Coat, welcoming the U.S. President George W. Bush at the Presidency in Islamabad in 2006

Since its establishment in 1947, the Pakistan Army has traditionally followed the British regimental system and culture, and currently there are six organized infantry regiments.

In the infantry branch, there are originally six regiments are in fact the administrative military organization that are not combat field formation, and the size of the regiments are vary as their rotation and deployments including assisting the federal government in civic administration.

In each of original six regiments, there are multiple battalions that are associated together to form an infantry regiment and such battalions do not fight together as one formation as they are all deployed over various formations in shape of being part of the brigade combat team (under a Brigadier), division, or a being part of much larger corps.

After the independence from the Great Britain in 1947, the Pakistan Army begin to follow the U.S. Army's standing formation of their Infantry Branch, having the infantry battalion serving for a time period under a different command zone before being deployed to another command zone, usually in another sector or terrain when its tenure is over

Special operations forces

The Pakistan Army has a military division dedicated towards conducting the unconventional and asymmetric warfare operations, established with the guidance provided by the United States Army in 1956. This competitive special operation force is known as the Special Services Group (Army SSG, distinguishing the Navy SSG), and is assembled in eight battalions, commanded by the Lieutenant-Colonel, with addition of three companies commanded by the Major or a Captain, depending on the availability.

The special operation forces training school is located in Cherat in Khyber-Pakhtunkhwa in Pakistan where the training and education on the philosophy of military arts and tactics take place by the army instructors.

Each battalion in the Pakistan Army Special Forces is specifically trained for a specific type of operation, and each battalion is a specialist in their nature of conducting the operation. Due to their distinctive service headgear, the Army

SSG is colloquially known as the **Maroon Berets.** In 2000, the Pakistan Army established the Army Strategic Forces Command that is charged with overseeing the operational readiness and various deployment of the Army SSG, Special Forces, Special Support Group, Army Rangers, and the Strategic Plans Division Force— the CBRN defense component of the department of army.

Besides the Army SSG and the Special Forces (SF), the Pakistan Army has trained a specific Rangers team that is especially trained in counter tactics, and is trained for carrying out the difficult counter-terrorism operation involving the civilian hostages in Karachi, and helping the state governments in Sindh and Punjab maintaining the law and order situation intact.

Implementing the counterterrorism tactics in 2004, the Army has been training the specific Army Ranger company, known as the Rangers Anti-terrorist Force (ATF), along with the Army SSG company, often conduct training with the U.S. Army Ranger in terror and infantry tactics.

Military philosophy

Combat doctrine (1947–2007)

The U.S.-Pakistan military relations: The group photo of the United States Army and the Pakistan Army after coordinating the joint operation in 2010.

In 1947, the Pakistan Army's war strategists developed a combat doctrine which was called "The Riposte", which featured a strategy of "offensive-defense". In 1989, the first and official implementation of this strategy was refined and featured in the major military exercise, Exercise Zab-e-Momin, organized under Lt-Gen. Hamid Gul– this combat doctrine was fully focused in engaging towards its primary adversary, Indian Army.

In 1989–99, the JS HQ, working with the Army GHQ to identify several key factors considering the large conventional attacks from the better equipped and numerically advantage adversary, the Indian Army, derived the combat doctrine to assess the vulnerability of Pakistan where its vast majority of population centers as well as political and military targets lies closer to the international border with India.

The national security strategists explored the controversial idea of strategic depth in form of fomenting friendly foreign relations with Afghanistan and Iran while India substantially enhancing its offensive capabilities designed in its doctrine, the Cold Start Doctrine. Due to the numerical advantage of Indian Army over its small adversary, the Pakistan Army, the Pakistani national security analysts noted that any counterattack on advancing Indian Army would be very tricky and miscalculated– the ideal response of countering the attacks from the Indian ground forces would be operationalizing the battle-ranged Hatf-IA/Hatf-IB missiles. The Pakistan Army Reserves, supported by the Army National Guard, and India's Territorial Army would eventually forward towards the defensive positions and fortifications in less than 24 hours. However, the Corps in both nation's commands with large stockpiles of ordnance will take between 24–72 hours to logistically mobilize its combat assets after the orders are authorized; therefore, both nation's armies will be evenly matched in the first 24 hours since the Pakistani units have to travel a shorter distance to their forward positions.

The war doctrine of "offensive-defense" entailed Pakistan not waiting to be attacked but instead launching an offense of its own, with an offense being a limited advance along with narrow fronts aiming towards occupying enemy territory near the border to a depth of 40–50 km. Pakistani national security calculated that since Indian forces will not reach their maximum strength near the border for another 48–72 hours, Pakistan might have parity or numerical superiority against India. Earlier studies in "Offensive-defense" doctrine validated results of finding and keeping the enemy forces off-balance as the Indian Army engage in containing the Pakistan Army forces into its territory rather than concentrating towards launching an attack onto Pakistan's territory. The strategic calculations by Pakistan Army's war strategists hoped that the

Pakistan Army's soldiers would keep the Indian Army soldiers engage in fighting on the Indian territory, therefore the collateral damage being suffered by the Indian Army at most. An important aspect in "offensive-defense" doctrine was to seize sizable Indian territory which gives Pakistan an issue to negotiate with India in the aftermath of a ceasefire brought about by international pressure after 3–4 weeks of fighting.

Due to fortification of LoC in Kashmir and difficult terrains in Northern Punjab, the Army created the Pakistan Army Reserves in the 1990s that is concentrated in the desert terrain of Sindh-Rajasthan sector, The Army Reserve South of the Pakistan Army Reserves is grouped in several powerful field-level corps and designed to provide defensive maneuvers in case of war with the Indian Army.

The limitation and constraint of the "offensive-defense" doctrine were eventually exposed by the Indian Army's performance in the Kargil war in 1999, as the Indian Army decided to take an action with full offense that forced Pakistan Army to go into full defense. Without the synergy between the Air Force, Navy, and Marines, the doctrine became redundant, and the Pakistan Army had to rely on international pressure on India to desist from an assault as it exactly happened, according to the Indian author, RSN Singh in 2011.

Threat Matrix (2010 – present)

Urban warfare near Afghanistan: Pakistan Army infantry troops engage in door-to-door clearance during N. Waziristan offense in 2016.

After the failure of the "Offensive-defense" in 1999, the national security institutions engaged in critical thinking to evaluate new doctrine that would provide a comprehensive grand strategy against the infiltrating enemy forces, and development began 2010–11 for the new combat doctrine. In 2013, the new combat doctrine, the Threat Matrix, was unveiled by the ISPR, that was the first time in its history that the army's national security analysts realized that Pakistan faces a real threat from within, a threat that is concentrated in areas along western borders. The Threat Matrix doctrine analyze the military's comprehensive operational priorities and goes beyond in comprehensively describing both existential and non-existential threats to the country.

Based on that strategy in 2013, the Pakistani military organized a four-tier joint military exercise, code-named: Exercise Azm-e-Nau, in which the aim was to update the military's "readiness strategy for dealing with the complex security threat environment." The objective of such exercises is to assess tactics, procedures, and techniques, and explore joint operations strategies involving all three branches of the military: the Army, Air Force, and Navy. In successive years, the Pakistani military combined all the branch-level exercises into joint warfare exercises, in which all four branches now participate, regardless of the terrain, platforms, and control of command.